W9-DJJ-919

DISCARDED

MIRRORS IN MIND

MIRRORS IN MIND

RICHARD GREGORY

W.H. FREEMAN
SPEKTRUM
OXFORD · NEW YORK · HEIDELBERG

W. H. Freeman and Company
41 Madison Avenue, New York, NY 10010
W. H. Freeman at Macmillan Press Limited
Houndmills, Basingstoke, RG21 6XS

British Library Cataloguing in Publication Data
A catalogue record for this book is available from the British Library.

Library of Congress Cataloging-in-Publication Data

Gregory, R. L. (Richard Langton)
Mirrors in mind/Richard Gregory.
p.   cm.
Includes bibliographical references and index.
ISBN 0–7167–4511–9 (hard cover)
1. Visual perception.   I. Title.
BF241.G735 1996   96-20953 152. 14—dc20   CIP

Copyright © Richard Gregory 1997

Acknowledgements for poetry extracts
The extracts from 'Before the World was Made' and 'The Hero, the Girl, and the Fool'
by W. B. Yeats are reproduced by kind permission of A. P. Watt Ltd on behalf of Michael
Yeats.
The extract from 'Before the World was Made' is reprinted with the permission of Simon
& Schuster from *The Poems of W. B. Yeats: A New Edition*, edited by Richard J. Finneran.
Copyright © 1933 by Macmillan Publishing Company, renewed 1961 by Bertha Georgie
Yeats.
The extract from 'The Hero, the Girl and the Fool' is reprinted with the permission of
Simon & Schuster from *The Poems of W. B. Yeats: A New Edition*, edited by Richard J.
Finneran. Copyright © 1928 by Macmillan Publishing Company, renewed 1956 by
Georgie Yeats.
The extract from 'Mirror' is reproduced from *Crossing the Water* by Sylvia Plath, by kind
permission of Faber and Faber Ltd.
The extract from 'Mirror' from *Crossing the Water* by Sylvia Plath is reprinted by
permission of HarperCollins Publishers, Inc. Copyright © 1963 by Ted Hughes.
Originally appeared in the *New Yorker*.

No part of this publication may be reproduced by any
mechanical, photographic, or electronic process, or
in the form of phonographic recording, nor may
it be stored in a retrieval system, transmitted, or
otherwise copied for public or private use without
written permission of the publisher

Set by Wyvern Typesetting Limited, Bristol.
Printed by Biddles Ltd., Guildford & Kings Lynn

To

DAVID SAINSBURY

❧

For his thoughtfulness and generosity
especially for funding the first exhibition
of the
Exploratory
Hands-on Science Centre

Contents

✦

Thanks

❧

THANKS are due to the many friends, students and colleagues who from time to time have put up with mirror talk for over thirty years. Much was written while staying with Dr V. S. Ramachandran and his delightful family, and with my first graduate student and old friend Professor Stuart Anstis at the University of Southern California.

An early version of the manuscript was read by the television producer Michael Croucher. Joanna, Lady Hilton, has advised on the Shakespeare quotations. The publisher Dr Michael Rodgers has shown his usual patience, and been of the greatest help in every way. Many of the photographs owe a great deal to Sara Waterson. Jane Gregory (no relation) edited the typescript with much skill, searching for, and finding, errors which I had missed (any remaining are of course entirely my responsibility).

The University of Bristol continues to give me an office following my 'sell-by-date'. The Department of Psychology of the University of Oxford gives me room, and Magdalen and Hertford Colleges Membership. The Leverhulme Foundation awarded an Emeritus Fellowship.

Mrs Janet John, for many years my secretary, has been the gold brick foundation of this as for other endeavours.

This book is dedicated to a former student at Cambridge: David Sainsbury, hinting at his thoughtful generosity in supporting many ventures and adventures which, unlike mirror images, are real though not visible.

Bristol 1996   R.L.G.

Preflections

The soul may be a mere pretense
The mind makes very little sense
So let us value the appeal
Of that which we can taste and feel.

PIET HEIN

MIRRORS are extraordinarily puzzling. Many years ago a philosopher friend had a house built in a village outside Cambridge, and he asked the architect for a mirror to be placed on the door of a cupboard at the end of the bath. From which side should it be hinged? My philosopher friend could not see an answer; the architect found that if the hinge was against the wall it was impossible to see the mirror when the door was opened, and if the hinge was on the near side it was impossible to get anything out of the cupboard, as the opened door got in the way. My friend ended up having to kneel in the bath to shave every morning.

A very different story: the owners of a New York skyscraper had a problem on their hands as people got dangerously impatient waiting for the elevators. A psychologist was called in, who advised that large mirrors be placed on the elevator doors so that people could see themselves as they waited. This stroke of brilliance solved the problem.

It is a strange quirk of biology that without mirrors we cannot see our own faces; for it is facial expressions that give the game away for reading minds. A puzzle here is how babies come to relate facial expressions of *other* people to their *own* feelings. For they can't see their own faces without a mirror. How do we come to read another's smile, or frown, in terms of our own pleasures and pains? Do we, as Leontes says in *The Winter's Tale*, discover by 'practis'd smiles as in a looking-glass' how to relate to other people, and they to us?[1] Do mirror images serve as bridges between minds. As Polixenes puts it:[2]

> Good Camillo,
> Your changed complexions are to me a mirror
> Which shows me mine, changed too

Mirrors have always been seen as magical. With our present understanding they remain puzzling and evocative. It is no wonder they are called 'magic glasses', as they deceive and they serve truth. They can be uniquely important windows of truth: we would know nothing of the distant reaches of the universe without the huge mirrors of astronomical telescopes. Yet they are also conjuror's friends, as they can delude and confuse with false ghostly worlds. Here we look into their mythology, their history, and the science of images and light — to see into the past and occasionally to scry the future.

Mirrors seem hardly to exist, apart from what they reflect, and most people notice only themselves in the glass as it satisfies and challenges vanity. How much and how we learn of ourselves from our mirror-image is just one of the puzzles. Very different is the puzzle of 'mirror writing'—everything reversed right-left, yet not upside down. Puzzling in its turn is why such a simple and universally experienced phenomenon is, for almost everyone, so hard to explain. Here there is astonishing confusion in the literatures of optics, perception, physics and philosophy.

This takes us to perceptual and to conceptual illusions. As mirrors present sight without touch, so we come to appreciate that children have to learn to see that objects are far more than first appearances: hard or soft, wet or dry, cold or hot, heavy or sharp, dangerous or safe—poisonous or good to eat or drink. For, as in mirrors, none of the important properties of things is in the images made by eyes, for these images are but patterns of light. What objects are, for use or to avoid, must be learnt from dangerous experiments. To learn to see effectively some things must be handled and picked up, dropped and tasted, shaken and stirred. The fingers must occasionally be burnt to learn of fire and matches. So very gradually—though never completely—we come to read objects from images, and to separate illusion from reality.

Thousands of years of questioning and experimenting have led to an ever more surprising understanding of light, of matter, and of mind. Each step has revealed new wonders and fresh puzzles. There is plenty still to learn. Who would have guessed that light is waves of electricity and magnetism? Who could have guessed that mirrors are like radio aerials, and like tuning forks; yet, through the strangeness of light, they are not quite like anything else at all.

Apart from some wonderful exceptions, some of which we will look at, mirrors figure surprisingly seldom in art; though they give evocative alternative views, and curious mixtures and stranger paradoxes.[3]

This book is not just about mirrors as objects. It is about *mirrors in mind*. Mirrors reflect ancient questions of what exists 'objectively' and what we create 'subjectively', by perceiving and thinking. So we are led to some curious questions of physics and psychology, and where they meet in perception and understanding. Mirrors present the opposite of blindness—sight without touch. As the mirror world is not checked by touch, or any of the other senses, it is less than a complete copy of the world we call reality. But it is also more, for our visual imagination is not constrained by counter-evidence. So, long before recorded history, reflections provided visual evidence of ghosts and demons drowned in still water, or buried in glassy rock. In the sacred lake one saw oneself as another self, staring up from the waters, looking as other people look, though silent and blind, with a unique face visible only in the reflection. Very likely it was mirror-images that suggested minds and souls separate from our bodies. No doubt, mirrors inspired the possessive *doppelgänger* of horror.

Mirrors are found in nature: they make cats' eyes shine, and help nocturnal animals see in the dark. The remarkable mirror scales of fish provide a cloak of invisibility for the shoals that swim in bright waters. Recently discovered eyes focus not with lenses but with mirrors, though there are no metal mirrors in nature. Evolution invented diffraction optics so sophisticated that it is right at the edge of our technology.

Though seldom considered, mirrors are uniquely surprising and fascinating in their many forms and functions. Evidently mirrors are puzzling because we can not interact with their images 'hands-on'. So when considered at all, we generally explain 'mirror reversals' in ways that are not appropriate. The brightest people can be and are misled—fooled by everyday ghosts of themselves. But once it is appreciated how to see and think, such puzzles drop away. Here I have taken the unusual step of not citing the many friends and colleagues who have other views of this puzzle; for it is, frankly, embarrassing to get it 'wrong' and have it pointed out. But of course if I am wrong, the embarrassment will be mine.

This takes us *through the mirror*, to the hands-on experience of children and of science. When Alice returned from her adventure to Looking-glass House, she *shook* the Red Queen. Scientists disturb things to shake out secrets of nature, much as children handle and sometimes break toys. Here we will journey through the mirror of appearance to try to see something of how children and science go behind appearances, discovering reality in play.

However this may be, we see through a glass darkly when we do not know where to look for an answer. So here we will try to understand puzzles and wonders of reflections, and something of ourselves, with mirrors in mind.

Notes

1. Shakespeare's *The Winter's Tale*, Act I, scene ii, lines 118–119. Camillo is a Lord of Leonte's court.

2. *The Winter's Tale*, Act I, scene ii, lines 379–381. Polixenes, King of Bohemia, is speaking.

3. Perhaps the only sculptures featuring mirrors are the bronzes of the English artist Michael Ayrton (1921–1975). He was a close friend through the last ten years of his life. He died before he could complete an ambitious television series *A Question of Mirrors*. We often discussed mirrors; I actually suggested the use of grey part-reflecting perspex for his evocative bronzes *Captive* and *Contained Heads*. His most ambitious sculpture was the huge (22 feet high) *Reflective Head*, later known as *Corporate Head*, for the Kresge Corportation building in Philadelphia. See Hopkins (1994).

1

Face to Face

Face-affecting lasses, Neglect their Graces,
to Attend their Glasses.

CROCKER

W E can't face ourselves without a looking-glass. It can be even harder with
it! Young people spend a lot of time discovering—creating?—themselves
through criticising and admiring their own reflections. We sometimes wish to
shut our eyes, but the mirror-image is inescapable. We need tolerance to tolerate
ourselves; but this is hard when we are comparing ourselves with the image of
ourselves. Of course, we sometimes cheat. It is said that changing-rooms of
clothes shops have slightly distorting, flattering mirrors. And as clothes and
make-up are designed to improve upon ungarnished truth, why not?

It is a jolt to look back to how mirrors appeared to Aristotle, two-and-a-half
millennia past. Aristotle has this to say: 'An example of the rapidity with which
the sense organs perceive even a slight difference is found in the behaviour of mirrors; a subject which, even considered by itself, would give scope for careful study
and investigation. At the same time it is quite clear from this instance that the
organ of sight not only is acted upon by its object, but acts reciprocally upon it.'
This is a totally different physics from ours. Aristotle continues with a very different physiology and psychology:[1]

If a woman looks into a highly polished mirror during the menstrual period, the surface of
the mirror becomes clouded with a blood-red colour (and if the mirror is a new one the
stain is not easy to remove, but if it is an old one there is less difficulty). The reason for this
is that, as we have said, the organ of sight not only is acted upon by the air, but also sets up
an active process, just as bright objects do; for the organ of sight is itself a bright object possessing colour. Now it is reasonable to suppose that at the menstrual periods the eyes are in
the same state as any other part of the body; and there is the additional fact that they are
naturally full of blood-vessels. Thus when menstruation takes place, as the result of a fever-
ish disorder of the blood, the difference of condition in the eyes, though invisible to us, is
none the less real (for the nature of the menses and of the semen is the same); and the eyes

set up a movement in the air. This imparts a certain quality to the layer of air extending over the mirror, and assimilates it to itself; and this layer affects the surface of the mirror. Now the cleaner one's clothes are, the more readily they become stained, because a clean object exhibits distinctly any mark which it receives; and the cleaner the object, the better it exhibits even the slightest effects produced upon it. In the same way the bronze surface of the mirror, being smooth, is peculiarly sensitive to any impact (and one must regard the impact of the air as a kind of friction or impression or washing); and because the surface is clean, any impact upon it is clearly apparent. The reason why the stain does not readily come off from a new mirror is that the surface is clean and smooth; in such cases the stain penetrates deeply all over, deeply because the surface is clean, and all over because it is smooth. The reason why it does not persist in old mirrors is that it does not penetrate so deeply, but is comparatively superficial. All this proves first that movement is produced even by minute differences, secondly that perception is very rapid, and thirdly that the sense organ which perceives colours is not only affected by colours, but also in turn affects them.

Jumping two and a half millennia, here are some mirror views. According to the American writer Benijoy La Belle, the pursuit of a beautiful face can even be 'not the worship of self but the worship of an ideal'.[2] W. B. Yeats's poem 'Before the World was Made'[3] reads:

> If I make the lashes dark
> And the eyes more bright
> And the lips more scarlet,
> Or ask if all be right
> From mirror after mirror,
> No vanity's displayed:
> I'm looking for the face I had
> Before the world was made.

Yeats's heroine in 'The Hero, the Girl, and the Fool' declares that those who love her for what is in the mirror are deceived:

> I rage at my own image in the glass,
> That's so unlike myself that when you praise it
> It is as though you praised another, or even
> Mocked me with praise of my mere opposite;
> And when I wake towards morn I dread myself,
> For the heart cries that what description wins Cruelty must keep;
>   therefore be warned and go
> If you have seen that image and not the woman.

Nancy Mitford comments: 'I have often noticed that when women look at themselves in every reflection, and take furtive peeps into their hand looking-glasses, it is hardly ever, as is generally supposed, from vanity, but much more often from a feeling that all is not quite as it should be.'[4] And Shakespeare's Henry V tells Kate that he is, 'a fellow . . . that never looks in his glass for love of anything he sees there.'[5] This literature confirms the view that where mirrors are concerned, all is not vanity.

Whether young children should be encouraged to look at themselves is controversial. Possibly it might lead to narcissism; but some child psychologists and teachers believe that experiencing mirrors helps children to gain confidence. A psychologist, Fritz Wittels, wrote of his own childhood:[6]

When I was still a small boy, I woke with the overwhelming realization that I was an 'I', that looked externally, to be sure, like other children but nonetheless was fundamentally different and tremendously more important. I stood before the mirror, observed myself attentively and often repeatedly addressed my image by my first name. In doing so, I evidently intended to create a bridge from the image in the external world over to me, across which I might penetrate into my unfathomable self. I do not know if I kissed my reflection, but I have seen other children kissing theirs; they come to terms with their ego by loving it.

People suffering from dissociative disorders such as multiple personality disorder may be disturbed by their mirror-images. As their self-image frequently changes, so it only occasionally matches what they see in the mirror. There are even more than the usual conflicts between how we see ourselves psychologically and physically.[7] This is illustrated in Figure 1.1.

Reading Minds

We spend a great deal of our time reading other's minds. We also spend a lot of time making up our own minds, wondering just what we ourselves think and feel. How do we know how we appear to others? Which of our thoughts and moods are revealed in our faces? How fully facial expressions let us see into other's minds, and give away our own, is an open question for art and literature and science. Lawrence Sterne, in his novel *Tristram Shandy* (1759–67), describes Tristram's difficulties in trying to describe his Uncle Toby's character.[8] Tristram regrets that the Greek god Momus—the critic of reality—was unavailable to explain why things are so created that we can not see directly into each other's minds. Tristram says that if Momus had his way:

Nothing more would have been wanting, in order to have taken a man's character, but to have taken a chair and gone softly, as you would a dioptrical bee-hive, and looked in,— viewed the soul stark naked; . . . then taken your pen and ink and set down nothing but what you had seen, and could have sworn to.

Lawrence Sterne complains that the biographer does not have this advantage:

. . . our minds shine not through the body, but we are wrapt up here in a dark covering of uncrystallised flesh and blood; so that, if we would come to the specific characters of them, we must go some other way to work.

FIGURE 1.1 *How multiple personalities appear in a mirror*
People with severe dissociative disorders frequently experience discomfort and disorientation
when they look at themselves in the mirror. In many cases, they are unlikely to see a
predictable reflection, due to the changeability of self-image in multiple personality disorder.
This picture concretises (at a clear level of meaning) some of what is known about the
patient's system of personalities, including various ages, genders and specifics of identity.
The more detailed each reflection in the mirror, the more crystallised that aspect is in
consciousness. The zigzag lines covering the mirror frame remind the observer of the fragile
nature of identity, particularly in this disorder. From Telling Without Talking: Art as a
Window into the World of Multiple Personality *by Barry M. Cohen and Carol Thayer*
Cox. © 1995 by Barry M. Cohen and Carol Thayer Cox. Reprinted by permission of
W. W. Norton & Company, Inc.

Tristram goes on to take a behaviourist tack to 'Draw my Uncle Toby's character
from his hobby-horse.' Yet behaviourism denied that anything goes on inside—
which we all know is wrong!

Presumably it is this difficulty of seeing into *another's* mind—this lack of a
'dioptrical' view—that makes us regard mind and body as essentially different.
For if we think of our *own* bodies and our sensations and actions, the difference is
not so clear. We *feel* when our fingers meet an object; *taste* when the tongue is

touched with food; *see* with our eyes open; *will* our hands to move and miraculously they do move. So one's own body is seen as a uniquely special object as experiences and willed actions are tied uniquely to it. To will another's actions is far more indirect, requiring persuasion or bribery or threat. For to feel another's sensations is impossible, though we believe that others have pains and pleasures much like our own.

Biologically speaking, it is almost inexplicable that we can not see our own facial expressions. This is like writing or drawing with our eyes shut. Facial expressions—of pleasure, boredom, hostility, rage and so on—are vital for reading others' minds, and so for predicting behaviour, to respond appropriately. There are even specialised regions of brain for the recognition of faces, and also for hands.[9] So it is extremely odd that the give-away expressions of faces are invisible to their owners. Mirrors can hardly be of help—except for actors practising— for one hardly ever sees one's own expressions in mirrors while one is in the various emotional states and moods one reads in others' faces. This leads to a curious puzzle: how do we know which *private* emotions correspond to which *public* expressions? And how did expressions of smiling and so on originate biologically?

The key notion for explaining this is one of the brilliant insights of Charles Darwin. Darwin suggested that the meanings of smiling and frowning, and so on, evolved from pre-human and very different functional uses of the facial muscles. This notion he developed with a great deal of evidence from animals, and also from children including his own, in his fascinating and very important book *Expression of the Emotions in Man and Animals* (1873).[10]

Darwin does not mention mirrors here, but these ideas are important for understanding how we read minds from faces. He considers the use of the muscle indicating mental reflection, the corrugator, that produces the furrows of the forehead when we are thinking hard. Here Darwin refers to an earlier writer, the Scottish anatomist Sir Charles Bell, who suggested, in his *Anatomy of Expression in Painting* (1806),[11] that this muscle of reflection ranks as '. . . the most remarkable muscle of the human face. It knits the eyebrows with an energetic effort, which unaccountably, but irresistibly, conveys the idea of mind.' Darwin disagrees somewhat, suggesting that frowning is not so much from mental reflection, but rather from a sense of unpleasantness—prolonged reflection being unpleasant. Paradoxically, this is precisely what Darwin spent his long and happy life doing!

Darwin's suggestion is that each facial muscle that now gives meaningful symbolic expressions has its origins in very different physiological functions that were directly important for survival. Thus, frowning made the eyes work best in situations of danger, and the muscles around the eyes limited the blood flow during exertion, to protect them from damage. Primates learned to read these functional changes of the face as predictive to behaviour. So they have become give-aways, to friends and foes, as signs of minds.

Blushing is particularly interesting. According to Darwin, blushing occurs only in humans, and not in children before they have considerable social understanding. He sees blushing as an outward sign of guilt, signalling that the individual is not to be trusted. The accompanying debilitating confusion of embarrassment makes covering up or inventing a plausible lie more difficult.

Darwin does refer to an infant's reaction to a mirror in a paper published in 1877, from notes made 37 years earlier, about his first child William:[12]

When four and a half months old, he repeatedly smiled at my image and his own in a mirror, and no doubt mistook them for real objects; but he showed sense in being evidently surprised at my voice coming from behind him. Like all infants he much enjoyed thus looking at himself, and in less than two months perfectly understood that it was an image; for if I made quite silently any odd grimace, he would suddenly turn around to look at me. He was, however, puzzled at the age of seven months, when being out of doors he saw me on the inside of a large plate-glass window, and seemed in doubt whether or not it was an image.

Darwin adds: 'When a few days under nine months old he associated his own name with his image in the looking-glass, and when called by name would turn towards the glass even when at some distance from it'. And: 'When a few days over nine months, he learnt spontaneously that a hand or other object causing a shadow to fall on the wall in front of him was to be looked at from behind'.

This raises the curious question: how does an infant appreciate emotions represented by facial expressions—for how does the baby know what he or she looks like when pleased or sad, angry, or whatever? This is not too mysterious where sounds are involved, such as laughing and crying; but many expressions are silent and subtle. Children can look impish, secretive, sly, excited, amused, sad: surely, these are not learned from a mirror?

The Cambridge philosopher C. D. Broad, in *Mind and Its Place in Nature* (1929),[13] was so puzzled by how children could come to relate their own feelings to others' expressions that he saw it as evidence for telepathy. Broad thought that reading others' facial expressions could not possibly arise by *inference* from our own feelings and expressions, because we can not see our own faces, except by looking in mirrors; so we have very little knowledge of what we look like when we feel angry or pleased, or in pain or whatever, to base the inference on. Broad offers two explanations for reading minds from others' expressions: *telepathy*, and what he calls *Natural Expression*. By this he meant inherited innate knowledge.

Broad justified his reference to telepathy as a possibility (he had a deep interest in psychical research[14]) in this way:[15]

If the reader will do what most philosophers are too proud and most scientists too prejudiced to do, and will study the evidence for 'telepathy' in *Phantasm of the Living* and the evidence which has accumulated since 1886 as marshalled by Mrs Sidgwick in the S.P.R [Society for Psychical Research] for October 1922, he will see that a large proportion of the cases are of the kind suggested.

Broad's conclusion was that, although he couldn't *prove* any power of telepathy, he considered it had a role to play in reading facial expressions—as mirrors are not adequate for discovering links from one mind to another. Since Broad was writing reliable evidence has not accumulated for telepathy: the earlier claims look more and more dubious as they are examined in detail.

Broad's other theory, that we have innate inherited responses to facial expressions, seems far more plausible. This could be 'wired in' inheritance. Looking at a sad face may make us sad, and a laughing face make us jolly—make us smile, and laugh in return, as innate responses. But this could, however, be only be the tip of the iceberg, for facial expressions are somewhat different in different cultures. Darwin's concept of innately inherited expressions, developed from functional muscle movements, seems to be the essential key. But there must be some later learning, as various social groups have characteristic expressions.[16]

The Self

Perhaps it is the difficulty of communicating with and trying to understand other people that urges us (though wrongly) to the philosophy of dualism, associated with the French rationalist philosopher René Descartes (1596–1650). As is very well known, he set out to doubt everything, ending with: *cogito ergo sum* (I think therefore I am). Descartes puts it as a dilemma:[17]

But immediately I noticed that while I was trying thus to think everything false, it was necessary that I, who was thinking this, was something. And observing that this truth 'I am thinking, therefore I exist' was so firm and sure that all the most extravagant suppositions of the sceptics were incapable of shaking it, I decided that I could accept it without scruple as the first principle of the philosophy I was seeking.

This has all sorts of difficulties. The argument is formally illegitimate as the 'I' appears both in the *definiens* and in the *defiendum*. And nowadays it is not too difficult to imagine a computer that thinks though it has no 'I', or 'Self'. Indeed, it is far harder to think of a computer that *does* have an I or a Self than one that does not. The status of Self among philosophers is controversial. Is the Self an internal entity—an internal eye? Or is the Self, perhaps, a construct—a hypothesis? Does an animal have a Self? Does a baby have a Self? It might be thought that such questions are beyond experiment; but quite recently an American social psychologist, Gordon Gallup, has devised a test for self-recognition—using a mirror.[18]

Starting with chimpanzees: having familiarised the chimps to mirrors, Gallup painted a red spot on one side of the animal's face, while it was anaesthetised. Then, he wondered, upon recovering from the anaesthetic would the animal touch the spot *in the mirror*—or *on its face*? The answer found was: 'higher' primates would touch the spot of paint on their faces; 'lower' animals would touch the mirror, not the mark on the face. Gallup interpreted this as showing that as only chimpanzees could pass the mirror test, only the highest primates have self-recognition (see Figure 1.2). Trying this on babies (applying the paint while they were asleep[19]) he found that very young babies would touch the mirror, not their faces; but after about two years of age they would touch the paint mark on their face and not the mirror. The results with babies might seem to show that human self-recognition is not present for the first two years of human life.

There are doubts over how these fascinating observations should be interpreted. Could an animal, or a baby, recognise itself in a mirror—even if it knows itself as a special individual? For how could it know what it looks like? Indeed, this is C. D. Broad's problem the other way round. No doubt it is by making movements, and seeing them reflected, that we come to realise that the mirror image is of oneself. This might take some time, for a baby or an intelligent non-human species, as some active experimenting is needed. This, indeed, makes mirror-watching essentially different from seeing oneself in still photographs, or in motion on film or TV, for only mirrors give immediate feedback from motion. If we had not learned to recognise ourselves in a mirror, I doubt whether we would know ourselves in still or moving pictures. We do not even recognise our own recorded voices initially. Again, we need correlated action to establish that it is oneself.

FIGURE 1.2 *Chimpanzee recognising itself in a mirror*
© *Kim A. Bard, Yerkes Regional Primate Center, Atlanta.*

All mobile animals avoid bumping into objects—so they must have a body image. This suggests that they have some sense of self. But this may be very different from conscious self-awareness. Here it is useful to think of robots. Fifty years ago, the pioneer brain scientist Grey Walter[20] made simple electro-mechanical 'tortoises', with headlights and photo-cell eyes, which would interact with each other—and so with themselves in a mirror.[21]

When a mirror or white surface is encountered the reflected light from the head-lamp is sufficient to operate the circuit controlling the robot's response to light, so that the machine makes its own reflection; but as it does so, the light is extinguished, which means the stimulus is cut off—but removal of the stimulus restores the light, which is again seen as a stimulus, and so on. The creature therefore lingers before a mirror, flickering, twittering and jigging like a clumsy Narcissus. The behaviour of a creature thus engaged with its own reflection is quite specific, and on a purely empirical basis, if it were observed in an animal, might be accepted as evidence for some degree of self-awareness. In this way the machine is superior to many 'high' animals who usually treat reflection as if it were another animal, if they accept it at all.

The question to ask is how the animal, or the baby, behaves that is essentially different from Grey Walter's mechanical 'animals', or from more sophisticated robots. One would be extremely surprised if a not-specially-programmed robot paid 'attention' to itself, rather than to the mirror. But surely this would only show that it treated itself as special, and this is what lowly creatures and quite simple robots do. The issue is what kind of 'special' does appropriate 'mirror behaviour' have to be to demonstrate a sense of Self?

For interpreting the baby experiments, one would like to know the importance (if any) of prior experience of mirrors. Would babies who had never seen themselves touch the mark on their face? If not, it should be asked: does it take a year or so to discover *mirrors*—rather than Self? Given how puzzling mirrors are to adults, it seems inconceivable that babies could easily interpret reflections and identify their source. This is beyond the capacity of the adult visual system (see page 78), and requires quite sophisticated judgement.[22]

The issue turns on what we mean by 'Self'.[23] Surely it is far more than body image. Like Descartes, one may be most aware of Self while thinking—but then surely one is least aware of one's body. This leads to issues of consciousness that we will glance at later (page 272).

Here is a mirror-experiment which shows that there is more to the psychology and philosophy of mind than behaviour. It was originally set up in the Exploratorium science centre, in San Francisco, and it allows one to experience one's Divided Self, when vision departs from kinaesthetic body image. The apparatus is simply a vertical mirror with a horizontal rod through its centre. On the rod there are two rings, one in front and the other behind the mirror. Hold the ring behind the mirror with, say, one's left hand, and the ring in front with one's right hand; then, slowly move the left hand—and there is an extraordinary experience of failed body image, as the wrong hand seems to move (see Chapter 9).

Where do we experience *ourselves*? Somewhere associated with the eyes, surely. A simple test, related to mirror images, may be used. Try writing a letter on the forehead of a friend, while his or her eyes are closed. Ask your friend: 'What letter do you 'see' in you mind? Is it seen as *normal*—or in *mirror-writing*?' If you write it the usual way round on the forehead and your friend 'sees' it as mirror-writing, the implication is that it is being 'seen' from a psychological Self inside the head. If it is 'seen' as normal writing, the psychological Self is in front of the face. If the writing on the forehead is drawn in mirror-writing, these are of course reversed.

A subtle version of this experiment, described by David Krech and Richard Crutchfield, is to use an ambiguous letter-number, such as Ɛ, as this is like a mirror-written 3. It can be 'seen' as the letter E or the number 3. In one experiment (with 202 students) 76% reported seeing a 3.[24] This is 'inside' perception. There is some evidence that more men than women 'see' themselves from outside—from in front of their faces—as though they have mirrors watching their own expressions, and how they appear to others.

It is possible that facial expressions are so important to humans because upright posture is biologically recent. Human lovers stare into each other's eyes. But face-to-face communication and love-making depend on the new (a few millions of years old) biological stance of primates, especially humans. Possibly this is why the eyes and the mouth provide evidence of intention, and the gamut of emotions from fear to love, though the face is invisible to its owner. Possibly, also, this lack of visual check makes dissimulation difficult, so emotional expression is reasonably reliable, and can generally be trusted. Fortunately, it is quite hard to be a convincing actor.

Mirror Therapy

There is a substantial psycho-analytic literature on the development in children of Self, and relation to Others, and mirrors are sometimes used.[25] Experiments have been carried out using distorting mirrors to estimate how people see themselves. Traub and Orbach (1964) made a flexible mirror that could be distorted, concave or convex, with four motor-driven clamps controlled by the subject of the experiment. The Adjustable Body-Distorting Mirror was designed to explore the visual perception of the physical appearance of the body. A full-length mirror was made that was adjustable to reflect the observer on a 'distortion continuum', ranging from extremely distorted to completely undistorted. The observer adjusted his or her reflection until it appeared undistorted. It was found that subjects tolerated quite large distortions—and they sometimes forgot what they looked like. They needed undistorted images, or pictures, to maintain calibration of themselves.

The head and shoulders were best identified as distorted or undistorted. One psychiatric subject 'recognised that her reflection was distorted but mislocated the distortion: "My legs are fine but my body is much too big." In fact her legs were too short and tapered down to tiny feet.' Some subjects were given drugs known to affect apparent body size—alcohol, for example, makes the head feel larger. Quite apart from the drugs, some subjects experienced nausea from their distorted images.

Looking-glasses have been used for psychiatric and weight-control therapy. A therapist, Daniel Cappon, got his over- or under-sized patients, who did not believe they had a problem, to look carefully at themselves for several minutes a day in a triple full-sized mirror.[26] Gradually the patients corrected their distorted mental images of themselves, and in some cases were able to change their eating habits so that they could achieve a healthy body weight.

What Happens when Sight is Lost or Gained?

What happens to the body image without sight? John Hull, who lost his sight at the age of 24, describes this in his remarkable book, *Touching the Rock: an Experience of Blindness*.[27] Following increasing and then total blindness his concept of visual space—including his body-image—was gradually lost:

I feel as if I am on the borders of conscious life, not just in the literal sense that I am slipping in and out of sleep, but in a deeper and more alarming sense. I feel as if I want to stop thinking, stop experiencing. The lack of a body image makes this worse: the fact that one can't glance down and see the reassuring continuing of one's consciousness in the outlines of one's body . . . I am dissolving. I am no longer concentrated in a particular location, which would be symbolized by the integrity of the body.

The changes of his experience, knowledge and perception were profound: 'Sometimes I am being carried deeper and deeper in. The weight presses me down. Such knowledge as I have is disappearing.' His body becomes his only reference: 'I come back to the one thing I know. There is my body, sitting here on the edge of the bed, trembling and sweating. There is tension in my stomach, the pounding of my temples. I hear my breathing. I feel my heart pounding. I do not know what is out there; I know what is in here.'

There are rare cases of babies blind from birth, or from infancy, then given sight when adult by operations to the eyes. These cases are of great interest; but they do need to be looked at with caution, for the adults are not like babies frozen in time. Unlike babies they have had years of experience of handling things, and of learning from others, which means that their new-found vision is based on infinitely more knowledge than is available at birth. It is also important to know just how blind they were before the operation.[28]

Until recently it has been thought that little or nothing is seen effectively for many months following the operation; but there are quite contrary findings. Cases have been reported for many hundreds of years, and were summarized by M. von Senden in 1932.[29] Blindness, in almost all cases, was due to cataract of the lenses of the eyes. But it is important to note—though not always realised—that removal of the lens disturbs the eye: it may be months before there is an effective retinal image. This is especially so in the primitive conditions of *schrieving*, an operation dating from the early Middle Ages in which the cornea was slit open and the eye lens pulled out. The more recent technique of corneal transplant, on the other hand, gives optically good eyes immediately. So it is only these cases, and those involving the even more recent techniques of implanting acrylic lenses, that should be looked at for evidence of rate of initial development of vision following operation for gaining sight.

I had the good fortune to study just such a case, with my colleague Jean Wallace, in the early 1960s.[30] 'SB' (Sidney Bradford) was 52 at the time of the operations. He was effectively blind by ten months, probably from birth, from an infection producing very dense opacity of the corneas of both eyes. We expected that he would temporarily remain effectively blind. However:

It was very soon apparent that his vision was far from rudimentary: he could name almost any object in the room. Much to our surprise, he could even tell the time by means of a large clock on the wall. We were so surprised at this that we did not at first believe that he could have been in any sense blind before the operation. However he proceeded to show us a large hunter watch with no glass, and he demonstrated his ability to tell the time very quickly and accurately by touching the hands. It appears that he always used this method of telling the time before the operation.

From the start of his visual life, SB was fascinated by mirrors. This became obvious the day after he left hospital. As we reported at the time:[31]

Next morning at breakfast, he [SB] sat for preference facing a very large wall mirror in which the room was reflected. This fascinated him, and mirrors continued to be chosen objects.

A year later: 'He was still fascinated by mirrors, and he still noted improvement in his ability to see.'[32] In his 'local' he preferred looking at his friends reflected in a long wall mirror to seeing them directly. Sadly he did not like the look of his own face in a mirror—or his wife's! In many ways he continued to live the life of a blind person; for example, he preferred to shave in the dark by touch.

There is a hazard to look out for in these cases: the people are intelligent. So they may guess correctly—making one think they see more than they do. When we first met SB, in the ward of the hospital just after the first transplant operation, it happened that I had a magazine in the pocket of my raincoat, sticking out so that its title was showing. He immediately named it correctly! We were already surprised by how much he could see, but this seemed too much:

We were even more surprised when he named correctly a magazine we had with us. It was in fact *Everybody's* (for January 17, 1959), and had a large picture of two musicians dressed in striped pullovers. Although he named the magazine correctly, he could make nothing of the picture. We at once asked him how he knew which magazine it was, and he said that although he could not read the name, he could recognise the first two letters, though not the rest, and guessed that the *Ev* belonged to *Everybody's*. Further questioning revealed that he could recognise any letter in upper case, though not in lower case, and it so happens that the title of the magazine was written with only the first two letters in upper case, thus:

EVerybody's

He then told us that he had learned capital letters by touch, these being inscribed on blocks and taught at the blind school. Lower case letters were not taught. This was particularly interesting, for it suggested direct transfer from touch experience. It also showed how he could guess correctly from comparatively little evidence. We were, after this early experience, continually on our guard for intelligent guessing covering up perceptual abnormality.

This ability to read upper case letters—and only upper case letters—followed learning only upper case by touch at the blind school. This finding was confirmed by an Italian psychologist, A. Valvo, in 1971. Valvo studied half a dozen cases (including a philosopher!), the front parts of whose eyes had never formed.[33] They were given artificial lenses, with a new technique.[34] Valvo also found that they could immediately read visually; and generally they could see what they had learned, especially from touch, when they were blind.

Our finding with SB, that previous experience from exploratory touch was immediately available for his new-found sight, is the basis of the philosophy of mind of this book. Mirror-confusions (which are so strikingly prevalent) highlight the point that effective seeing depends on interactive experience of objects— which is not available in mirrors. It seems we would be effectively blind in a museum-world of protective glass cases, or a media-world of film and television, or Plato's world of shadows. We would be blind if brought up in a mirror-world of sight without touch.[35]

There are new studies of such cases being undertaken in Japan.[36] Toshiko Mochizuki and Shuko Torii (1992) have made a study of perception of mirrors, following operations to restore the sight of a girl ('MO') aged 13 years (in 1992). She, like SB, received corneal transplants. She had a series of operations from the age of 4 years 9 months when, according to her mother, she could only see light, not form or colours.

Toshiko Mochizuki and Shuko Torii report:[37]

Our experiment started about 3 years ago (1989.10.10), just after she had received the second corneal transplantation. Since that time, she has continued visual learning with us, and up to now she had gradually gained the ability to identify colour, 2-dimensional shapes on a white ground and 3-dimensional solids on a table.

But it was still difficult for her to locate an object in visual space, especially the images in a mirror . . . . We examined where MO searched and whether she could orient the mirror images of herself and/or other persons with herself and the mirror-images of objects in her hand or on the table as well. . . . MO was guided to a full-length mirror situated 10–15 cm away from her in an experimental room. She was standing up facing the mirror and was asked to look at it without being told that it is a mirror. Her behaviour was observed by experimenters and recorded by VTR. Records were kept of the amount of time spent viewing the mirror, the number and description of social responses directed at the reflection, and the incidence of any behaviours directed at the self with the aid of the mirror. . . .

When she looked at the mirror-image of herself for the first time ('89.12.28) she searched not only the surface of the mirror by touching and seeing, but also the space behind the mirror by going to the back of it. She could not locate objects (e.g. herself) reflected by the mirror. The behaviour of searching behind the mirror continued for about 15 months from 1989.12.28 to 1991.6.20. It was after 7 months that she succeeded in locating reflected images of herself or images of herself with an experimenter.

Eventually she stopped searching behind the mirror (1991.10.15), and the searching spaced enlarged into the area behind her. For example, when she found something green in the mirror, she looked back and recognized that the reflection was from a tree.

When she succeeded in locating an object reflected in the mirror for the first time ('91.3.1), it was not her own body, but that of another person.

When she looked at her mirror-image of herself for the first time ('89.12.28), she could neither locate it in space nor could she recognize is as herself . . . . When we had her move her arms and hands in front of the mirror, she observed the movement on the surface of the mirror, but seemed to think that the mirror was moving. She said 'Mr. Mirror', and 'I don't know who you are'.

This condition, in which location and identification of her mirror-image were difficult, continued to the fourth experiment ('90.8.31). But at the fifth experiment 7 months later ('91.3.12), she repeated 5 times that a change had happened. When an experimenter pointed to her image and asked who it was, she repeated 'I don't know' 5 times, and 'Who is she?' 22 times.

But then she said 'It imitates my movement' 3 times. So we asked her 'Which is yourself?' After carefully observing the image, she said 'Is this me?' pointing to the image of herself. She looked puzzled.

The experiment studying MO's perception of the mirror images of other persons began on March 12. On that day, regarding the experimenter's image with suspicion, she asked us if the mirror-image was of herself. When she found something black in the mirror, she searched around and behind her. At first, she said twice that 'Someone is here' and she asked 'Who is it?' Then she found the experimenter and asked 'Who is it?', 'Is he Mr. S.?' She compared the real image and the mirror-image and recognised that the black part of the mirror-image was the experimenter's hair. Then she said, 'I realized it by his hair'.

Since then, she has succeeded in locating mirror images of others (experimenters I, II) standing beside her, and almost always succeeded in identifying the images by the colours of their clothes. When the experimenter moved his hands in the 3rd experiment ('91.10.15), it became easier for her to correctly point to the part of the image in the mirror.

When she identified others in a mirror-image, hair, colours of clothes and height of the person were used as cues. She never reported using facial features as cues.

In the 5th experiment ('91. 6.21), to assist her in identifying the mirror-image of herself, we gave her one or two coloured papers (e.g. red, yellow, or green). She moved the coloured papers in her hands and observed their movement . . . . It was not easy for her to understand that she had coloured papers in her hand. She was able to call the correct names of these colours when she saw them directly. At first, she confused the coloured papers with her dress or her hand. She said, 'My dress is white, but why do I see me yellow?' and 'My hand isn't red, is it?'

After that interpretation, she supposed that the coloured part is another person wearing the same coloured clothes. She said 'I see a tall yellow person . . . ', and 'Green person is hanging down from the mirror'. In the third step she extinguished the possibility that the coloured part is another person existing in the room by deduction. For example, she said 'it is not me. It is not my mother' . . . .

In the 6th experiment ('91.10.15) to make clear whether she understood the problem of optics in the mirror itself, we had her observe a ball or balls on a table . . . . At first, she could not distinguish between a real object and its image in the mirror, and so counted twice as many objects as existed. But, on the 3rd trial, she put a ball behind the mirror and found that its image disappeared in synchrony with the movement. On the 4th trial, an experimenter arranged two balls side by side on the table in front of the mirror and asked, 'How many real balls on the table?' She answered, 'Two and the other two balls are mirror-images, as the mirror reflects objects'.

Through a series of experiments on the cognition of images in a mirror, we found four factors . . . :

1. Space where the subject searches
2. Mode of observation
3. Object which can be recognized in the mirror, and
4. Part of the body which can be recognized in the mirror.

In the case of MO, at first, the space where she searched was the area between her and the mirror. Then, it changed to the space behind the mirror, and later the space behind her. At that time she compared the image in the mirror and the real object, and was able to associate the image to the real object. . . .

The most difficult thing to recognize was the reflection of herself in the mirror.

The easiest part of a person to recognize was the clothes. Head and hands were the next easiest and the face was the most difficult.

These results explain why perception of her own image in a mirror was most difficult for her. When we recognize the image of ourselves in a mirror, we must use facial features as cues. Even now, however, she cannot visually recognize human faces.

Unusual situations can throw light on the usual. These detailed mirror studies of recovery from blindness, from Japan, are providing new evidence which may be significant for understanding the origins and development of perception. But just because special cases are not typical they must be interpreted with special care. Even for perception, what is important lies beneath appearances and so is hard to see. This, surely, is why science offers such special challenges and opportunities for coming face-to-face with hidden depths of nature and ourselves.

Let's end with a face-to-face mirror experiment. Look at your own eyes in the looking-glass and shift your gaze back and forth from eye to eye. Can you see your eyes move? Then ask a friend to look alternately at your eyes, while you watch theirs. The difference is incredible. Your friend's eyes clearly move from side to side. Your eyes appear *fixed*—though they move exactly as the eyes of your friend. Why can't you see your own eyes moving in a mirror? We'll leave this as a question.

Notes

1. Aristotle (384–322 BC).
2. La Belle (1988).
3. Both 'Before the World was Made' and 'The Hero, the Girl, and the Fool' can be found in Yeats (1983).
4. Mitford (1945).
5. Shakespeare's *Henry V*, Act V, scene ii, lines 147–148.
6. Quoted in Goldberg (1958) page 249.
7. This is discussed by Cohen and Cox (1995).
8. Laurence Sterne (1713–68), the son of an infantryman, grandson of an Archbishop of York, led an adventurous, somewhat dissolute life—writing the first stream-of-consciousness novel in *The Life and Opinions of Tristram Shandy*. The origin of 'Shandy' is not known but it meant crack-brained, half-crazy,eccentric.
9. Perrett, Mistlin and Chitty (1987).
10. Further research over the following century is described with comments in Ekman (1973). The conclusion is that Darwin's ideas were sound. Ekman (1972) reports interesting experiments.
11. Bell (1806).
12. Darwin (1877). It includes a delightful photograph of Charles Darwin and his eldest child William aged about three years.
13. Broad (1929).
14. Professor C. D. Broad lived for many years in Newton's rooms in Trinity College, Cambridge. There was a legend that he would try to communicate with Newton's ghost, with elaborate rituals. Whether he succeeded is not on record.
15. Broad (1929). The reference to *Phantasm of the Living* is to Myers (1915).
16. This is discussed informatively and entertainingly by Desmond Morris: see Morris (1967, 1977).
17. Descartes (1637).
18. Gallup (1970, 1977, 1979), Suarez and Gallup (1986).
19. Amsterdam (1972) and Brooks-Gun and Lewis (1975).
20. Grey Walter (Walter William Grey) (1910–76) was Anglo-American; a physiologist who pioneered electrical recording from the brain. He discovered that there is brain activity just before a decision is made. His mechanical 'tortoises' of the early 1950s showed life-like behaviour from just a few active components.
21. Grey Walter (1953) page 84.

22. Parker, Mitchell and Boccia (1994).

23. From the huge literature: Williams (1973), Rorty (1976), Locke (1968), Churchland, (1988), Dennett (1991).

24. Krech and Crutchfield (1962).

25. Especially by Berman (1989). Morris Berman discusses the ideas of Balint (1968), Goldstein (1957), Stern (1983, 1985), Verney (1981), Winnicott (1957); and for a useful review, Anderson (1984).

26. Cappon (1973), Bennett (1956).

27. Hull (1991). This and related examples and issues are well described by Rosenfield (1992).

28. Total absence of light at the retina does not occur with cataract or corneal opacity, and a non-functional retina or optic nerve cannot be repaired or replaced, so the operable blindness is not strictly complete, though it can be profound.

29. Senden, M. (1932) *Raum-und Gestaltauffassung bei operierten Blindgeborenen*. The copies were destroyed by air raid in the Second World War. The English translation is Heath (1960).

30. Gregory and Wallace (1963).

31. Gregory and Wallace (1963), page 32.

32. Gregory and Wallace (1963), page 35.

33. Valvo (1971).

34. Their operations were delayed until adulthood, because the technique did not exist when they were children. In the case of SB, corneas were in too short supply to risk on his eyes, which seemed beyond help; but corneas suddenly became far more available when corneal banks were established.

35. We would also be blind if we were brought up in Searle's Chinese Room. The distinguished American philosopher John Searle suggested that an allegedly intelligent computer robot machine could no more learn to understand English writing, than an English non-Chinese-speaking man would learn the meanings of Chinese characters by watching them being used by Chinese speakers in a closed room. In my view a baby wouldn't learn to see in Searle's Chinese Room. See Searle (1984) and Gregory (1987).

36. Umezu, Torii and Uemura (1975).

37. Toshiko Mochizuki and Shuko Torii (1992).

2

Mirrors in Art

The mirror is the master of painters

LEONARDO DA VINCI

*United with reason, imagination is the mother of the arts
and the source of their wonders*

FRANCISCO GOYA

PAINTERS present subtleties of reflections—perhaps especially on water—with such wonderful skill that it is surprising to find so few pictures featuring mirrors.[1] No doubt painters felt superior to mirrors, as only they could capture a moment for eternity. This completely changed in 1840 with the incredible 'memory mirrors' of photographs which challenged and informed painters. At first photographs needed exposures of many minutes; but when a fraction of a second sufficed for creating a finely detailed picture, the intricacies of light flashing from ripples and waves were at last revealed to the eye, to be captured in painting. But there was a danger of capturing more than the eye could see: destroying art's images of the mind's eye with excessive realism. For centuries mirrors had been a special challenge for painters as people wrongly saw them as pictures; now photography set impossible and in some ways irrelevant standards for portraying reality in paint.

As Rene Hughe says in *Discovery of Art*, under the heading 'Beyond Natural Appearance':[2]

Realism has its fascination and its justification: it would be presumptuous to exclude it from art. One must, however, be clear of its rightful place. And it is precisely the mirror that raises this question: to look in a painting solely for the reproduction of the object it represents is like mistaking the ephemeral image in the mirror for the mirror itself. The mirror as such, with its substance and qualities, is not the deceptive image it reflects. It is not this face, these flowers whose forms strike its surface and rebound into our eyes. The mirror exists behind this semblance, behind the phenomenon of reflection of which it is merely the vehicle.

As we have said, apart from notable exceptions (some illustrated here) there are surprisingly few paintings featuring mirrors, which is odd given that mirrors provide extra views and extensions of space—ambiguities of illusion and reality—that delight artists.

Rene Hughe continues:

The painting is a flat surface covered with a certain substance, the pictorial medium, which forms lines and colours 'assembled in a certain order' to quote Maurice Denis's famous formula. But it is much more than that. Unlike the mirror, it has, behind its visible surface, a psychological context—the life of the mind out of which the artist drew it, and of which these lines and colours are the visible sign. The background, the seeming depth in which the mirror-image is imbedded, is illusory, reflecting only the space in front of the mirror; in the painting the background leads into another 'dimension', another world, to which the work invites us. The painting is in this sense the artist's soul.

Some artists stress the 'reality' in the illusion of a painting representing other objects; others are concerned with the impact of its patterns and colours, as a special object in its own right. Variations on this double reality hold endless interest for paintings, which photography cannot match.

Although natural reflections enormously enhance pictures, possibly paintings and photographs of mirrors are somewhat disappointing, as they lack the stereoscopic depth needed for their tunnel-like probing into another space. And until recently mirrors themselves were generally small and, by modern standards, lacklustre. Perhaps more important is the fact that generally their images are smaller than whatever is reflected; so artists often have to 'cheat' to make mirror images effective in a painting. This is a privilege photographers do not enjoy.

Mirrors have been used extensively as *aids* for painting—especially for self-portraits. It is a snag that the artist sees himself right-left reversed. Wouldn't compensating, with optically reversing mirrors, solve this problem? All that is needed is a pair of looking-glasses at right angles forming a corner (see page 82). This simple solution does not seem to be used by artists. For this and other reasons, there are many right-left confusions in drawings and paintings. An interesting example is preserved in Rembrandt's self-portrait of 1668 which is shown in Plate 1. Evidently realising he appeared left-handed, Rembrandt painted out and changed over his hands and arms. This is clearly visible in an X-ray of the painting.

Engravings generally have to be made right-left reversed, for they are switched in the printing process, when the paper is lifted and turned face up from the copper or wood or stone. The print maker does not always know whether the work was done reversed or what to do about it; so engravings have often been reproduced reversed by mistake. The reversed-print problem can occur in photography; but unlike print-making, it is a simple matter to rotate the negative to correct it. Artists have been upset by confusions of this kind. Van Gogh wrote to his art dealer brother, Theo, complaining that the print of *The Potato Eaters* came out the wrong way round. The effect is that people look left-handed when they are not, and the composition is changed, which matters perhaps especially where there is action.

Bad actions are generally shown happening from right to left, and good actions moving towards the right. However, an English psychologist, Chris MacManus, showed a number of people well-known pictures mirror-reversed. Perhaps surprisingly, few could tell they were reversed.[3] Left-handedness is considerably more common for painters and architects than for the general population. Famous left-handed artists included: Leonardo da Vinci, who wrote his *Notebooks* in mirror-writing; Raphael; Holbein; Paul Klee; and Pablo Piccaso. It is found that about twice the general proportion of art students are left-handed.[4]

Brief History

The best known painting that features a mirror is the early Flemish painter Jan van Eyck's (1386–1441) *The Marriage of Arnolfini*, with its large convex mirror behind the couple (see Plate 2). This is one of the first full-length portraits. The figures are a merchant, Giovanni Arnolfini, and his daughter-of-a-merchant wife Giovanna Cenami, probably in their home at Bruges. The mirror reflects two people, one most likely being the artist. The Latin inscription on the rear wall, 'Johannes de Eyck fuit hic', may mean that the artist identified himself with the mirror—'Jan van Eyck was here,' perhaps meaning: 'Jan van Eyck was in this mirror.'

The Italian painter Michelangelo da Caravaggio (1569–1609), noted for dramatic themes and extreme perspective foreshortening, gives a frightening image of the Gorgon, Medusa, reflected in Perseus's shield (see Plate 3). The Spanish painter Diego Rodríguez de Silva y Velázquez (1599–1660) achieved astonishing and not always flattering realism, though he was a court painter. Velázquez's *Las Meninas* has an extremely complicated, highly unusual composition, making central use of a mirror (Plate 4). The artist is facing the viewer, and part of the back of his canvas is visible on the left side. A mirror in the middle shows the two principal persons—the King and Queen—surrounded by the Court, including the Infanta. But where are the King and Queen? They should be with their backs to us in the centre of the picture—but they are not there. So evidently their mirror image is imaginary. Although the mirror is huge for the time (and it is known that Velázquez owned a number of very expensive mirrors), its image is rather small to be fully dramatic.

Sir Michael Levey describes this most puzzling picture:[5]

The trick effect of a mirror at the end of a recessed room, reflecting spectators who stand where the actual spectators stand to see the picture, may even have been inspired by van Eyck's Arnolfini group, then in the Spanish Royal collection. But here the room is filled by

PLATE 1
REMBRANDT *Self Portrait* (1661–2)
Kenwood House, Iveagh Bequest / English Heritage

Evidently realizing he appeared left-handed, Rembrandt (1606–69) painted out and changed over his hands and arms. This is visible in an X-Ray of the painting. *See page 19*

PLATE 2
VAN EYCK *Marriage of Arnolfini* (1434)
National Gallery, London / Bridgeman Art Library

Perhaps the most famous painting featuring a mirror, by Jan van Eyck (1390–1441). *See page 20*

PLATE 3
CARAVAGGIO *Medusa* (1596–8)
Uffizi Galleries, Florence / Visual Art Library

Here the Italian painter Caravaggio
(1573–1610), noted for dramatic themes
and extreme perspective foreshortening,
gives a frightening image of the Gorgon
Medusa reflected in Perseus's mirror-
shield, which protected him from being
turned to stone. *See page 20*

PLATE 4
VELÁZQUEZ
Las Meninas (*c.*1650)
*Prado Museum, Madrid /
Visual Arts Library*

This most enigmatic mirror
picture, by Velázquez
(1599–1660), shows the
Spanish court and also the
painter; but how are they
reflected? *See pages 20–21*

PLATE 5
VELÁZQUEZ *The Rokeby Venus* (*c.*1648–51)

National Gallery, London / Visual Arts Library

Her reflection is necessarily painted too large: so here art triumphs over science. *See page 21*

PLATE 6
RUBENS *Toilet of Venus*

Private Collection / Bridgeman Art Library

The colour of the earring is different in the mirror. The Flemish artist and international statesman Peter Paul Rubens (1577–1640) painted over a thousand pictures, in very different styles. *See page 21*

PLATE 7
BURNE-JONES *The Baleful Head* **(1886–7)**

Staatsgalerie, Stuttgart/Bridgeman Art Library

The pre-Raphaelite artist Sir Edward Burne-Jones (1833–98) shows the Gorgon Medusa reflected in water in a surprisingly quiet garden scene. *See page 21*

PLATE 8
MANET *Bar at the Folies Bergères*

Courtauld Institute Galleries/Visual Arts Library

The pre-Impressionist French artist Édouard Manet (1832–83), influenced by Goya and Velázquez, portrayed lively scenes, here enhanced with a large mirror. *See page 21*

PLATE 9
DALI *Swans Reflecting Elephants* (1937)

Private Collection / Bridgeman Art Library
© DEMART PRO ARTE BV / DACS 1996

The Surrealist Spanish painter and sculptor,
Salvador Dali (1904–89) made good use of
scientific experiments and demonstrations of
visual phenomena, including illusions of several
kinds, and he painted some 3-D stereo pictures.
Here is a most ingenious ambiguity, reflected in
a lake. Try turning the picture upside down.
See page 23

PLATE 10
HOOGSTRATEN *View Down a Corridor*
(*c.*1662)

Dyrham Park / National Trust Photo Library / Derek Witty

Student of Rembrandt, Samuel van Hoogstraten
(1627–78) wrote on techniques of painting, and
was an expert in *trompe l'oeil* of which this is a
splendid example. Although at first sight looking
like a mirror, *trompe l'oeil* is perceptually very
different, having the paradox of depth on a flat
surface, and rotating bizarrely *with* the observer's
movements—oppositely to the real world, and to
images of a mirror. *See page 28*

PLATE 11 *The 'sky mirror' at Blagdon, designed by Lutyens*

By kind permission of Viscount Ridley. Photographed by John Robinson

This was Sir Edwin Lutyens's (1869–1944) appropriate name for this delightful formal lake, linking the sky to the trees and the house (which is in the North of England). *See page 46*

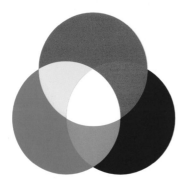

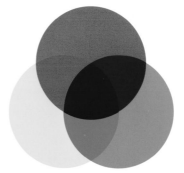

Adding lights   Subtracting lights

PLATE 12 *Adding coloured lights and colour printing by taking away from white*

Thomas Young produced (in 1801) all spectral colours and white by combining only three coloured lights, in various proportions. James Clerk Maxwell was the first (1861) to make 'memory-mirror' colour pictures, by combining photographs taken and projected through red, green and blue filters—surprisingly also giving non-spectral colours, such as brown. For colour printing, special filters are used to subtract colours from white. The filters are: *cyan* (blue-green); *magenta* (red-green) and *yellow* (stimulating red and green receptors of the eyes). The cyan subtracts red; the magenta subtracts green; the yellow subtracts blue. Subtraction of all colours gives black. *See page 138*

PLATE 13 *Reflection from a soap film*

Science Photo Library / © David Parker

These are diffraction colours, seen in thin films such as soap bubbles and oil floating on water. Why only for *thin* films? *See pages 138–9*

PLATE 14 *Galerie des glaces, Château de Versailles*

Visual Arts Library / Edimédia / J. C. Maillard

Built by Louis XIV (*r.*1643–1715). Astonishing for the mirror technology of the time, it remains extremely impressive to this day. *See page 156*

PLATE 15
***The Birth of Stars—revealed
by the mirror of the Hubble
Space Telescope***
*NASA / Photri USA / Barnaby's Picture
Library*

The distant Universe—distant in
space and time—is known only
by reflections from large
telescope mirrors—here from the
Hubble telescope in orbit around
the Earth. *See page 162*

PLATE 16
An original praxinoscope
From the author's collection

Invented by Emile Reynaud, in
Paris in 1877. The inner ring of
mirrors has half the radius of the
outer ring of slightly different
pictures, which remain flat-on to
the observer as the simple apparatus
rotates—showing the sequence of
pictures as moving. They are
brighter and the movement is
smoother than in the earlier slotted
drum of the zootrope, invented by
William George Horner in 1834,
in Bristol. *See page 185*

the maids around the Infanta Margarita Teresa and the painter himself at work, conceivably on a double portrait of the King and Queen whose reflections are seen in the mirror. Amid the complicated game of appearances and illusion there remains firm this group, not obviously posed for portraiture, but seized in a moment of action: a maid kneels before the Infanta, a boy caresses a dog with his foot; in the background a door opens and a man is seen framed by it in the light beyond. Not only is the paint applied expressionistically but the picture might seem at a casual glance an 'impression' of court life. Nothing is known of how it originated; it remains unique in Velázquez's work and was probably intended to be kept, like the royal treasures of ancient Egypt, from ordinary men's eyes.

Equally well known is Velázquez's only existing female nude, *The Rokeby Venus*, painted around 1647–1651.[6] Showing the back of a Goya-like reclining young woman, her face is seen in a looking-glass supported by a cherub. As the mirror is further away than her face, the image is with legitimate artistic licence at least twice the size it should be (Plate 5). This is a problem with using mirrors for painting or photography, as the image is disappointingly small when the glass is behind the subject.

The great Flemish artist Peter Paul Rubens (1577–1640) produced more than 1200 paintings, yet he was more than an artist—he was also a diplomat with exceptional tact and linguistic skills, and with outstanding international cultural accomplishments. He produced important work in London, for Buckingham Palace and the Banqueting Hall at Whitehall, and was knighted by Charles I. Although perhaps best known for his voluptuous female figures, in later life he excelled at landscapes. A mirror appears in his *Toilet of Venus* (Plate 6), where an earring is a different colour in its reflection.

By the nineteenth century mirrors had become more frequent. Holman Hunt's *Lady of Shallot* (known as the last Pre-Raphaelite painting) refers to Tennyson's poem (1850) of the same name (Figure 2.1). It reflects the beginning of women's emancipation. In Edmund Swinglehurst's words: 'Perhaps it was this that made Hunt choose to paint the moment when the Lady of Shalott, condemned to see life only as a reflection in a mirror, decides to rebel and looks out of the window at Sir Lancelot.'[7] Hunt worked for twenty years on this, his most celebrated painting. In *The Baleful Head* (Plate 7) Burne-Jones reveals the Gorgon Medusa, reflected in water in a surprisingly quiet garden scene.

The French impressionist Edgar Degas (1834–1917) was fascinated by women, especially dancers. As mirrors are very important for dancers they quite often feature in his pictures—which have so captured the popular imagination that they have lost the vitality of surprise. Mirrors also appealed to Manet (see Plate 8).

Extremely different are René Magritte's remarkable experiments with multiple representations of many kinds, including mirrors. We are so used to mirror reversals that when they don't occur it is disturbing, as in Magritte's non-reversing mirror in *La reproduction interdite* (Figure 2.2).

FIGURE 2.1 *William Holman Hunt, 'The Lady of Shalott' (1886–1905)*
By kind permission of Manchester City Art Galleries.

FIGURE 2.2 *René Magritte, 'La reproduction interdite' (1937)*
(or 'Not to be reproduced') By kind permission of Museum Boymans-van Beuningen, Rotterdam.
© ADAGP, Paris and DACS, London 1996

The Spanish surrealist Salvador Dali (1904–1989) projects his fascination with perceptual illusions in many paintings—including changes of appearance with rotation of the picture. For *Swans Reflecting Elephants* (Plate 9), try turning the book upside down: then elephants reflect swans. Dali's *Metamorphosis of Narcissus*

(Figure 2.3) shows Narcissus fascinated by his own reflection in a lake, with a decaying stone hand holding an egg from which a narcissus flower is growing.

There are pictures from classical times to the present day of women using mirrors for titivating face and hair. How do women artists respond to mirrors? In her painting *At the Psyché* (1891), the French impressionist painter Berthe Morisot (wife of Edouard Manet's brother, Eugène) paints herself reflected in a large mirror—including a right-left reversed portrait of herself by Manet, *Berthe Morisot Reclining* (Figure 2.4). 'Psyché' was the charming and evocative name for a mirror in a lady's private dressing room, or boudoir. Manet's portrait appears, quite small and left-right reversed, top left in the mirror. An analysis of Berthe Morisot's painting *At the Psyché* (Figure 2.5) is given by Anne Higgonet (1990):

This apparition of Manet's portrait of Morisot is uncanny indeed, in the same sense that Freud defined 'uncanny' in his essay of that name [see page 43] and Neil Hertz refined it in his essay on Freud and the uncanny in 'Freud and the Sandman'; the imagined resurgence of one's past as one's double. . .

At the Psyche initially appears to be an image of a nude model, seen twice, once as an ostensibly real figure and again as a mirror image. But the mirror image itself has a reflection, Manet's portrait.

The female nude—passive object of a masculine sexual gaze—seen in the mirror is juxtaposed with herself seen by Manet, but, thus juxtaposed, Morisot can bring neither into

FIGURE 2.3 *Salvador Dali, 'Metamorphosis of Narcissus' (1937)*
By kind permission of the Tate Gallery, London.
© DEMART PRO ARTE BV/DACS 1996

FIGURE 2.4 *Edouard Manet, 'Berthe Morisot Reclining' (1873)*
From a private collection; © Witt Library, Courtauld Institute.

focus. Both are visions of a female self seen with masculine eyes, and neither, in Morisot's vision, can be resolved. They are reminders of the contradiction between being the one who looks and being the one who is looked at, and remain as ghosts to haunt her paintings.

In sculpture, mirrors are very rare. A major exception is the bronzes of the English artist Michael Ayrton (1921–1975), who introduced large metal mirrors in a huge maze leading to figures from Greek mythology, and part-reflecting (neutral density perspex) mirrors between small figures mounted on turntables—especially *Captive* and *Contained Heads* and *Mirror Twins* (Figure 2.6). This, indeed, is to play reality against illusion; evoking in Alfred Friendly's words:[8]

a brooding search in which man's image both appears in a glass darkly and is reflected from it, sometimes from some angles completed, at other times left fractured, and at all times occupied by beings or forces that have intruded from the outside.

Michael Ayrton was a close friend of mine and a relative by marriage over the last ten years of his remarkably creative life. He died just as he was about to present a major television series to be called *A Question of Mirrors*. It is tragic that *A Question of Mirrors* died with Michael Ayrton.[9] No doubt I learnt a great deal from him. In any case, this book would have been very different and no doubt much better had he lived. I hope that at least it recalls his memory to his friends.

FIGURE 2.5 *Berthe Morisot, 'At the Psyché' (1891)*
From a private collection.

Reflecting Perspective

Any painting of a scene or objects is curiously paradoxical, for it shows three dimensions on the two dimensions of its visible surface. And apart from three-dimensional stereo pictures (which are very rare in art, though Dali tried it) there is only a one eye view—so perspective, and other 'monocular' cues to depth, are very important.

The view in a mirror has perfect perspective; but this is not a helpful statement, for perspective as defined and used by painters refers to how the *three*-dimensional world of objects can be represented on the *two* dimensions of a flat surface. True, the plane mirror is a *flat surface*, but this is entirely unlike a drawing or a painting, as the mirror's reflection is not constrained to the glass. Its perspective is exactly as for seeing a scene directly—so a mirror does not solve the artist's problem, though it can help in various ways.

A mirror is like a window, except that it presents a fully three-dimensional

FIGURE 2.6 *Michael Ayrton, 'Mirror Twins' (1973)*
A reflecting, reflective, sculpture. By kind permission of the estate of Michael Ayrton;
© G. F. Faiers.

visual world *in a wrong place*. This is so, also, for a painting; but in a painting the picture is also not in 'real time', and may be more or less imaginary. Only in stereoscopic pictures are features lifted above or sunk below the surface realistically; though the 'monocular' visual clues of shadows and so on can be remarkably effective, especially in a finely executed *trompe-l'oeil* painting (Plate 8). Mirror images change with movements of the viewer—rotating against the observer's motion, as for objects seen directly.[10] But this is not so for paintings, or other pictures including drawings or photographs. Interestingly, when depth is shown very realistically in a painting or other picture, the absence of the usual motion-parallax and object rotation, as the observer moves, can be highly disturbing. The picture seems to rotate (oppositely to the direction of normal motion-parallax), to follow the observer's every movement. This only occurs when depth is shown realistically in a picture.[11] Usually pictures are paradoxically in depth at the same time as their surface is seen as flat. This quasi-semi-depth is not quite compelling; but it is more comfortable than fully realistically represented depth in a picture. Occasionally though—especially for internal architecture, even for creating huge missing parts of churches, rooms of palaces, or complete statues—the artist goes all out to create the most real illusion possible. This tradition goes back to ancient Greek painting. But often, admiration is barbed with criticism, that 'this is not quite art'. Thus Lucas de Here said of van Eyck's work: 'They are mirrors, yes, mirrors, not paintings.'[12]

Such mirror-like perfection in painting is disturbing when one moves around it. For it appears to rotate to follow one, with one's every move. This is opposite to the motion parallax of objects seen directly, or in mirrors. In a painting we see objects depicted with unchanging view, though we move, which normally occurs only when objects (such as people) follow our movements. In normal paintings perceived depth is not sufficiently clear to make this effect dramatic; but in *trompe-l'oeil*, especially when the surface of the picture is not visible, a normal painting's paradoxical and rather unimpressive depth is replaced with a frozen mirror-like image which goes through weird transformations with motion. (This is so when the observer moves, rather than when the painting itself is rotated, though the change at the eye is the same.)

For the full effect, the painting itself needs to be seen, not a reproduction; but an example of *trompe-l'oeil* is shown in Plate 10. *Trompe-l'oeil* works best with rich shadow detail and accurate or exaggerated perspective. No doubt the changing distortions and reversed motion would be too disturbing for pictures in a gallery. So artists generally gain more by settling for less realism than it is possible to attain. Although an extremely important discovery, optically or geometrically correct perspective can be a mixed blessing for art, and very often is not used to full effect—or is even completely abandoned.

Using Mirrors for Painting

Geometrical perspective was first achieved with a mirror. The great Italian engineer-architect-inventor, Filippo Brunelleschi (1377–1446), invented the principle in Florence just before 1413.[13] This is not to say that earlier artists did not develop systems for representing objects in three dimensions: they certainly did, and with considerable success. But prior to Brunelleschi, the key concept, that objects shrink linearly at the eye with increasing distance, was not fully appreciated or applied. And before Leonardo it was not clear that a *plane* can intercept the *cone* of rays from objects to the eye, a perspective picture being just such a plane across the cone of sight (see Figure 2.8, below). Distances *along* the lines of sight are totally ambiguous, for distance or depth; so depth from perspective always depends on (unconscious) assumptions—which may not be correct. Though very useful, perspective is a great source of illusions in pictures.

Geometrical perspective was first used to show how the then unbuilt Cathedral of Florence would appear amid its surrounding buildings. Brunelleschi achieved this by piercing a peephole in a picture of the planned Cathedral, and viewing it reflected from a mirror, placing the picture in the existing buildings, to see how it would look (Figure 2.7). This was fifteenth century virtual reality— of a planned future, set in present context. With his mirror and a peephole in a picture, Brunelleschi could paint existing buildings and scenes in perspective, even though he did not know the rules for *creating* perspective. These rules followed later. According to Martin Kemp,[14] Brunelleschi's method was of little

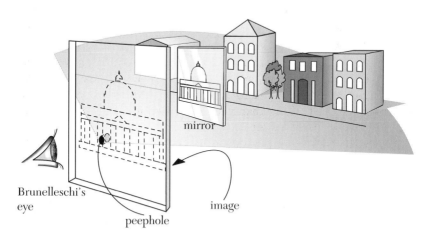

FIGURE 2.7 *Brunelleschi's virtual reality in perspective*
Looking through the peep-hole in the picture of the planned cathedral, into the mirror, the cathedral appeared surrounded by the existing Baptistery and Palazzo de' Signori—much as it would appear when built.

use to artists, who had to wait some time before they could use geometrical perspective in the portrayal of scenes from their imaginations.

Brunelleschi's use of a mirror is well described by John White in *The Birth and Rebirth of Pictorial Space* (1957) with quotations from Antonio Menetti's *Life of Brunelleschi*,[15] describing this very first (and now long lost) example of true perspective, *S. Giovanni and the Piazza del Duomo*:

And this matter of perspective, in the first thing in which he showed it, was a small panel about half a braccio[16] square, on which he made an exact picture (from the outside) of the church of Santo Giovanni de Firenze, and of that church he portrayed, as much as can be seen at a glance from the outside: and it seems in order to portray it as he placed himself inside the middle door of Santa Maria del Fiore, some three braccia, done with such care and delicacy, and with such accuracy in the colours of the white and black marbles, that there is not a miniaturist who could have done better; picturing before one's face that part of the piazza which the eye takes in, and so towards the side over against the Misericordia as far as the arch and corner of the Pecorori, and so of the side of the column of the miracle of Santo Zenobio as far as the Canto alla Paglia; as much of that place as is seen in the distance, and for as much of the sky as he had to show, that is where the walls in the picture vanish into the air, he put burnished silver, so the air and the natural skies might be reflected in it; and thus also the clouds, which are seen in that silver, are moved by the wind when it blows.

Manetti describes how it was arranged to be seen:

In which painting, because the painter needs to preserve a single place, whence his picture is to be seen, fixed in height and depth and in relation to the sides, as well as in distance, so that it is impossible to get distortions in looking at it, such as appears in the eye at any place which differs from that particular one, he had made a hole in the panel on which there was this painting, which came to be situated in the part of the church of San Giovanni, where the eye struck, directly opposite anyone who looked out from that place inside the central door of the Santa Maria del Fiore, where he would have been positioned, if he had portrayed it; which hole was as small as a lentil on the side of the painting, and on the back of it opened out pyramidally, like a woman's straw hat, to the size of a ducat or a little more. And he wished the eye to be placed at the back, where it was large, by whoever had it to see, with the one hand bringing it close to the eye, and with the other holding a mirror opposite, so that there the painting came to be reflected back; and the distance of the mirror in the other hand, came to about the length of a small braccio; up to that of a true braccio, from the place where he showed that he had been to paint it, as far as the church of Santo Giovanni, which on being seen, with the other circumstances already mentioned of the burnished silver and the piazza etc. and of the perforation, it seemed as if the real thing was seen: and I have had it in my hand, and I can give testimony.

Leonardo da Vinci (1452–1519) described perspective—and the use of mirrors and windows as optical aids—in his *Discourse on Painting*:

Perspective is a rational demonstration by which experience confirms that all things send their semblances to the eye by pyramidal lines. Bodies of equal size will make greater or lesser angles with their pyramids according to the distances between one and the other. By pyramidal lines I mean those which depart from the surface edges of bodies and travelling over a distance are drawn together towards a single point.

This is illustrated in Figure 2.8. Leonardo explains:

All things send their semblances to the eye by means of pyramids. The image of the original object will be smaller to the extent that the pyramid is intersected nearer the eye. Therefore you may cut the pyramid with an intersection that touches the base of the pyramid . . .

Leonardo compares pictures with images in a mirror:

When you wish to see whether your whole picture accords with what you have portrayed from nature take a mirror and reflect the actual object in it. Compare what is reflected with your painting and carefully consider whether both likenesses of the subject correspond, particularly in regard to the mirror. You should take the mirror as your master, that is a flat mirror, because on its surface things in many ways bear a resemblance to a painting. That it is to say, you see a picture which is painted on a flat surface showing things as if in relief: the mirror on a flat surface does the same. The picture has but one surface, the mirror the same. Your picture is intangible in as much as something which appears round and detached cannot be braced by the hands, and the mirror does the same. And if you recognise that the mirror by means of outlines and shades and lights makes things appear to stand out, you, who have among your colours stronger light and shade than those in the mirror, will certainly, if you know how to put them together well, make your picture, also, look like something from nature seen in a large mirror.

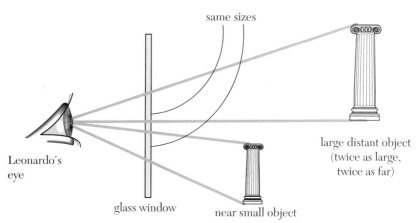

same sizes

large distant object
(twice as large,
twice as far)

Leonardo's
eye

glass window   near small object

FIGURE 2.8 *Leonardo's 'pyramidal lines' cut by a glass*
*This shows that a large distant object can present the same angle to the eye—and so give
the same retinal image—as a nearer smaller object. A perfect perspective picture is produced
by drawing on the glass. But this only works for existing objects.*

Leonardo also advises artists to look at their part-finished work in a mirror:

I say that when you are painting you ought to have by you a flat mirror in which you should often look at your work. The work will appear to you in reverse and will seem to be by the hand of another master and thereby you will better judge its faults.

Perspective is geometrical, but it is also *psychological*—for it depends upon visual *assumptions*. These are not conscious. As the assumptions are not at all fully checked, the eye is very easily fooled. Indeed, perspective in pictures would not work were not this so! Perspective in pictures works because we continue to follow normal-object assumptions into the abnormal world of depth portrayed on a flat surface. This is not unlike the psychological component of virtual images (page 78), though the perspective assumptions of shapes of objects are far richer than the simple (false) assumption that light rays continue through the mirror, to where the virtual image of reflected objects is (wrongly) seen.

False visual assumptions on which perspective depends produce the wonder of realistic painting. They can also produce dramatic and sometimes funny illusions. The earliest perspective-joke picture is William Hogarth's engraving of a fisherman (1754). This is an amalgam of conflicting visual clues to depth (Figure 2.9). Striking illusions, such as these, tell us a great deal about the art and science of perception and deception.

Illusions of Perspective

Striking visual effects are produced when three-dimensional objects themselves have markedly perspective shapes. This is the basis of the wonderful demonstrations of the American painter-psychologist, Adelbert Ames.[17] Most famous are the rotating *Trapezoid Window*, and the *Distorted Room*. The Ames Window, especially, cannot be adequately experienced in static pictures or described in words. But it is quite easy to make, and to experience at first hand, eyes-on (see Figures 2.10 and 2.11). The queerly-shaped room looks like a normal rectangular room, because features such as the windows of the further (right-hand) wall are expanded with increasing distance, keeping the retinal image the same as for a normal room.

The Ames Demonstrations were for many years ignored by visual psychologists. But they impressed visitors including Albert Einstein. Ames's friend Hadley Cantril complained to Einstein of: 'stimulus bound' psychologists who refused to look at the demonstrations. When Cantril showed him the Ames Window, Einstein smiled broadly, and said: 'I learned many years ago never to waste time trying to convince my colleagues.'[18]

Ames had predecessors, especially the founder of modern studies of perception, Hermann von Helmholtz (1821–1894). Helmholtz also saw that perception is not 'stimulus bound', but readily takes off on its own. Helmholtz fully appreciated the significance of perspective for depth perception, as indeed had Leonardo before him, and he described the basis of the Distorted Room almost a century before Ames—as he realised that any such 'distortions', giving the *same* retinal image as a *normal* rectangular room (or whatever), must look like a normal

FIGURE 2.9 *William Hogarth, 'The Fisherman' (1754)*
This plays with conflicting visual cues of perspective and occlusion to produce evocative paradoxes of perception. By kind permission of the Trustees of the British Museum.

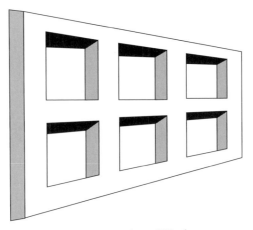

FIGURE 2.10 *Ames Window*
This has the perspective shape of a normal rectangular window, viewed from the side. So, when rotated (slowly) it does not go through the usual perspective transformations at the eye. The brain misinterprets what is going on, so it looks bizarre beyond belief.

rectangular room. This, indeed, is why a perspective painting of a room looks like a room. But it seems that Helmholtz did not actually make a Distorted Room, to try it out in practice. In Ames's term, he did not enter into *transactions* with it, and so did not discover its full potentials.

Helmholtz's description follows a discussion of how and why a normal familiar room appears rectangular in dim light, with no abrupt transition to full vision in brighter light. Helmholtz wrote (1866):[19]

But even when we look around a room of this sort flooded with sunshine, a little reflection shows us that under these conditions too large a part of our perceptual-image [perception] may be due to factors of memory and experience. The fact that we are accustomed to the perspective distortions of pictures of parallelepipeds and to the form of the shadows they cast has much to do with the estimation of the shape and dimensions of the room, as will be seen hereafter. Looking at the room with one eye shut, we think we see it just as distinctly and definitely as with both eyes.

He then says:

And yet we should get exactly the same view in case every point in the room were shifted arbitrarily to a different distance from the eye, provided they all remained on the same lines of sight.

This is a precise general description of the Distorted Room, written almost a century earlier than Ames. But as Helmholtz almost certainly did not make such a Room, he did not realise that familiar-sized objects in the Room introduced interesting conflicts. Could a child appear ten feet tall—or would the Room be written

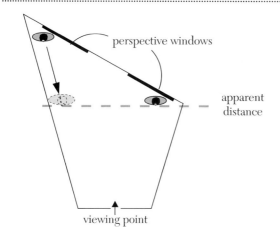

FIGURE 2.11 *Ames Room*

This is simplified—all the walls and the floor and ceiling should expand with distance. An interesting question: when familiar objects are placed inside, does the room now look distorted, or do the objects (such as people) look the wrong sizes? Generally, the room wins.

off as a cheat, to preserve the child? This is a high-level cognitive issue far removed from the retinal images of 'distorted' Rooms; but almost all of vision is far removed from optical images—and indeed from objects.

It is surprising, as Ames showed, that even familiar laws of physics may be violated. Thus in the Distorted Room, a ball rolling down a trough can appear to run up against gravity. This makes one question the power of knowledge, or cultural experience, to modify vision. But it is biologically important that we are able to see the unusual (even to see what is accepted as impossible) for unlikely events may occur, perhaps to be useful or dangerous. So, it could bring disaster to be blind to the unusual, or to what seems impossible.

In Film and Literature

It is tempting, here, to cite a range of references to mirrors in poetry, novels, horror stories, and films. Indeed, there are many examples, some of considerable interest; but regrettably this would take us too far from the central flow of our theme. So for films we must be content to remember the very funny mirror sequence in the Marx Brother's film *Duck Soup* (1933), the terrifying sequence in Jean Cocteau's *Orphée* (1950), the drama unfolding in 'The Haunted Mirror', one of five episodes of Michael Balcon's *Dead of Night* (1945), directed by Robert Hamer. To extend this to literature would again take us too far afield; but Oscar Wilde's long short story *The Picture of Dorian Gray* can not be ignored. Comparing an early picture of oneself frozen in time with each day's inevitably changing mirror-image is a trauma almost unknown before photography. Oscar Wilde simply but powerfully reversed this situation that now we all experience. Year after year, the young Dorian Gray remained beautiful and unblemished, in spite of a life of vice including driving a girl to suicide, and murdering Basil Hallward, the painter of his portrait. This is how Dorian first discovered the change in the picture:

In the dim arrested light that struggled through the cream-coloured silk blinds, the face appeared to him to be a little changed. The expression looked different. One would have said that there was a touch of cruelty in the mouth. It was certainly strange. . . . He winced, and taking up from the table an oval glass framed in ivory Cupids, one of Lord Henry's many presents to him, glanced hurriedly into its polished depths. No line like that warped his red lips. What did it mean? . . . Suddenly there flashed across his mind what he had said in Basil Hallward's studio the day that picture had been finished. Yes, he remembered it perfectly. He had uttered a mad wish that he himself might remain young, and the portrait grow old; that his own beauty might be untarnished, and the face on the canvas bear the brunt of his passions and his sins.

So, locked in an unused upper room, the portrait grew ever more ugly while Dorian kept his youth—until finally, he picked up the murder-knife that killed the painter, plunged it into the portrait, and:

There was loud cry heard, and a crash. The cry was so horrible in its agony that the frightened servants woke, and crept out of their rooms. . . . When they entered they found, hanging upon the wall, a splendid portrait of their master as they had last seen him, in all the wonder of his exquisite youth and beauty. Lying on the floor was a dead man, in evening dress, with a knife in his heart. He was withered, wrinkled, and loathsome of visage. It was not until they had examined the rings that they recognised who he was.

Let's end this chapter with conceptual mirror-images of our greatest poet. In Shakespeare's time, mirrors were still quite small and very expensive, though with improved clarity; so at last rich men and women could see themselves whenever they wished. Evidently this had profound effects on self-image, self-criticism, and self-identity. The looking-glass evoked introspective thoughts. Scrying glasses, for occult visions, were taken seriously. Mirrors were seen as symbols evoking ambiguities of life and death—captured and nurtured by the poets, especially John Donne and Shakespeare's genius.

Richard II (1597) is full of mirror associations and reflections of introspection. Much of the plot of the play is based on the collection of stories of Kings and Nobles, often coming to ignoble ends, assembled by William Baldwin between 1555 and 1587 and called *The Mirror for Magistrates*. When Richard is in prison, he comes to terms with himself through the mirror. According to Peter Ure, editor of the Arden edition:[20]

There is something deliberately unexplained, something therefore impulsive and compulsive, about his wish to have the mirror at this moment, and something intense and private in his act at looking at it. . . . The sending for the mirror is a movement towards asking the question 'What am I like now I have given everything away' but has behind it, perhaps, the question 'Am I anything at all?'. . . When the mirror lies to him he smashes it.

This is Richard's prison soliloquy:

> Give me that glass, and therein will I read.
> No deeper wrinkles yet? Hath sorrow struck
> So many blows upon this face of mine
> And made no deeper wounds? O flatt'ring glass,
> Like to my followers in prosperity,
> Thou dost beguile me! Was this face the face
> That every day under his household roof
> Did keep ten thousand men? Was this the face
> That like the sun did make beholders wink?
> Is this the face which faced so many follies,
> That was at last outfaced by Bolingbroke?
> A brittle glory shineth in this face—
> As brittle as the glory is the face.
>   (Dashes the glass upon the ground)
> For there it is, cracked in an hundred shivers.

> Mark, silent King, the moral of this sport,
> How soon my sorrow hath destroyed my face.

There are far too many Shakespeare mirror references for completeness here; but a small selection is suggestive and delightful:[21]

The Winter's Tale: *Act I, scene ii, lines 380–382*

KING POLIXENES: Good Camillo,
Your changed complexions are to me a mirror
Which shows me mine, changed too.

Comedy of Errors: *Act V, scene i, lines 420–421*

DROMIO OF EPHESUS (to his twin, Dromio of Syracuse):
Methinks you are my glass and not my brother
I see by you I am a sweet-faced youth.

Within only five lines, Shakespeare uses the three different words 'mirror', 'looking glass' and 'glass':

Richard II: *Act IV, scene i, lines 254–259*

RICHARD II: If my word be sterling yet in England
Let it command a mirror hither straight
That it may show me what a face I have
Since it is bankrupt of majesty.

BOLINGBROKE: Go some of you and fetch a looking-glass.

NORTHUMBERLAND: Read o'er this paper while the glass doth come.

Henry V: *Act V, scene ii, lines 146–149*

HENRY V: If thou canst love a fellow of this temper, Kate, ...
that never looks in his glass for love of anything
he sees there—

Henry VI, Part 2: *Act V, scene i, lines 139–140*

CLIFFORD: Why, what a brood of traitors have we here
YORK: Look in a glass and call thy image so.

Below, the Duchess of York is speaking of her dead husband and of her two sons who resemble him, and who are also dead—they are 'cracked in pieces'; the 'false glass' is Richard Duke of Gloucester, later Richard III. Here, as *Richard II*, Act IV, scene i, 254–259, there are three words for mirror—'images', 'mirrors' and 'glass'—in five lines.

Richard III: *Act II, scene ii, lines 49–54*

DUCHESS OF YORK: I have bewept a worthy husband's death
And lived with looking on his images;
But now two mirrors of his princely semblance
Are cracked in pieces by malignant death,

And I for comfort have but one false glass,
That grieves me when I see my shame in him.

Troilus and Cressida:	*Act III, scene iii, lines 47–49*
ULYSSES:	Pride hath no other glass
	To show itself but pride: for supple knees
	Feed arrogance and are the proud man's fees.

Julius Caesar:	*Act I, scene ii, lines 53–60*
CASSIUS:	Tell me, good Brutus, can you see your face?
BRUTUS:	No, Cassius, for the eye sees not itself
	But by reflection, by some other things.
CASSIUS:	'Tis just;
	And it is very much lamented, Brutus,
	That you have no such mirrors as will turn
	Your hidden worthiness into your eye,
	That you might see your shadow.

Hamlet:	*Act III, scene i, lines 153–157 (nunnery scene)*
OPHELIA:	Oh what a noble mind is here o'erthrown,
	. . . The glass of fashion and the mould of form,
	Th' observed of all observers, quite, quite down.

Hamlet:	*Act III, scene ii, lines 20–25*
HAMLET	The purpose of playing,
(to the actors, of acting):	Whose end,
	Both at the first and now,
	Was and is to hold,
	As 'twere the mirror up to nature:
	To show virtue her own feature,
	Scorn her own image
	And the very age and body of the time
	His form and pressure.

Hamlet:	*Act III, scene iv, lines 18 –20 (closet scene)*
HAMLET *(to Gertrude):*	You shall not budge.
	You go not till I set you up a glass
	Where you may see the inmost part of you.

In *Measure for Measure*, Angelo seems to be speaking of a scrying glass:

Measure for Measure:	*Act II, scene ii, lines 96 –101*
ANGELO:	(The law) like a prophet
	Looks in a glass that shows what future evils,
	Either raw, or by remissness new-conceived
	And so in progress to be hatched and born,

> Are now to have no sucessive degrees,
> But ere they live, to end.

Sonnet 3   Look in thy glass and tell the face thou viewest
> Now is the time that face should form another.

Sonnet 22   My glass shall not persuade me I am old,
> As long as youth and thou are of one date.

At the very least, these quotations show that rich implications of mirrors were seen by Shakespeare and, as always, his poetic powers open our eyes to timeless reflections.

Notes

1. Of the 549 paintings cited in Sir Michael Levey's *From Giotto to Cézanne: A Concise History of Painting* (1962) only two show mirrors: Jan van Eyck's *Marriage of Arnolfini (*or *Giovanni Arnolfini and Giovanna Cenami*), dated 1437 (Plate 2), and Diego Velázquez's *Las Meninas* painted in about 1650 (Plate 3). Herbert Read's *A Concise History of Modern Painting* has no mirror examples.
2. Hughe (1959) pages 70–71.
3. Mentioned by Galloway (1992).
4. See Coran (1992) page 131.
5. Levey (1962) page 190.
6. The subject was taboo in Spain during the Inquisition, so it is believed to have been painted for someone close to the King, probably its first owner, the Marqués del Carpio. Its name comes from having been in the Moritt Collection, at Rokeby Hall in Yorkshire.
7. Swingelhurst (1994).
8. Quoted by Hopkins (1994).
9. Produced by Karl Sabbagh for the BBC. This series was to follow Kenneth Clark's *Civilisation* and Jacob Bronowski's *The Ascent of Man*, all organised by Philip Daly. Ayrton was played by Hugh Burden. I am grateful to Karl Sabbagh for lending me the tape of a programme outlining what should have been in the series, which was undertaken shortly after Michael Ayrton's death.
10. When travelling on a train, it is interesting to look at various distances: the scenery appears to rotate around the 'point of fixation', counter to your movement. In a room every object rotates against your movements, and nearer objects shift against more distant objects (motion parallax), though this is not usually noticed.
11. For students of visual perception, this is a fascinating, important, under-researched bunch of dramatic phenomena. See Gregory (1970).
12. See Hughe (1959) page 68.
13. Filippo Brunelleschi (1377–1446) was born and died in Florence. He was goldsmith, sculptor, architect, engineer and inventor. His great dome (1420–1461), completing the Cathedral, has the greatest diameter of any in the world.
14. Kemp (1990) page 14.
15. The exact date does not seem to be known. It must have been a few decades after 1446, the year of Brunelleschi's death.
16. There is doubt here, as the Florentine braccio varied over time and according to what was

being measured. It must have been less than the 0.5836 metres adopted later for the metrical system. In the next passage, he refers to a 'true' and a smaller braccio.

17. They began to appear in 1938, at Hanover. They were later set up and investigated by Ames with several colleagues at the University of Princeton. See Ames (1951).

18. Cantril (1960).

19. Helmoholtz (1866); see also Helmholtz (1867).

20. Peter Ure (1956).

21. I am most grateful to Joanna, Lady Hilton, for finding and for writing out these quotations by hand. The comments are hers. Lady Hilton made use of Mrs Clarke's *Concordance to Shakespeare*, 1847 but for the convenience of modern readers I have used *The Oxford Shakespeare* (Wells and Taylor (1986)).

3

Histories and Mysteries

Man is a history-making creature
WYSTEN HUGH AUDEN

Imagination deserted by reason produces impossible monsters
FRANCISCO GOYA

THE history of mirrors is a rich amalgam of crafts and technologies, of ancient and modern science, and of the occult—for mirrors were used for peering into the future, and into souls of gods and men. It has not always been accepted that women have souls, but absence of reflections of women in mirrors does not seem to have been reported. No doubt this demonstrates the illogicality of men, at least where women are concerned.

The wonder of mirrors is reflected in their name, 'mirror' being closely related to 'miracle' in Latin: *miratorium* means 'mirror' and *miraculum* means 'object of wonder', exceeding the known powers of nature. The later 'speculum' is appropriately related to 'speculate'—for indeed we do speculate, and contemplate, on what mirrors reflect. The origin of 'window' is quite different, coming from the Scandinavian for 'wind + eye'.

As mirrors are so evocative and puzzling it is hardly surprising that they figure in myth and legend and poetry—and indeed in the mystique of science. Mirrors *look* magical! Very possibly it was reflections that inspired the first pictures inscribed on sand, then the superb paintings of life and magic in sacred caves, as early as thirty thousand years ago. It is a remarkable fact, of biology and of evolution, that of all species it is only humans who make pictures and have structured language. Representing in symbols is what makes us human; it is also the basis of myth and of science.

Both myth and science seek to understand and control supposed realities behind appearances. Control by magic is persuasion by words and by gestures—it assumes an intelligence behind nature—an intelligence which generally is roughly human in form, though intangible. In mirrors lie ghostly copies of our world, peopled with silent, sometimes transparent, yet life-like beings. Looking down into still water, one's head is a ghost in the sky, living with the gods. Perhaps reflections suggested mind as separate from body; for in a mirror, we see our bodies separate from our sensations, in a different place from where we know we are. So we are double, though our mirror-double is not quite alive.

No doubt horror stories reflect very ancient fears; and there is very often a moral side to them, which is hardly surprising as behaviour has always been controlled with threats of disaster and death, and of punishment of the soul after death. The myth-theory for absence of mirror-reflections for soulless beings, such as Dracula, is that an *image* cannot cast a shadow, or form an image of *itself*. If it is one's soul one sees in the mirror, isn't this perfectly logical? It is a fearful thought: one's own mirror reflection is un-dead.

There is a rich mythology, in folk tales and literature, of a personal *double*— more-or-less identical to oneself, more-or-less living. In modern times, this is a theme particularly of German literature and of psychoanalysis. Sigmund Freud discusses the double or *doppelgänger* in an interesting essay, *The Uncanny* (1919).[1] Freud starts by saying that *uncanny* means frightening—but a special kind of frightening. He points to the ambiguity of the German *Heimlich* which can mean uncanny or its opposite: 'friendly', 'intimate', 'familiar'. In English a *familiar* is synonymous with a *doppelgänger*: a double, both frightening and protecting.

Freud considers Jentsch's view, that the double is uncanny because of its uncertainty: 'whether an apparently animate being is really alive; or conversely, whether a lifeless object might not be in fact animate'. This refers to 'waxwork figures, ingeniously constructed dolls and automata'. Freud relates this to the half-living doll in Offenbach's opera *Tales of Hoffman*. But Freud looks to more than uncertainty or ambiguity. He sees this theme as secondary to the nightmare of the 'sand man', who blinded children by throwing sand in their eyes; and he sees the fear of losing their eyes as a symbol of castration-fear. But surely, this looks like an arbitrary anatomical priority of psychoanalysts. It could not possibly be a general theory as it could only apply to half of children. And why shouldn't there be simply a straightforward fear of losing one's eyes? This illustrates the power of symbols in dream and myth—and perhaps their power to mislead even great thinkers and scientists.

Freud refers to a paper by the psychoanalyst Otto Rank, *Der Doppelgänger* (1914), in his book *The Double* (1971), saying of Rank's work:[2]

He has gone into the connections which the 'double' has with reflections in mirrors, with shadows, with guardian spirits, with the belief in the soul and with the fear of death; but he also lets in a flood of light on the surprising evolution of the idea. For the 'double' was originally an insurance against the destruction of the ego, and 'energetic denial of the power of death', as Rank says; and probably the 'immortal soul' was the first 'double' of the body.

Otto Rank (1914), and also Ralph Tymms (1949), discuss doubles in literature from the psychoanalytical viewpoint, with examples such as Dostoyevsky's *The Brothers Karamasov* where the Devil appears to Karamasov as his double; also Oscar Wilde's *Picture of Dorian Gray* which separates the Self from conscience (see page 36). The double in literature often exposes moral lapses, or worse. References to mirrors and paintings are frequent in this connection. More obscure is Maupassant's *The Oval Mirror*. The obsessive artist paints his young and beautiful adoring wife, hour after hour for days on end, cloistered in a turret room. As the picture grows, in life-like colour, she fades. With the last brush stroke, she dies.

Reflections can be uncanny—their absence even more so—as in Maupassant's powerful story *The Horla*:

Behind me stands a tall wardrobe with a mirror, which daily assisted me in shaving and getting dressed and in which I looked at myself from head to toe every time I walked past it. I was pretending to write, to deceive him, for he was watching me also. And suddenly I felt—I knew very well what I was doing—that he was bending over my shoulder and reading, that he was there, and that he brushed against my ear. I stood up, stretched out my hands, and turned around so quickly that I almost fell. What now? One could see as well here as if the sun were shining, and *I did not see myself in the mirror.* The glass was empty, clear, deep, brightly lit, but my reflection was missing, though I was standing where it would be cast. I looked at the large, clear, mirrored surface from top to bottom, looked at it with horrified eye! I no longer dared to step forward; I dared make no movement; I felt that he was there but that again he would escape me, he whose opaque body prevented my reflecting myself. And—how terrible!—suddenly I saw myself in a mist in the centre of the mirror, through a sort of watery veil; and it seemed to me as if this water were slipping from left to right, very slowly, so that my image appeared more sharply outlined from second to second. . . . Finally I could recognise myself as fully as I do every day when glancing into the mirror. I had seen him; and even now I am still trembling with fright.

A mirror-experience where even the existence of the mirror is ambiguous ends Edgar Alan Poe's story, *William Wilson*. The rich and evil William Wilson recounts the events in the first person. He has a double of the same name, looking in every way identical, including his clothes; but the double's voice is limited to a whisper. The evil 'hero' is a wealthy dissolute, first at Eton and then at Oxford, where the double rushes into a gaming party at the moment the 'hero' has cheated a noble friend out of a great deal of money. The double flings open the door—the candles blow out—and all is plunged into darkness. Then he (or it) gives the game away in rather interesting detail:

'Gentlemen,' he said, in a low, distinct, and never-to-be-forgotten *whisper* which thrilled to the very marrow of my bones, 'Gentlemen, I make no apology for this behaviour, because in thus behaving, I am fulfilling a duty. You are, beyond doubt, uninformed of the true character of the person who has to-night won at *écarté* a large sum of money from Lord Glendinning. . . . Please to examine, at your leisure, the inner lining of the cuff of his left sleeve, and the several little packages which may be found in the somewhat capacious pockets of his embroidered morning wrapper.'. . . Can I—shall I describe my sensations? Must I say that I felt all the horrors of the damned! . . . In the lining of my sleeve were found all the court cards essential in *écarté*, and, in the pockets of my wrapper, a number of packs, facsimiles of those used at our sittings, with the single exception that mine were of a species called, technically, *arrondees*; the honours being slightly convex at the ends, the lower cards slightly convex at the sides. In this disposition, the dupe who cuts, as customary, at the length of the pack, will invariably find that he cuts his antagonist an honour; while the gambler, cutting at the breadth, will, as certainly, cut nothing for his victim which may count in the records of the game.

When the double appears—dressed identically—at a masked ball and approaches the young wife of an infirm husband, William Wilson challenges his double to a duel, plunging his sword into his moral-tormentor's heart. Someone tries the latch at the door. Wilson looks away for moment:

A large mirror—so at first it seemed to me in my confusion—now stood where none had been perceptible before; and as I stepped up to it in extremity of terror, mine own image, but with the features all pale and dabbled in blood, advanced to meet me with a feeble and tottering gait. Thus it appeared, I say, but was not. It was my antagonist—it was Wilson who then stood before me in the agonies of his dissolution. His mask and cloak lay where he had thrown them upon the floor. Not a thread in all his raiment—not a line in all the marked and singular lineaments of his face—which was not, even in the most absolute identity, *mine own*! It was Wilson; but he spoke no longer in a whisper, and I could have fancied that I myself was speaking while he said: '*You have conquered, and I yield. Yet henceforward art thou also dead—dead to the world, to Heaven, and to Hope! In me didst thou exist; and in my death, see by this image, which is thine own, how utterly thou hast murdered thyself!*'

Surely it is plausible that supposed doubles and visible mirror images are uncanny simply because they are, ambiguously, not alive and not dead. Life or death must have been of central concern and puzzlement from the beginnings of human curiosity. It is this not-quite-alive-not-quite-dead status that makes Dracula uncannily frightening. For many people the scientific attempt of artificial intelligence, to put mind into machines, is disturbing in this kind of way. What could be more uncanny than seeing a transparent silent ghost of *one's own face* moving, smiling and frowning, as a mocking mask registering one's inner thoughts and feelings, though it is not alive. In early times, reflections were quite rare and were startling. We are so familiar with our mirror-double, we seldom stop to think that in our looking-glass we face the life-death ambiguity of the soul.

According to Frazer's classic of anthropology, *The Golden Bough*,[3] mirror myths start from concepts of the soul. These are the basis of the 'common sense' and religious account of mind as having a separate identity from the body. In 'primitive' thought the soul is generally seen as a manikin in every respect like its owner (except that it may, for example, be the size of the thumb). Frazer says:[4]

As the savage commonly explains the processes of inanimate nature by supposing that they are produced by living beings working in or behind phenomena, so he explains the phenomena of life itself. If an animal lives and moves, it can only be, he thinks, because there is a little animal inside which moves it: if a man lives and moves, it can only be because he has a little man or animal inside who moves him. The animal inside the animal, the man inside the man, is the soul.

Sleep is the temporary death, and death itself the permanent absence of the soul. Warriors would take their souls out of their bodies for safe keeping during periods of danger. In illness, the soul was apt to float away. It was most important to prevent this happening; so mirrors were very dangerous as they might capture the weakened soul. They were covered up until the patient recovered or passed away. Shadows and reflections were seen as part of the man—as his soul. So it was dangerous to look for a long time into a pool. It could be an omen of death, to dream of seeing one's reflection. This fear extended to portraits, and later to photographs, as pictures might steal the soul.

Mirror-image puzzles are found in still water. One's own image is as far beneath the surface as one is above it. Semi-immersed, one's limbs look bent—broken—as now we know, by refraction. And objects beneath are displaced; so they disagree with touch, and they appear nearer than normally. Then, winking one's *left* eye—it is the reflection's *right* eye that winks back. Yet looking up to the further side at the scene of what lies beyond, it looks upside-down and not sideways reversed. Did these observations puzzle our pre-historic ancestors? Now we may be more sceptical of mermaids and of monsters of the deep; yet Scotland's Loch Ness Monster is not far from public consciousness.

There is a beautiful 'sky mirror'—as its architect Edwin Lutyens called it—at the seat of the Ridley family, Blagdon, in the North of England (Plate 11). No doubt, the first mirrors were calm pools of water. But it is quite hard to see oneself in a pool, or a lake, for one must look directly down, which is quite uncomfortable even with a steep firm bank. Then, one sees oneself deep below the surface of the water, as though drowned. Mirror-pools have always been secret-sacred, watery alloys of reality and illusion. Stepping into the water-mirror of distorted monsters mixed with the sky, one stands upon the rocks and sand beneath and touches living things in its depths. As for any mirror, not *all* is illusion. This is why it is so hard to disentangle histories and mysteries. The slightest invisible wind ruffles and destroys this optical echo; but sacred lakes or pools were in sheltered groves protected from disturbance or disruption.

In the second verse of her poem 'Mirror', the American writer Sylvia Plath adds this view of the sacred lake itself:[5]

> I am silver and exact. I have no preconceptions.
> Whatever I see I swallow immediately
> Just as it is unmisted by love or dislike.
> I am not cruel, only truthful—

The eye of a little god, four-cornered.
Most of the time I meditate on the opposite wall.
It is pink, with speckles. I have looked at it so long
I think it is a part of my heart. But it flickers.
Faces and darkness separate us over and over.
Now I am a lake. A woman bends over me,
Searching my reaches for what she really is.
Then she turns to those liars, the candles or the moon.
I see her back, and reflect it faithfully.
She rewards me with tears and an agitation of hands.
I am important to her. She comes and goes.
Each morning it is her face that replaces the darkness.
In me she has drowned a young girl, and in me an old woman
Rises toward her day after day, like a terrible fish.

The Greek goddess for the sacred groves was Nemetona. Now cathedrals are forest groves realised in arching stone. The baptismal font is the sacred water-mirror. The word 'font' comes from the Latin *fons*—'fountain', or 'spring'. There are pagan references in fonts, such as at Ottrava in Sweden, with its carving of Thor. In the Middle Ages, it was a practice to steal holy water from Christian fonts, for sorcery. One can still see marks in the stone of old fonts where there had been locks for a protective lid: sometimes these survive in English churches. In 1236 Edmund, Archbishop of Canterbury, ordered that all fonts be locked (*Fontes baptismales seb sera clausi teneantur propter sortilegia*) to guard the water-mirror against evil magic.

Now let's take a look at mirrors in various cultures from pre-history.

Brief History through Times and Places

Egypt

Recorded Egyptian history goes back to 3100 BC. Mirrors appear throughout as useful, valuable and symbolically rich possessions. Before metal and then glass mirrors, the first portable mirrors were bowls filled with water. These were inconvenient, as it was necessary to look down to see oneself, so one never saw one's whole body, and clothes. The trouble, of course, was that water is horizontal. But in pre-dynastic Egypt, some water was occasionally turned on its side—to be vertical! A wetted slate was hung on a wall, as a pre-metal or glass looking-glass.

The Egyptians were expert at polishing copper, silver and gold, with carefully graded quartz sand. Copper and sometimes gold were used for mirrors; but silver is best for facial make-up, as silver gives the most neutral-coloured image. Make-up was invented in Egypt, originally as protection from the burning Sun, especially around the eyes. Eye-shadow started as necessity, before becoming adornment. So developed an extremely elaborate ritual with the 'see-face' mirror as the centre piece. (The longer name, incorporating *ankh*, the symbol of life, was *ankh-en-maa-her*, 'mirror for seeing the face', abbreviated to 'see-face'.)

The first known metal mirror is from an Egyptian grave of the First Dynasty (2920–2770 BC). Made of copper, it is pear-shaped, with a handle. Though found in Egypt, it has been suggested that this mirror was in origin Hittite, as its pear-shaped form is not found in later Egyptian mirrors but is seen in Hittite engravings and in later examples from this region.[6] Egyptian mirrors from the Fourth Dynasty (2575–2415 BC) and later were often slightly flattened copper disks, representing the rising or setting Sun as it appears on the horizon, distorted by atmospheric refraction. (The flattening is about one fifth, which is just about the vertical-to-horizontal ratio of typical Egyptian hand-mirrors.)

Mirrors were used to direct the light of the Sun into dark places such as tombs. The burnished discs were almost as bright as the Sun—like the god Ra, so it is not surprising that mirrors were sacred, and were buried with the dead. And a sarcophagus ('flesh-eating stone'[7]) had painted eyes so the dead could see.

Perhaps as the face is seen through the mirror, it was believed that a mirror placed under the head of the dead person in the tomb allowed the soul—the *Ka* or Double—to pass through the mirror, to visit the gods. For poorer tombs the precious metal mirror was replaced with a model of wood (a *hypocephalus* disc), which generally was decorated with texts of rebirth and pictures of the solar disc.

The handles of Egyptian mirrors were often papyrus plants; they were supposed to combat decline with age by referring to youth and to the symbol of the rising Sun and light—the Falcon god, Horus. Some mirror handles were in the form of human figures. When naked these figures represented female servants, perhaps servants of the disc of the mirror—of the Sun and the soul. (The *hem-club* stood for the 'servant', as servant of the god, demonstrating the divinity of the disc.) The mirror disc was especially sacred to Hathor, mother of the Sun god Ra, and goddess of love and beauty.

Almost all ancient Egyptian pictures are drawn in profile. There can be very odd combinations of various parts of the body as each is shown in its distinctive view, so the shoulders, breasts, knees and feet may together be anatomically impossible. Faces are virtually always simple profiles. But Hathor is a rare exception: she pops out from a sea of profile hieroglyphs as looking at one full-face (see Figure 3.1).

It seems to me likely (though following an amateurish perusal I have not seen this in the Egyptological literature) that the exceptional full-face of Hathor, her variant Qetesh,[8] and the dwarf god Bes who was associated with childbirth, were represented as *mirror images* of these intimate gods. So, perhaps we see their faces as in an ancient Egyptian mirror. The hieroglyph for 'face' is a *front facing* simple drawing of a face set above a single vertical line, which as for us is the Egyptian sign for 'one'.

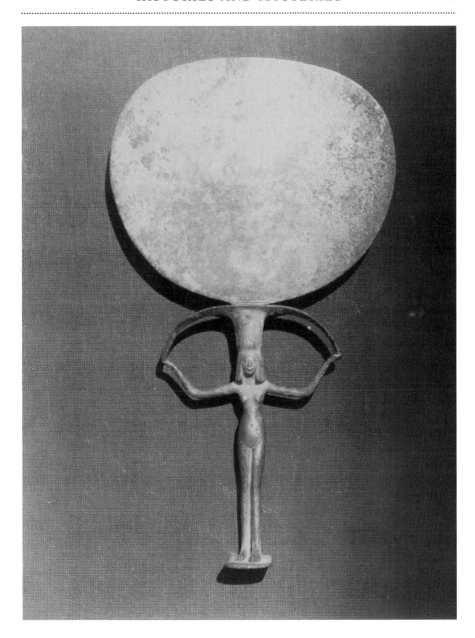

FIGURE 3.1 *Hathor, the goddess of love and beauty*

Hathor appears full-face on the front and back of the handle of this fine mirror, which belonged to a princess. Full-face pictures were only used for Hathor, her variant Qetesh, and the dwarf god Bes. By kind permission of the Werner Forman archive.

China

The Chinese combined superb metallurgy and craftsmanship with myth and magic. This reflects the origins of science universally, but in Chinese civilisation science never broke free from magic. The Chinese, however, understood the essentials of the optics of mirrors before the Greeks. A technical document from the fourth century BC—the *Mo Ching*—describes the optics of plane, convex, and concave mirrors. It says: 'Standing on a plane mirror and looking downwards, one finds that one's image is inverted.' And:

A plane mirror has only one image. Its shape, bearing, colour, white or black; distance, far or near; and position, slanting or upright—all depend on the position of the object or the source of light. If now two plane mirrors be placed at an angle there will be two images. If the two mirrors are closed, or opened (as if on a hinge), the two images will reflect each other. The reflected images are all on the opposite side (from where the eye is).

The properties of both concave and convex mirrors are described in such detail there must have been quite a sophisticated technology based on experiments. From very early times, the Chinese used concave mirrors as searchlights for illuminating distant places, with a lamp. Burning mirrors were used to make fires, and they were used to capture the light of the Moon. There were systematic experiments in China as early as the fourth century BC, entirely separate from Greece. From the great work of Joseph Needham, *Science and Civilization in China*, we learn that before Greek civilisation the Chinese had many advanced technologies, especially in bronze. They made astronomical as well as many other observations, and they had ingenious inventions including remarkable clocks. They made superb bronze mirrors—seen as symbols of the universe—from the Shang dynasty of about 1200 BC and continuing for twenty-one centuries. These mirrors were cast as slightly convex discs, with philosophical or religious symbols on the back. The roundness of the mirror represented the cosmic world of the sky; its brilliance, the intelligence of the universe. These 'cosmic' mirrors often represented space and time—the yang and the yin principles of harmony, given by a balance of light against darkness, warmth against cold, positive against negative, female against male.

The symbolism and the history of mirrors in China is described in considerable detail by Benjamin Goldberg (1985) in *The Mirror and Man*.[9] Here we learn that mirrors were a feature of temples and were presented as treasured gifts. Thus in 673 BC the emperor gave his queen a 'large girdle with a mirror in it.' Mirrors were especially important to men of high social standing who wore extremely elaborate head dresses needing frequent attention.[10] Ancient Chinese mirror inscriptions have been catalogued by Bernhard Karlgren (1934). They range through astronomical and astrological symbolisms, to moral and personal precepts. Some mirrors are symbols of marriage, and magpies are frequently present: they refer to an old legend of a mirror owned by a loving couple, which broke when they had to part. Each took half the mirror, as a promise of fidelity; but when the wife became unfaithful, her half of the mirror changed into a magpie, which flew to her husband and spilled the beans.[11]

It appears that the mirror as a symbol of fidelity derives from ancient philosophers who held that the mirror reveals the mask with which a person faces the world. So, contemplating a mirror leads to self-knowledge and so, hopefully, to self-control and faithfulness. Something of this is represented in a poem by Li Po.[12]

I

Bright, bright, the gilded mirror,
Absolutely perfect in front of me on the jade dressing stand.
Wiped, rubbed, splendid as the winter moon;
Its light and brilliance, how clear and round!
The rose-red face is older than it was yesterday,
The hair is whiter than it was last year.
The white-lead powder is neglected,
It is useless to look into the mirror. I am utterly miserable.

II

When my lord went away, he gave me this precious mirror coiled with dragons
That I might gaze at my golden-threaded dress of silken gauze.
Again and again I take my red sleeve and polish the bright moon.
Because I love to see its splendour lighting everything.
In its centre is my reflection, and the golden magpie which does not fly away.
I sit at my dressing-stand, and I am like the green fire-bird who, thinking of its
    mate, died alone.
My husband is parted from me as an arrow from the bow string.
I know the day he left; I do not know the year when he will return.
The cruel wind blows—truly the heart of the Unworthy One is cut to pieces.
My tears, like white jade chop-sticks fall in a
single piece before the water-chestnut mirror.

Chinese philosophers compared reflections of mirrors with mental contemplative reflections. Chuang Tzu (*c.* 350 BC) compared the mirror to calmness of mind; the philosopher's mind, like a mirror, is neither forward nor backward: it reflects anger, beauty and ugliness, yet is itself entirely neutral and unaffected by what it reflects.

The Manichean 'Religion of Light' was celebrated with mirrors. Its founder, Manichaeus (213–276 AD), proclaimed the new religion at the court of the Persian king Shahpur I; but Shahpur abandoned Manichaeus to his enemies, who crucified him. So Manichaeus, certainly, was not neutral or unaffected by events. The elaborate backs of Manichaen mirrors have grapes, 'fruits of light,' which were the only acceptable food for the pious; but despite the protection of these sacred symbols, the Chinese were full of fears, which in those troubled times were too often justified.

Mirrors were seen as possessing 'the vital essence of creation', and were venerated in temples. It was even believed that mirrors could show the internal organs of the body. The emperor Shih Huang-ti (*c.* 220 BC) had a mirror called *chau-ku-pau* ('the precious mirror that would illuminate the bones of the body') and there were other mirrors believed capable of 'X-ray' reflection, with powers to heal. Mirrors were used to discover evil spectres, in the form of grotesque animals (*sie*, or *mei*). They are described by Wang Tu (Sui dynasty) in *Record of His Antique Mirror*. Wang Tu received a mirror from the scholar Heu Shing, who declared: 'Wherever you bear it in your hands, hundreds of *sie* will run away from men.' Wang Tu tested its powers on a journey in 606 AD:[13]

At an inn the innkeeper complained to him of a slave girl of great beauty, whom a lodger had abandoned because she was strangely ill. Suspecting something odd about her abandonment, Wang Tu thought she might be a *mei*. When he fetched the mirror, she screamed pitiably, 'Do not kill me,' showing herself immediately in her spectral form. Wang Tu put away the mirror, and the girl prostrated herself before him, confessing that she was a vixen a thousand years old who lived in a large willow in front of the temple of a mountain god. Having committed a crime, and to avoid this god's punishment, she escaped, assumed a human form, and married. After travelling for years with her unsuspecting husband, she arrived in this inn where her illness drove her husband away. Now, discovered and deserving to die, she asked to do so in a state of drunkenness. Wang Tu called for wine and invited the whole neighbourhood to witness the event. In a short time the beauty was so intoxicated that she began to dance and sing ever more wildly and, after changing into a vixen, died.

This mirror has a long history. Shining in darkness, it went on to cure people of the plague, and it subdued the sea in a storm. This was indeed a powerful *magic mirror* (*theon-kouang-kien*: mirrors that let light pass through them). When Wang Tu was given the mirror, the scholar Heu Shing said: 'Whenever the sun shines on this mirror, the ink of these inscriptions [on its back] permeates the images which it reflects.' We now know what this means (see page 54).

What are called TLV mirrors link magic and science. Joseph Needham[14] presents the back of a splendid bronze mirror of the Hsin dynasty, showing cosmic symbolism, with a design made up of what look to us like the letters T, L and V (see Figure 3.2). The Ls mean the four points of the compass, Vs the four corners of the universe and the beginnings of the four seasons. The Ts may represent screens inside the gates leading to the emperor. Similar TVL designs are found on ancient Chinese sundials. They are also found on a game of divination, *lui-po*. Evidently for the Chinese, science and the occult are entwined. But it is *generally* true that science emerges from magic.[15] Practical successes of science and technology challenge, and may exorcise, magic. This myth-science alloy is seen in the poem inscribed on a Chinese bronze mirror:

FIGURE 3.2 *Chinese TLV mirror*

The Hsin have excellent copper mined at Tan-yang,
Refined and alloyed with silver and tin, it is pure and bright.
This imperial mirror from the Shang-fang [state workshops] is wholly flawless:
Dragon on the East and Tiger on the West ward off ill-luck;
Scarlet bird and Sombre warrior accord with Ying and Yang.
May descendants in ample line occupy the centre,
May your parents long be preserved, may you enjoy wealth and distinction,
May your longevity endure like metal and stone,
May your lot match that of nobles and kings.

(Tr. Yetts)

The famous and for a very long time mysterious magic mirrors, of China and Japan, have the remarkable property of projecting invisible designs onto a distant wall or screen. Right up to the end of the nineteenth century this was generally seen as light penetrating the metal. Thus, an eleventh century Chinese account reads:[16]

There exist certain 'light-penetration mirrors' (*thou kuang chien*), which have about twenty characters inscribed on them in an ancient style which cannot be interpreted. If such a mirror is exposed to the sunshine, although the characters are all on the back, they 'pass through' and are reflected on the wall of a house, where they can be read most distinctly.

Those who discuss the reason for this say that at the time the mirror was cast, the thinner part became cold first, while the (raised part of the) design on the back, being thicker, became cold later, so that the bronze formed (minute) wrinkles. Thus although the characters are on the back, the face has faint lines (*chi*) too faint to be seen with the naked eye. . . .

I have three of these inscribed 'light-penetration' mirrors in my own family, and I have seen others treasured in other families, which are closely similar and very ancient; all of them 'let the light through', but I do not understand why other mirrors, though extremely thin, do not 'let light through'. The ancients must indeed have had some special art.

In the fifth century AD, Wuchhiu Yen thought it due to invisible irregularities of the surface, given by the use of two kinds of bronze. In 1832, Sir David Brewster also thought it due to density differences. Finally, two British physicists, W. E. Ayrton and J. Perry (who introduced electricity into Japan), saw them being made and discovered the secret.[17] The back of the mirror has a deep engraving, which appears on the distant wall. The front was worked with a scraper. The thinner regions being more flexible, they were less affected by the scraper, and so become very slightly concave.[18] The minute changes of angle serve as 'light levers', bending the reflected light sufficiently to project the picture at a distance, though the irregularities are too small to be visible on the polished bronze surface (see Figure 3.3). Magic mirrors were sometimes made as a 'sandwich' so the engraving is hidden in the middle of the mirror. Modern versions can be obtained from China.

Japan

Early Japanese mirrors were influenced by Chinese designs. They came to represent the Shinto concept of awe, and gratitude to nature. Metal mirrors were made until the nineteenth century, when the previously isolated Japan opened its ports to the rest of the world. Then, as elsewhere, glass took over from metal for mirrors.

Japanese mirror-legends reflect the domination of the Shinto religion. Shinto lacks both ideology and official theology; its practices are aimed to evoke awe and gratitude. The tangible token of the presence of a god was the mirror of Amerasuomikami—the sun goddess. According to Benjamin Goldberg, its origin is in this legend:[20]

Once Amaterasu was so outraged by the adulterous behaviour of the God-ruler of the netherworld that she shut herself into the Rock Cave of heaven, thus putting earth in darkness. Greatly disturbed by this, the many gods of Japan on the plain of High Heaven came together to devise ways of luring the goddess from her hiding place. They lighted fires, danced and frolicked, recited liturgies, but to no avail. Finally they ordered two of the gods to make a mirror of metal taken from the sacred mountain. Then tantalizingly, they spoke

FIGURE 3.3 *A Chinese magic mirror*
A similar principle is easy to demonstrate with an ordinary mirror and a felt pen. When illuminated by a small source or the Sun, marks made on the mirror's surface are seen clearly on a distant screen. What is surprising about Chinese and later Japanese magic mirrors is that their surfaces appear free of irregularities, and yet these are sufficient to cast a distant ghostly pattern.[19]

before the cave: 'The august mirror in our hands is spotless and indescribably beautiful as though it was thine own august person. Pray open the cave door and behold it.' Whereupon Amaterasu said to herself: 'how is it that the Gods can enjoy such merry making even when the world is wrapt in darkness, since I concealed myself in the cave?' And so saying she slightly opened the cave door to peep out. At that moment the mirror was pushed through the opening, and when the goddess paused, seeing her brilliant reflection in it, a muscular God took hold of her and led her out of the cave to light up the earth again.

The goddess Amaterasu decreed to her descendants that the mirror should be regarded 'exactly as if it were our August Spirit; reverence it as if reverencing us and rule the country with a pure lustre such as radiates from its surface.' This legend was passed down orally until writing was introduced in the sixth century. The mirror is preserved at Isle in Japan as a most sacred relic.

Greece

The mirror, or *speculum*, of the Greeks was a thin metal disc, usually of bronze with specially added tin. It was slightly convex, polished on one side, and with the other side left plain or with an incised design. Pliny the Elder mentions mirrors in his *Historiae Naturalis*, which lists inventions and discusses fine art.[21] Glass mirrors of this time—coated with tin and sometimes with silver—were found in Pompeii.

Early Greek mirrors seemingly were derived from Egyptian designs. The handle is usually in the form of a statuette, especially of Aphrodite, supported on a pedestal. Another kind of Greek mirror was two discs fastened with a hinge. Called 'box mirrors', one disk was a cover, often ornamented in low relief. The best date from around 400 BC. A good example of these shows 'Ganymede carried away by the eagle.' Another, found at Corinth, shows Eros with two girls and a nymph seated on a bench and playing a game with Pan. On the back of another mirror (in the British Museum) is a figure of Eros, which has been silvered over, with a bronze case on the back of which is a group of Aphrodite and Eros in repoussé. An example of a Greek mirror is shown in Figure 3.4.

FIGURE 3.4 *A Greek mirror*
From Roche (1957). By kind permission of the Musée du Louvre;
© Réunion des Musées Nationaux.

Mirrors figured in the prolonged and important initiation rites of the Dionysus mysteries, especially, perhaps, *obscura* mirrors which were so poor optically that they stimulated the imagination more than the eye.[22] Hence, looking through a glass darkly?

Pausanias describes a ceremony in Patrae of a mirror let down into a well by means of a string, until its rim grazed the surface of the water. After a while it was pulled up. When looked into, it showed the face of the sick person, alive or dead, for whom the ceremony took place.[23]

But the best known of all mirror-myths must be that of the Greek youth Narcissus, who became enamoured with his own reflection in a pool, and of Echo, the nymph he spurned. In his lighthearted account of myths and legends Thomas Bulfinch (1796–1867) tells us:[24]

But Echo had one failing; she was fond of talking and, whether in chat or argument, would have the last word. One day Juno was seeking her husband, who, she had reason to fear, was amusing himself with the nymphs. Echo by her talk contrived to detain the goddess till the nymphs made their escape. When Juno discovered it, she passed sentence upon Echo in these words: 'You shall forfeit the use of that tongue with which you have cheated me, except for that one purpose you are so fond of—*reply*. You shall have the last word, but no power to speak first.

Seeing Narcissus, separated from his friends while hunting, Echo was unable to address him; but when he called out 'Who's here?', she replied 'Here.' Narcissus looked around and, seeing no-one, called 'Come.' Echo answered 'Come.' As no-one came, Narcissus called again, 'Why do you shun me?' Echo asked the same question. When Narcissus said 'Let us join one another' she answered in the same words—and came out to fling her arms around his neck. But he started back, exclaiming: 'Hands off! I would rather die than you should have me!' 'Have me,' said she. But he rejected her, leaving the nymph Echo to die through grief.

These reflections of ear and eye echo to this day in Ovid's *Metamorphoses*:[25]

> Echo was still a body, not a voice,
> But talkative as now, and with the same
> Power of speaking, only to repeat,
> As best she could, the last of many words.
>
> . . .
>
> Now when she saw Narcissus wandering
> In the green byways, Echo's heart was fired;
> And stealthily she followed, and the more
> She followed him, the nearer flamed her love,
> As when a torch is lit and from the tip
> The leaping sulphur grasps the offered flame.
>
> . . .

He bolted, shouting 'Keep your arms from me!
Be off! I'll die before I yield to you'.
And all she answered was 'I yield to you'.
Shamed and rejected in the woods she hides
And has her dwelling in the lonely caves;
Yet still her love endures and grows on grief.

. . .

Only her voice and bones are left; at last
Only her voice, her bones are turned to stone.
So in the woods she hides and hills around,
For all to hear, alive, but just a sound.

. . .

There was a pool, limpid and silvery.

. . .

Here—for the chase and heat had wearied him—
The boy lay down, charmed by the quiet pool,
And, while he slaked his thirst, another thirst
Grew; as he drank he saw before his eyes
A form, a face, and loved with leaping heart
A hope unreal and thought the shape was real.
Spellbound he saw himself, and motionless
Lay like a marble statue staring down.

. . .

Not knowing what he sees, he adores the sight;
That false face fools and fuels his delight.
You simple boy, why strive in vain to catch
A fleeting image? What you see is nowhere;
And what you love—but turn away—you lose!
You see a phantom of a mirrored shape;
Nothing itself; with you it came and stays;
With you it too will go, if you can go!

. . .

A little water sunders us. He longs
For my embrace. Why, every time I reach
My lips towards the gleaming pool, he strains
His upturned face to mine. I surely could
Touch him, so light the thing that thwarts our love.

. . .

You smile, and when I weep, I've often seen
Your tears, and to my nod your nod replies,
And your sweet lips appear to move in speech,

Though to my ears your answer cannot reach.
O, I am he! Oh, now I know for sure
The image is my own; it's for myself
I burn with love; I fan the flames I feel.
What now? Woo or be wooed? Why woo at all?
My love's myself—my riches beggar me.
Would I might leave my body!
. . .

But as wax melts before a gentle fire,
Or morning frosts beneath the rising sun,
So, by love wasted, slowly he dissolves
By hidden fire consumed.
. . .

Nor longer lasts the body Echo loved.
But she, though angry still and unforgetting,
Grieved for the hapless boy, and when he moaned
'Alas', with answering sob she moaned 'alas',
And when he beat his hands upon his breast,
She gave again the same sad sounds of woe.
His latest words, gazing and gazing still,
He sighed 'alas! the boy I loved in vain!'
And these the place repeats, and then 'farewell',
And Echo said 'farewell'. On the green grass
He drooped his weary head, and those bright eyes
That loved their master's beauty closed in death.
Then still, received into the Underworld,
He gazed upon himself in Styx's pool.
His Naiad sisters wailed and sheared their locks
In mourning for their brother; the Dryads too
Wailed and sad Echo wailed in answering woe.
And then the brandished torches, bier and pyre
Were ready—but no body anywhere;
And in its stead they found a flower—behold,
White petals clustered round a cup of gold.

Poet John Milton (1608–1674) alludes to Narcissus, in *Comus*; and William
Cowper (1731–1800) does something to redress Echo's hurt:

On An Ugly Fellow

Beware, my friend, of crystal brook
Or fountain, lest that hideous hook,
    Thy nose, thou chance to see;
Narcissus' fate would then be thine,
And self-defeated thou would'st pine,
    As self-enamoured he.

Reflections and echoes were not only of poetic interest to the Greeks. Aristotle asks:

Why is it that a voice, which is air that has taken a certain form and is carried along, often loses its form by dissolution, but an echo, which is caused by such air striking something hard, does not become dissolved, but we hear it distinctly? Is it because in an echo refraction takes place and not dispersion? This being so, the whole continues to exist and there are two parts of it of similar form; for refraction takes place at the same angle. So the voice of the echo is similar to the original voice.

As pointed out by Carl Boyer, Aristotle's account of acoustics must have been inspired by optical phenomena; the 'dissolution' or 'dispersion' of the voice being a striking parallel to optical reflection from small irregular mirrors, in which form is not preserved.[26] Boyer thinks that the voice and its echo were accepted as analogous to the visual and reflected rays of mirrors, in which: 'the forms of things are reflected. And the echo angle is, surely, derived from the much more easily observed angle of light from a mirror.' This has taken us from myth to early science: but no doubt science has its origins in myth and poetry.

The Greeks had a magic-technology of mirrors. By looking in his mirror shield when he cut off her head, Perseus was protected from the power of Medusa to turn the beholder to stone (see Plate 3). His magic armoury also included the cap of invisibility, winged shoes, and a magic wallet in which he put the severed head. These he obtained by blackmailing the Graeae, the grey-headed sisters, and stealing the single eye and tooth that the three old women shared between them.[27] Clearly, the Greeks spurned the blandness of untarnished heroes.

Etruria

Etruscan mirrors of the fourth and third centuries BC (in what is now Tuscany) resemble Greek mirrors and often feature subjects from Greek mythology and legend—the Trojan War, the birth of Athena, Aphrodite and Adonis—but the lettering is generally Etruscan. Many have beautiful engraved scenes on the back—freely drawn vignettes of intimate life—such as shown in Figure 3.5.

The Roman Empire

Roman mirrors are austere, having simple decorative patterns, often of circles, but not scenes. Looking-glasses were generally small, though according to Seneca the Younger, some may have been large enough to show the whole figure, and it is known that some could be moved up and down.[28] There is an early description of such a mirror in Athens of the fourth century BC—a hairdresser's mirror that could be pushed up or down to suit adults or children.[29] The Romans made mirrors from cast glass, as well as from metals including Cornish tin.

FIGURE 3.5 *An Etruscan mirror.*
Reproduced with the permission of the Masters and Fellows of Corpus Christi
College and of the Fitzwilliam Museum, Cambridge; © Fitzwilliam Museum.

Mesoamerica

Tezcatlipoca, the 'Smoking Mirror', was one of the four creation-gods of
Mesoamerican religions, who set the cosmic ages in motion through battles. The
Smoking Mirror stood for the contradictory forces of youthful vitality and fero-

cious darkness. This god drew his uncanny powers from an obsidian mirror, which cast a magical spell over a Toltec king, Quetzalcoatl, resulting in the downfall of the kingdom and the reintroduction of ceremonial human sacrifice. This tradition greatly influenced the Aztecs, whose high priests were called Quetzalcoatl. They identified the Spanish invader Cortes (1485–1547) as the returning Toltec king who, they believed, would restore the jewelled wonders of Tollan. They were sadly wrong.

Europe

By definition, we know little of the Dark Ages. Towards the end of the Roman occupation of Britain and for the following five centuries there is almost no recorded British history. But there were the Picts. They were called 'Picts' by the Romans, meaning 'painted people'. They lived as various tribes in Scotland and further north in the Orkney Islands. Although their language is lost, the Picts left remarkable pictures of animals and monsters, and of technical and magical tools, on hundreds of wonderfully carved symbol stones. Frequently found is a carved hand-mirror (see Figure 3.6). An example is the stone from the Knowe of Burrian in Harry on the main Island of Orkney.[30] It shows a bird, a crescent, and a mirror. Another example is the Lindores stone at Abdie in north-east Fife; on one side is a triple disc, a crescent, and 'V-rod' symbols overlaid with an elaborate sundial; on the other a lone mirror. A large clear mirror also appears on a stone from Dunrobin, now in the Sutherland Dunrobin Castle Museum. Mirrors occur most frequently in the early symbol stones of the fourth to the ninth centuries. The interpretation of the symbols, including the role of the mirror, has largely been speculation; but they are grist to the mill of general questions of the origins of science and mathematics and how they arose from magic. And, of course, science and mathematics create their own magic.

Mirrors were virtually banned by the early Christian Church. This gradually changed during the Middle Ages when small hand mirrors were used by ladies. Carried on a belt, they were made of steel or silver, with cases of ivory sometimes with lavish carving. There was a guild of glass mirror-makers in Nuremberg in 1373; and convex 'bulls' eyes' were made in southern Germany from the sixteenth century. They were made by blowing globes of glass, into which a mixture of tin, antimony and resin or tar was passed through a pipe while the glass was still hot. When cool, the globe was cut into small convex mirrors and also lenses.

Throughout medieval Europe, mirrors were associated with witchcraft, soothsaying, and generally with 'black' magic. Mirrors captured souls and—with their usual ambiguity—they also frightened off evil spirits. Hence the large silvered spheres ('witches' balls'), hung in the window to prevent spirits of evil entering the room.

The breaking of a mirror, associated with ill-luck, is expressed by Tennyson

FIGURE 3.6 *A fine example of a Pictish symbol stone, showing a mirror*
From Jackson (1984); © Trustees of the Sutherland Estate, Dunrobin Castle.

in 'The Lady of Shalott' (pt. iii):

> She left the web, she left the loom,
> She made three paces through the room
> She saw the water lilly bloom,
> She saw the helmet and the plume,
> She look'd down to Camelot.
> Out flew the web and floated wide;
> The mirror cracked from side to side;
> 'The curse has come upon me,' cried
> The Lady of Shalott.

Byron adopts powerful mirror-imagery in *Childe Harold* (clxxiii):

> Thou glorious mirror, where the Almighty's form
> Glasses itself in tempests.

Mirrors were used in trials of witchcraft. Around the sixteenth century in England there was 'A thief-magic of village wizards, who employed mirrors and polished stones in which their clients might discern the features of those who had stolen their goods.'[31] Keith Thomas comments:

The verdicts of the witch-detectors . . . must be 'in line with general expectations' . . . . As when identifying thieves, the wizard would show the client a mirror or a piece of polished stone, and ask if he recognised the face he saw in it. Or he might ask the client for a list of suspects, and carry out a series of tests designed to isolate the guilty one, carefully watching for his customer's reaction as each name was pronounced. A contemporary preacher summarised the procedure: 'A man is taken lame; he suspecteth that he is bewitched; he sendeth to the cunning man; he demandeth whom they suspect, and then sheweth the image of the party in a glass.'

The gradual loss of confidence in witchcraft, and of magical practices for identifying criminals, are quite fully recorded. This is part of the gradual acceptance of what grew into scientific method, as set out formally by Francis Bacon in his *Novum Organum* of 1620.[32] The role of established religion, in separating truth from illusion, is complicated and no doubt controversial. Keith Thomas writes:[33]

By the thirteenth century it had become customary for the clergy to pronounce an annual excommunication of all sorcerers *in genere*, and parish priests were expected to use the confessional as a means of coercing their flock into abandoning their time-honoured recourse to magic. The various magical practices which were current in the sixteenth and seventeenth centuries had all been listed in such earlier mandates as that of Ralph Baldock, Bishop of London, who in 1311 ordered his archdeacon to proceed against those who practised sorcery for recovering lost goods and foretelling the future, and who conjured spirits or made use of stones or mirrors.

Thomas continues:

In the later Middle Ages preachers inveighed against the practice of magic by the laity, while the ecclesiastical courts regularly proceeded against wizards and those who had recourse to them.

He concludes:

The theory underlying such a prohibition was coherent enough. There was no objection to attempts to heal the sick or foretell the future by purely natural means. The Church never discouraged the use of medicine, for example, or the attempt to predict the weather on the basis of observable natural phenomena. But any claim to have achieved some effect greater than that which could be shown to have arisen from known natural causes was immediately suspect. If a healing power was claimed for charms or written words, or if the weather was foretold by reference to such unconnected data as the day of the week on which Christmas had fallen, then the matter needed to be closely scrutinized. The Church did not deny that supernatural action was possible, but it stressed that it could emanate from only two possible sources: God and the Devil.

Here we can only skim the surface of these issues, where deeper reflection is needed for exploring how what is accepted as real in one age or culture, is illusion in another. But we will look at the use of mirrors for necromancy—scrying—in more detail in the next part of this chapter.

Scrying

Throughout history, it would seem that in all cultures there have been professional and amateur scryers claiming to see reflected destinies, fears and expectations. *Crystallomancy* is staring into a mirror; *hydromancy* is staring into bowls of water. Wine or blood were also used for scrying, as well as animal entrails.

Rituals for looking from shiny surfaces to the future were practised from earliest recorded times: especially by the Chinese, by the Egyptians, and of course by the Greeks with their oracles. From before Greek history, oracles were situated in certain centres, especially Delphi. A woman known as Pythogenes was a particular focus of inspiration. She underwent something like an epileptic seizure, supposedly being under the control of the gods. Plato distinguished between the 'sane' forms of divination and the ecstatic or 'insane' form. As we learn from the extremely interesting Dialogue the *Phaedrus*, Plato had a surprising preference for the latter:[34]

... in reality the greatest of blessings come to us through madness, when it is a gift of the gods. For prophesies of Delphi and the priestesses of Dodona [a principle shrine of Zeus] when they have been mad have conferred many splendid benefits upon Greece both in private and public affairs, but few or none when they have been in their right minds; and if we should speak of the Sibyl and all the others who by prophetic inspiration have foretold many things to many persons and thereby made them fortunate afterwards, anyone can see that we should speak for a long time. And it is worth while to adduce also the fact that those men of old who invented names thought that madness was neither shameful nor disgraceful; otherwise they would not have connected the very word mania with the noblest of arts, that which foretells the future, by calling it the manic art.

Plato complains that recently people had 'tastelessly inserted a T in the word', making it 'mantic' for divination or prophesy. Plato continues:

The ancients, then testify that a proportion of prophesy (mantike) is superior to augury, both in name and in fact, in the same proportion madness, which comes from god, is superior to sanity, which is of human origin.

This leads to the Muses:

And a third kind of possession and madness comes from the Muses. This takes hold upon a gentle and pure soul, arouses it and inspires it to songs and other poetry, and thus by adorning countless deeds of the ancients educates later generations. But he who without the divine madness comes to the doors of the Muse, confident that he will be a good poet by art, meets not success, and the poetry of the sane man vanishes into nothingness before that of the inspired madman.

Scrying was a feature of all pre-Christian cultures.[35] Mirrors of special power were attributed to the magician Merlin, in the court of King Arthur. Spenser in *The Faerie Queene* tells the story of King Arthur's daughter Britomart seeing her lover in the mirror:

> Whatever thing was in the world contaynd,
> Betwixt the lowest earth and heavens hight,
> So that it to the looker appertayned
> Whatever foe had wrought or friend had fayned.

Most scrying mirrors were rare and special, some requiring lengthy magical rituals for their manufacture. John of Salisbury (*c.* 1115–1180), however, believed that everyday objects could be used: he described scrying as divining in 'objects which are polished and shining, like a kettle of good brass, cups and different kinds of mirrors'.[36] Scrying became a profession of specularii travelling through Europe, but it fell foul of the church. As Goldberg writes:

To further condemn scrying, the church associated it with witchcraft, a crime of the vilest sort and punished in the most fearful ways. One edict pronounced: 'if ever you have . . . given rewards to anyone to raise the devil in order to discover lost goods, you have sinned. If you have looked in a sword, or basin, or thumb[nail], or crystal (or cause a child to do so)—all that sort of thing is called witchcraft.

Somewhat less controversial was the astrologer's use of the mirror. Since astrology and mirrors were separately used for predicting the future, the combination appeared to be ideal for many soothsayers. The cabalists, whose art was based on numerology and astrology, used seven metal mirrors, each of which bore the name of one of the then-known planets. The mirror of the sun was made of gold, the solar metal. It could be consulted with advantage only on a Sunday. The mirror of the moon was made of silver and could be consulted only on a Monday, and so on for every day of the week: iron (Mars) on Tuesday, mercury on Wednesday, tin (Jupiter) on Thursday, copper (Venus) on Friday, and lead (Saturn) on Saturday. Copying from the cabalists, many astrologers made divining mirrors from an Alloy of the seven metals known as the electrum.

Golberg continues:

With the aid of such a mirror you undoubtedly became all-knowing , for it was said that you could see events of the past and present; see absent friends or enemies; and all doings of men, day and night. You could also see in it everything that has ever been written down, or said, and by whom; and you could see anything however secret it may have been.

Several princes of the church objected to scrying as theologically and, we would now say, medically evil, including Bishop Baldock, who set up an investigation in 1311. Nicole Oresme (1330?–1382), Bishop of Lisieux, objected to the practice of young boys being made to look for long periods at a shiny surface, as this could make them blind, as also noted by John of Salisbury. Oresme commented on the terrible changes that the scryer's face underwent during his conjurations and invocations. Often he seemed to lose all identity. He appeared to be so disturbed mentally that it is small wonder he experienced so many fantasies.[37] The church never conquered the scryers, and adapted and adopted their practices: one such was that children would report messages from the angels.[38]

The most famous scryer, John Dee (1527–1608), was an alchemist, mathematician, traveller, and collector of marvels. He earned the reputation of a sorcerer at Trinity College Cambridge, where he was among the first Fellows, because he owned a mechanical beetle. Though greatly favoured by Queen Elizabeth, he was imprisoned on suspicion of compassing Queen Mary's death by magic. Dr Dee's obsidian magic mirror was venerated for many years after his death and is now to be seen in the British Museum (Figure 3.7).

Mirror Phantasms—Explained?

There were some people early on who doubted the occult status of scrying. In the fourteenth century, the Arabian historian Ibn-Khahaldun wrote: 'Sight is the most noble of all the senses, and is therefore preferred by those practising divination; fixing their gaze on a [mirror] they regard it attentively until they see that which they declare. The persons are mistaken in thinking they behold objects and visions in the mirror; a kind of misty curtain intervenes between their eyes and the bright mirror and on this appears the phantasms of their imagination.'[39] Later, scrying was related to hypnotism: the curious and still not entirely understood hypnotic state, when the subject is susceptible to suggestion, was produced when the subject gazed on a shiny object. Critical experiments were undertaken late in the nineteenth century, by A. Goodrich-Freer for the Society for Psychical Research.[40] She concluded that after-images or suppressed memories are brought back from subconsciousness; that ideas or images are externalized; that (less critically) visions, possibly telepathic or clairvoyant, are acquired by supernormal means. These she left for others to investigate.

It is very well known that we see 'faces in the fire', 'the man in the moon', and a great variety of forms and more or less bizarre objects in inkblots (see Figure 3.8). Vision and the other senses *project* visual reality as *hypotheses* of what may be out there. Just as hypotheses in science are richer than the available data, so perceptions fill in gaps, and create what might or 'ought' to be there. So it is easy to see forms and objects in vague ambiguous shapes such as inkblots, or in minimalist paintings, allowing many possible perceptual hypotheses. There is no clear relation between strength of stimulus and clarity of such perceptions. This depends very much on the state of the observer. Thus dreams (especially hypnogogic dream images, when half-awake/half-asleep) can be abnormally vivid with

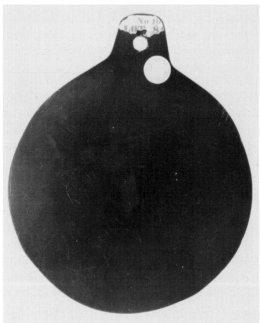

FIGURE 3.7 *Dr Dee's mirror*
By kind permission of the British Museum.

FIGURE 3.8 *Inkblot*

As one looks at the pattern, it may change into all manner of forms. This is because vision is highly active—always looking for what might be out there, sometimes generating wild fantasies.

supersaturated colours, though there is no external stimulus. Visual perception is an active process, making effective use of limited and not always strictly relevant information from the eyes and the other senses. Perception calls upon knowledge and assumptions which are not always appropriate or correct. Thus there are rich sources here of phantasms of vision.

Very striking visual effects of this kind occur when the eyes have incompatible images. This is associated with stereoscopic vision. Historically it is strange indeed that stereoscopic vision by the two eyes was not recognised until quite recently. Wheatstone discovered (1832, first published in 1838) that the brain combines the slightly different retinal images from their two views into a single perception. But this has its limits. When the angular difference between features in the eyes' images exceeds about one degree (Panum's limit), 'fusion' of the eyes' images fails. When this happens, we experience the curious unstable phenomena of 'retinal rivalry', which occurs when the brain is unable to combine the images of the eyes into a single stable perception. Ever-changing bits and pieces from regions in each eye combine and switch in and out, giving bizarre visual experiences—including, surely, much of the weird experience of the scryers.

Let's look at this in more detail. We seem to see from a single point in our heads, between the eyes. This is known as the 'Cyclopean eye'. In his important book *Foundations of Cyclopean Perception* (1971), Bela Julesz says:[41]

The mythical Cyclops looked out on the world through a single eye in the middle of his forehead. We too, in a sense, perceive the world with a single eye in the middle of the head. But our cyclopean eye sits not in the forehead, but rather some distance behind it in the areas of the brain that are devoted to visual perception. One can even specify a certain site in the visual system as being the location of the cyclopean eye.

Try looking at some near object, while noticing a more distant object, with one eye and then the other open. When 'fixating' the near object, the further object will shift from side to side each time the eyes are switched, alternately, open and shut. Now fixate the further object—and the *nearer* will move. When the distance in depth between the objects is too great, the brain will fail to achieve cyclopean vision.

Looking in a blemished mirror reveals *either* the pattern of blemishes on its surface, *or* the objects it is reflecting—only one or other of these is seen clearly, according to how the eyes are converged and accommodated (focused) for depth. With the mirror close to, either its blemishes or the reflected scene will appear double, according to where the eyes are directed. It was this double vision of reflections that suggested the concept of stereopsis to Sir Charles Wheatstone, and inspired his invention of the stereoscope (see page 166).

With prolonged viewing of a somewhat textured mirror—or the undulating surface of obsidian or a crystal ball (Figure 3.9)—there will be alternating mixtures of the textured surface and what it reflects, as various regions are rejected and combined into ever-changing patterns and new scenes. So failure of stereopsis when disparity is too great—together with the hypothesis-generating power of vision—might create all manner of monsters in mirrors. Or is this just another mythology? The reader can see for her- or himself.

Are the scryers' notions *entirely* different from science? In any case, their ideas are not dead. As perhaps most people today prefer the occult to science, why has science not altogether triumphed? It has to be admitted that science has too little to say about the dramas, hopes and fears of individual lives, or of what lies in the future. It simply does not address most people's concerns—so it leaves gaps to be filled by *non*-science, including *anti*-science.

The beliefs and hypotheses of the sciences are gap-filling. This is also a powerful principle in perception (see page 224). Indeed, this is very much what perceptions and scientific hypotheses do—bridge gaps in data, to predict unsensed properties of things, and predict at least the immediate future for survival. It seems that the mind abhors gaps: presumably because perceptual and conceptual gaps

FIGURE 3.9 *A crystal ball*
It presents conflicting realities of internal structures and reflections.

block action, which is dangerous. It takes unusual discipline to live by questions and admit ignorance, yet this is very necessary for science. Surely this is a major difference between science and myth. Science draws its strength from admitting and examining sometimes frightening gaps in perception and understanding. Myths do the same—but fill the gaps in very different ways. Mirroring reality remains difficult and controversial, greatly depending on how eye and brain are focused.

Notes

1. Freud (1919).
2. Rank (1914).
3. James Frazer (1854–1941) spent all of his life at Cambridge, collecting and interpreting myths from around the world. *The Golden Bough* (named after the ritual plucking of the Golden Bough of a tree in a sacred grove in Africa) grew from two volumes in 1890, to twelve in 1911–1915. Here I refer to the abridged edition of 1923.
4. Frazer (1923) page 178.
5. Plath (1985).
6. Goldberg (1985) page 27.
7. Bodies were naturally mummified in the dry sand, but the flesh disappears in damp stone

tombs. This contributed to Stone Worship, as it was thought that the body and soul enters and lives in the stone.

8. Budge (1904).

9. Goldberg (1985) pages 37–66.

10. There is a fine collection in the Museum of Far Eastern Antiquities of the Hallwyl Museum in Stockholm.

11. Goldberg (1985) page 47.

12. Li Po (1921, 1949).

13. Goldberg (1985) page 53.

14. Needham (1962) Vol. III page 305.

15. Sarton (1952), Thomas (1971).

16. From the *Hou Shan Tan Tshung* (*Collected discussions at Hou-Shan*) by Chen-Tao Shen Kua.

17. Ayrton and Perry (1878).

18. This is described by Bragg (1933) in his superb *The Universe of Light*.

19. Lewis Carroll would paint on the face of a convex mirror a simple shape in a solution of weak gum arabic. In normal daylight this would be invisible, but when the sun fell on it, it would project a strong shadow on the opposite wall (see Fisher (1973) page 75). This works surprisingly well.

20. Fisher (1973) pages 67–68.

21. Gaius Plinius Secundus, 23–79 AD, of Como, in North Italy. Pliny died while approaching the eruption of Vesuvius, succumbing to the noxious vapours rolling down the hill of the volcano before he reached the stricken city of Pompei, in which all life was lost, yet preserved by dust.

22. See Seaford (1984) and (1987).

23. The Greek geographer and historian Pausanias (2nd century AD) is trusted as an accurate historian and eye-witness of Greek customs and art.

24. This is quoted from *The Golden Age of Myth and Legend* (1993), which is a recent version of *The Age of Fable* by Thomas Bulfinch (1796–1867).

25. Quoted from Ovid (1987).

26. Boyer (1959) page 40.

27. Kirk (1970) page 181.

28. Annaeus (*c.* 5 BC– AD 65).

29. To protect it from moving too fast, it had a piston in an air-damping cylinder. This is the first account of a piston and cylinder. Apart from Hero's toy engine, which worked like a steam rocket, most of the essentials of a modern steam engine were known to the Greeks.

30. This is now in Tankerness House Museum at Kirkwall.

31. Thomas (1971) pages 117 and 549.

32. It might be argued that the use of scientific method has failed to come to full flower in legal procedures, perhaps because of lack of adequate time or available evidence—although Bacon was a lawyer!

33. Thomas (1971) page 255.

34. Plato's dialogue *Phaedrus*.

35. Here I am greatly indebted to Goldberg (1985), especially Chapter 1. Goldberg gives extensive references.

36. Besterman (1924).

37. Thorndyke (1923–1958); see also Goldberg (1985).
38. Welton (1884).
39. Bolton (1893); see also Goldberg (1985) page 15.
40. Goodrich-Freer (1889).
41. Julesz (1971).

4

<hr>

Puzzles of Images

<hr>

*Nothing puzzles me more than time and space; and yet
nothing troubles me less, as I never think about them*

CHARLES LAMB

T HE first puzzle is why it took so long for images of light to be discovered.
They were unknown to Greek philosophers, or artists, or to those we would
now call scientists. What is puzzling is the historical fact that it was not appreciated until a few hundred years ago that light paints pictures in eyes. As it is the light-
paintings of images in the eyes that give visual knowledge of objects, all early
writings on vision look very odd to us now. The Greeks generally thought of eyes
as working by light shooting out of them, to touch objects. This made vision
appear to give direct reliable knowledge—which was central to Greek and to
much of later philosophy, as it seemed to give a certain basis for secure beliefs.
Now we know that this is not so, for the eye's images are but tenuously related to
objects; they are inherently ambiguous, and they depend upon some active exploration to be read effectively for signifying objects.

Plato (*c.* 427–*c.* 347 BC) was not impressed by perception as the window to
truth. For he was concerned not so much with objects of sense, as with what he
took to be deeper, much more important realities of mathematics, and his heav-
enly 'ideal forms' of objects. Yet for Plato the eyes were created as a priority by
the gods:[1]

And the first organs they [the gods] fashioned were those that give us light, which they fastened there in the following way. They arranged that all fire which had not the property of
burning, but gave out a gentle light, should form the body of each day's light. The pure fire
within us that is akin to this they caused to flow through the eyes, making the whole eye-
ball, and particularly its central part, smooth and close-textured so that it would keep in
anything of a coarser nature, and filter through only this pure fire. So when there is daylight round the visual stream, it falls on its like and coalesces with it, forming a single uni-
form body in the line of sight, along which the stream from within strikes the external
object. Because the stream and daylight are similar, the whole so formed is homogeneous,

and the motions caused by the stream coming into contact with an object or an object coming into contact with the stream penetrate right through the body and produce in the soul the sensation which we call sight. But when the kindred fire disappears at nightfall, the visual stream is cut off; for what it encounters is unlike itself and so it is changed and quenched, finding nothing with which it can coalesce in the surrounding air which contains no fire. It ceases therefore to see and induces sleep. For then the eyelids, designed by the gods to protect the sight, are shut, they confine the activity of the fire within, and this smoothes and diffuses the internal motions, and produces a calm; when this calm is profound the resultant sleep has few dreams, but when rather more motion remains images, corresponding in quality and number to the type and location of the residual motions, are formed internally and remembered as external events when we wake.

Aristotle (384–322 BC) did think of light as most likely entering the eyes, and he described many visual phenomena with remarkable prescience. But he did not appreciate that light forms *images* within eyes.[2]

The simplest way of producing a real image is not with a lens or a curved mirror, but with a pinhole.[3] This depends on light travelling in straight lines, so that each point of the object projects a corresponding point to the image. This was demonstrated in the tenth century by the Arab mathematician and experimentalist Al Hazen (Ibn Al-Haytham, *c.* 965–1038). He described this and much more in his *Optics*.[4] Al Hazen's laboratory consisted of large white rooms with holes of various sizes and positions pierced in the walls. He found that light from a particular star, shining through one of the holes, would cast an image on the wall in the exact place where he would have to stand in order to see the star through the hole. So he realised that light travels in straight lines. A distant fire was seen as a moving fire on the wall, as each point projected a ray contributing to the image. This is the first account of 'real' images. Al Hazen had an essentially modern account of perception, almost as Helmholtz saw seeing, a thousand years later.

The pinhole image is very dim. The next trick was to replace the pinhole with a positive lens or a concave mirror (see Figure 4.1). The first description of a lens *camera obscura* is given by the sixteenth century Italian scientist-architect-showman, Giovanni Battista della Porta, in his fascinating compilation of science and old wives' tales and witchcraft—which was the knowledge of his time—*Natural Magic* (1558). He was fascinated by 'images hanging in the air'. Thus: 'In a tempestuous night the Image of anything may be represented hanging in the middle of the Chamber, that will terrify the beholders.' He recommends screening plays with children and animals which will be seen 'so plainly, that they cannot tell whether they be true or delusions: Swords drawn will glister in at the hole, that they will make people almost afraid.' In the chapter 'Of Strange Glasses' della Porta tells us a lot about how concave mirrors can be used. To find the principal focus, or as he says 'point of Inversion':

Do thus: hold your glass against the Sun, and where you see the beams unite, know that to be the point of inversion. If you cannot well perceive that, breathe a thick vapour from

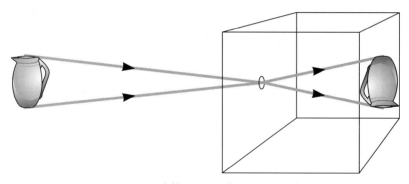

FIGURE 4.1 *della Porta's lens camera obscura*
This camera obscura was used extensively by artists in the eighteenth century, and later, for drawing in precise perspective.[6]

your mouth upon it, and you shall presently see where the coincidence is of the reflected beams; or set under it a vessel of boiling water. When you have found the point of inversion, if you will Set your head below that point, and you shall see a huge Face like a monstrous Baccus, and your finger as great as your arm; so women pull hair off their eyebrows, for they will shew as great as fingers. *Seneca* ['the Younger' *c.* 5 BC—*c.* 40 AD] reports that *Hostins* made such concave-glasses, that they might make things shew greater. He was a great provoker to lust: so ordering his Glasses, that when he was abused by Sodomy, he might see all the motions of the Sodomites behind him, and delighted himself with a false representation of his privy parts that shewed so great.[5]

della Porta gives a graphic description of looking into a large glass: 'you cannot but wonder; for if any man run at the Glass with a drawn sword, another man will seem to meet him, and to run him through his hand. If you shew a Candle, you will think a candle is pendulous in the Air'. He describes how with a concave mirror one can read by starlight; or, by using it as a burning glass, set an enemy's stores on fire, explode gunpowder or, very usefully, melt metals. Perhaps most interesting is focusing *cold*:

If a man put a Candle in a place, where the visible Object is to be set, the Candle will come to your very eyes, and will offend them with its light and heat. But this is more wonderful, that as heat, so cold, should be reflected: if you put snow in that place, if it came to the eye, because it is sensible, it will presently feel the cold.

Using the eye's sensitivity to cold is clever. It seems possible, though, that 'focusing cold' confirmed the false notion that heat is a fluid. What happens is: the surrounding warmth is *not* present at the focus of the snow, so it feels *relatively* cold. This is like the local absence of light of a dark region of an optical image. It looks dark by contrast to nearby brightness; so the snow feels cold by contrast to the surrounding heat.

A pinhole allows light to travel from each point of the object to a corresponding point of the wall—forming an upside down and sideways reversed image. Replacing the pinhole with a positive focusing lens gives a much brighter real image. It is important historically that della Porta realised that this is how the eye works:

The image is let in by the pupil, as by the hole of a window; and that part of the Sphere, that is set in the middle of the eye, stands instead of a crystal Table. I know ingenuous people will be much delighted by this.

He adds quite fairly: 'Others that undertook to teach this, have uttered nothing but toyes, and I think none before knew it.'[7]

This idea was taken up as the key to vision by the German astronomer-mathematician-physicist Johannes Kepler (1571–1630), who described the optics of the eye very accurately. He realised that 'mirror images' are not really images. He called real images on a screen, including retinal images in the eyes, 'pictures'. Those seen with plane mirrors he called 'images of things'. These are what we now call, respectively, *real* and *virtual* images. A looking-glass gives virtual images, as do convex mirrors. Concave mirrors may produce real images, as for convex lenses. How can we recognise whether an image is real or virtual? A simple test is whether the image can be projected on a screen. If you hold a sheet of paper in front of a plane (or a convex) mirror, the mirror does not give an image on the paper. So the image is *virtual*. On the other hand, when a slide projector or a camera lens casts an image on a screen, it gives a *real* image. The convex cornea and the lentil-shaped lens of the eye together cast a real image on the retina at the back of the eye—sending neural signals to the brain, from which we perceive objects. A virtual image is *nothing* until made real with a focusing convex lens or a concave mirror.

That we see objects *through* a mirror is due to our visual brain's inability to appreciate that light is bent by reflection. If our visual systems were brighter we would not see objects *through* mirrors—but where they are, in front. As it is, mirrors are paradoxical. For we *see* ourselves through a mirror though we *know* we are in front of it. This is a dramatic case of where seeing and knowing are separate. We appreciate intellectually that light is bent between object and eye, but this intellectual understanding is not available for vision. We do not automatically see what we know, or know what we see. It was clear to Newton that virtual images have a psychological component. He writes in *Opticks* (1704):

AXIOM VIII

An object seen by Reflexion or Refraction, appears in that place from whence the Rays after their last Reflexion or Refraction diverge in falling on the Spectator's Eye.

If the Object A [Figure 4.2] be seen by Reflexion of a Looking-glass *mn*, it shall appear, not in its proper place A, but behind the Glass at *a*, from whence any Rays AB, AC, AD, which flow from one and the same Point of the Object, do after their Reflexion made in the Points B, C, D, diverge in going from the Glass to E, F, G, where they are incident on the Spectator's Eyes.

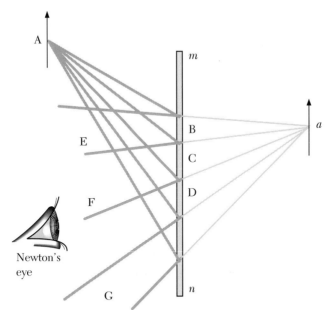

FIGURE 4.2 *Newton's diagram of a virtual mirror image,*
from **Opticks** *(1704)*

Newton gives the psychological component of what is going on:

For these Rays do make the same picture in the bottom of the Eyes as if they had come
from the Object really placed at *a* without the Interposition of the Looking-glass; and all
Vision is made according to the place and shape of that Picture.

This statement is an important *psychological* feature of vision, and of mirrors: that
our knowledge of the situation does not correct or compensate for the bending of
the light even when this is extremely obvious to the intellect. Sometimes knowledge does effect vision; in other situations it does not. This is a matter of *psychology*, not of optics. If our brains had been differently constructed (or programmed)
we might have been able to locate reflected objects where they are, when it is clear
that a mirror is involved. Some diving birds catching fish on the wing do correct
for the bending of light by refraction; but this is a simple situation with which we
can learn to cope.

Figure 4.3 extends Newton's diagram, to show why the virtual image is the
same way up as the object. Light rays are reflected from the mirror into the eye—
to form an image in the eye. Without the eye and its imaging power there is no
image from a mirror. (The dotted lines past the mirror to the object are not light
rays: they are visually assumed projections of the light rays, returned from the
mirror.) The object is seen *through* the mirror, *not* inverted. Since the *visual* brain

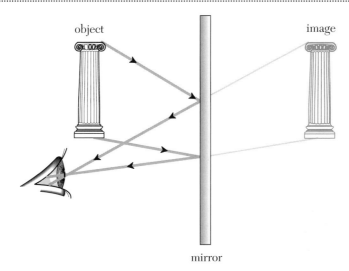

object

image

mirror

FIGURE 4.3 *The virtual image of a looking-glass*

does not know that light is reflected or otherwise bent, the object appears to lie along these projected lines—through the mirror. What lies optically behind a mirror? *Nothing*. So how—if there is nothing there without an eye—can a mirror's virtual image be reflected by a second mirror? This takes us to:

Multiple Reflections

Standing between a pair of parallel looking-glasses, one sees a repetition of images, which with perfect reflectance would continue for ever. Literally to infinity? One can see that this could not be quite so, for in practice mirrors are not perfect reflectors, and they are not perfectly flat. With each reflection the errors get magnified, so the (virtual) images gradually degenerate. This multiplication of errors is not entirely predictable—it is chaotic, related to fractal patterns.[8] Also, as light travels at finite velocity, one would have to wait an infinite time for an infinite number of reflections. So, as usual, infinity is beyond us.

The practical snag about standing between parallel mirrors is that one's head gets in the way. To avoid oneself, it is a simple matter to make a small hole (preferably two holes, one for each eye) in the backing of one of the mirrors. For an object placed between the mirrors, we see alternately its back—its front—its back—its front for thirty or more reflections. A coin is seen alternately head—tail—head—tail as it is seen alternately from mirror-positions in front and behind it. When the coin is tilted, the angle of tilt reverses each time in depth.

How can a second mirror reflect a merely *virtual* image from the first? What

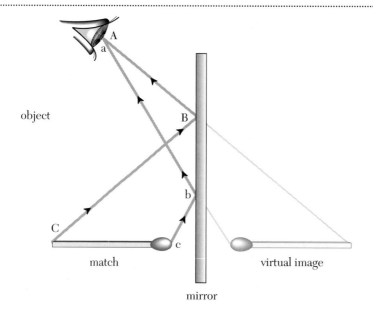

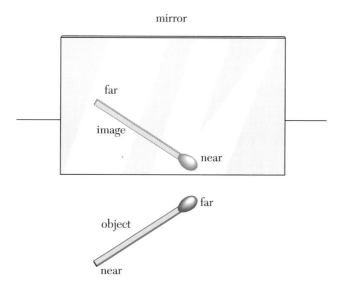

FIGURE 4.4 *Depth-reversal of a (virtual) mirror image*

In the upper part of the diagram, A, B, C, is longer than a, b, c—so the further away match-head appears nearer in the mirror. The lower part of the diagram shows how the match appears. The head appears nearer in the mirror even though it is further from the eye, as its optical path is shorter. (This is the only optical reversal of a mirror.)

causes the alternate depth reversals? That objects are depth-reversed in a single mirror is easily demonstrated with a match, as illustrated in Figure 4.4. The more *distant* match-head looks *nearer* in the mirror, because its optical path to the eye is shorter than from the tail end of the match. When a second mirror faces this image, the match is reversed again—so now its head faces the observer. This is because now the optical path from the head to the eye is shorter than the path from the match's tail. This is only puzzling if one thinks of the second mirror as reflecting the (non-existent) virtual image of the first mirror. It doesn't—it receives light from the object, via the first mirror, with no image involved (see Figure 4.5). For there is no image, apart from the real image in the eye. And as the optical path length from the head of the match to the eye is longer in the second reflection, the match looks further away. This depth-reversal—no-depth-reversal continues as a sequence for ever in a pair of ideal parallel facing mirrors.

Although the virtual image is not inverted vertically, it does (usually) appear right-left reversed. Why this happens may not be obvious. The reason is not to be seen in Newton's diagram (Figure 4.2), or in *any* ray diagram. Newton does not mention this mirror puzzle (which probably was no puzzle for him), which we

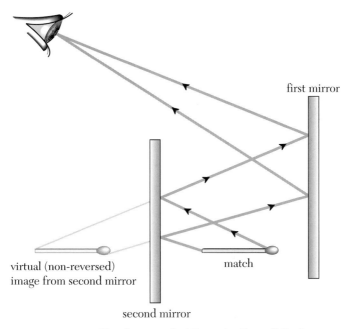

first mirror

virtual (non-reversed)
image from second mirror

match

second mirror

FIGURE 4.5 *Depth reversal with a pair of parallel mirrors*
The second mirror does not 'see' a virtual image from the first mirror. It receives light from the object via the first mirror. (The longer path length is now from the head of the match.)

will go on to discuss at length (pages 84–103). Meanwhile, we will look at some curious phenomena to be seen in pairs of mirrors hinged at various angles.

Hinged Mirrors

What happens when the two mirrors are not parallel? Here there are many possibilities for experiments with a pair of small looking-glasses or mirror tiles. They may be hinged at one side with sticky tape to open and shut like a book.

Set the mirrors at right angles—what do you see? When the 'spine' of the right-angle mirror 'book' is vertical you see yourself *non-reversed*—as others see you. Writing appears as though seen directly with no mirror. Right-angle mirrors can be used on a dressing table; but it is curiously confusing to shave or comb one's hair or make up one's face without the usual right-left reversal. One is so used to being confused by mirror reversal that one is confused by its absence!

If the right-angle mirrors are picked up, and rotated around the line of sight, the world and oneself swings around—in the same direction, at twice the rate of rotation of the mirrors. Figure 4.6 shows the reason for the reversal, with a ray diagram.

Very odd things happen when the mirrors are at certain angles less than a right-angle. When they are set to 60°, objects (including one's own face) appear as for a single mirror looking-glass—and amazingly when the 60° mirrors are rotated there is *no* image rotation. At 60° they are just like a single looking-glass.

What happens with other angles? This makes a nice experiment. Try looking into the mirrors hinged at 90°. Then reduce the angle, slowly, until your nose doubles—and then becomes a single nose. Now rotate the mirrors around the line of sight—turn them clockwise or anti-clockwise in front of you. Remarkably, you are *not* reversed, and your face remains upright as the mirrors are rotated. At 60°, as said above, the pair of mirrors acts like a single looking-glass.[9]

If you carry on reducing the angle, a series of outer images appear. And for the central image a sequence emerges. At the next critical angle (when you have a single nose again) the central image rotates twice as much as the mirrors—as for 90°. This sequence continues as the angle is decreased. Also as the angle is decreased, more and more faces appear either side of the central image of your face, and these are alternately reversed and not reversed, outward from the centre. They rotate—then don't rotate—through the series. So one can see opposite reversals and opposite rotations at the same time in the mirrors! Figure 4.7 shows what is happening as a ray diagram.

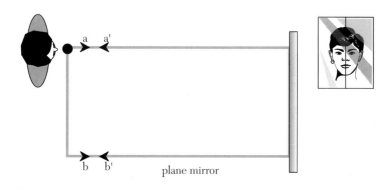

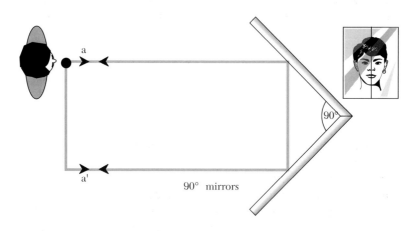

FIGURE 4.6 *Right-angle mirrors*

Looking into a pair of mirrors set at right angles one can see oneself as others see one—not right-left reversed. This is the case when the corner is vertical. When the mirrors are rotated around the line of sight, the image rotates in the same direction, at twice the rate.

How Much do you See?

Do you see more and more of yourself as you move away from a looking-glass? Can you ever see your whole body from head to toe? Most people will say 'yes.' But that is only true if the mirror is at least half your height. If the mirror is less than half your height, you will never be able to see all of yourself—however far

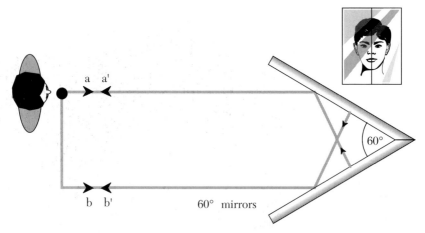

FIGURE 4.7 *60° 'book mirrors'*

At the critical angle of 60°, light from each point of the object meets the second mirror at right angles. This is the same for a single plane mirror. So—surprisingly—the image appears exactly as for a normal looking glass: reversed right-left and not rotating when the mirrors are rotated. (This is essentially different from 90° corner mirrors.)

away from the mirror you stand. This is well worth trying. Although it is commonly experienced in clothes shops, what is happening is not always realised. You do, however, see more of the *room* as you *approach* a looking-glass. But your head will always appear the same distance behind the mirror as you are in front of it; as optically, the mirror is always half-way between yourself and your image.

Here is a related experiment: with a crayon (or a lipstick) draw the outline of your head on the glass of a mirror. Then walk back. Does the image of your head shrink? No: it continues to fit the outline drawing on the glass. You will find that the drawing of your head is always half the size of your head.

Why are Looking-glass Images Right-Left Reversed?

This most famous mirror puzzle has confused bright people for centuries. So, why is everything in a looking-glass right-left reversed yet not reversed up-down? For example, why does *writing* appear as horizontally reversed though not upside down—as 'mirror writing'? The reader may find this simply obvious. Most people, however, go through their lives without ever considering it. Once considered, it can remain a puzzle for life.

How can a mere *mirror* distinguish right-left from up-down, even though many *people* don't know their right from their left? One's first thought is likely to be that *there is no problem*—because the top of the object is reflected from the top of the mirror, the bottom from bottom of the mirror, the left from the left and the right from the right. But this is just where the puzzle (if it is a puzzle for the reader) starts: the mirror is optically symmetrical—up-down and right-left—yet the reflected image is only reversed one way: right-left.

Handling Symmetries

In order to solve the puzzle of left-right reversal, it may be useful to look briefly at some notions of symmetry and asymmetry. If an object or a shape remains the same after it is *rotated*, or *shifted*, or *reflected*—it is symmetrical. It may be symmetrical on just one axis, or on many axes. A gear wheel looks just the same when it is rotated by one or a multiple of tooth-spacings. The more teeth, the larger the number of *axes of symmetry*. A repeated wallpaper design looks the same with each shifted repetition. So symmetry is defined by performing operations—by physical (or mental) *handling*.

Reflection is rotation through the third dimension. An extra dimension is always needed for reflection. As there are only three spatial dimensions, a four-dimensional object cannot be reflected in practice—though it can be reflected mathematically, as mathematicians can conjure up any number of conceptual dimensions.

The French physicist Pierre Curie (1856–1906)[10] suggested as a general principle that *asymmetry cannot arise from symmetry*. Curie's principle sets the puzzle of mirror reversal. For where does the asymmetry come from?

One might say that there are many apparent exceptions to Curie's principle—including some illusions. The 'Café Wall' visual illusion (Figure 4.8) seems to violate the principle, for its chess board-like patterns of squares (or rectangles) is symmetrical on the small scale, and yet produces long asymmetrical (illusory) wedges. The answer is: the visual distortion is generated by two processes; first, a series of small scale distortions, in which little wedges are produced across the 'mortar' lines where the 'tiles' have opposite contrast. Here there *is* local asymmetry in the figure, so there is no problem. The second stage is integration of these small illusion-distorted wedges into the long wedges.[11] Curie's principle is not violated, as there *are* small scale asymmetries in the pattern (which produce the small-scale illusory wedges), which then integrate to produce the long wedges, which seem to be impossible as at this scale the figure is symmetrical. It is often important to recognise that more than one process can be at work.

There is a very different way in which asymmetry can come from symmetry, which at first or even second sight seems to violate Curie's principle. This is well discussed by Ian Stewart and Martin Golubitsky in their interesting book *Fearful Symmetry*.[12] Consider a symmetrical bullet hitting a mirror and breaking it. The

FIGURE 4.8 *The Café Wall illusion*
The long horizontal wedges are visual distortions, for the 'mortar' lines are parallel. This distortion seems to violate Curie's principle that asymmetry cannot be generated from symmetry. The answer is: there are small-scale asymmetries, producing small wedge-shaped distortions—which add cumulatively to produce the long, clearly visible wedges.

broken pieces are not symmetrical. These asymmetries may be due to slight local variations in the strength of the glass. But what is more interesting is that if the glass were perfect, there could still be asymmetry. But if lots of mirrors are broken, on average there will be symmetry. So what Curie's principle is really saying is that it is not one instance that must always be symmetrical, but there must be symmetry in the long run from lots of instances.

Plane mirrors, however, seem to violate Curie's principle. We will look at this in more detail later. Meanwhile let's check with a simple experiment that a looking-glass does have symmetry—although the reversal seems asymmetrical.[13]

To make sure that a plane mirror is indeed optically symmetrical (up-down and right-left), we may rotate it around its centre. There is no change of the image: one's face remains upright, and right-left reversed. Words continue to be upright in 'mirror writing', like this:

words in a mirror *(right-left reversed)*

But they are not not-reversed:

words in a mirror

nor upside down only:

words in a mirror *(upside down)*

nor right-left reversed and upside down:

words in a mirror *(right-left reversed and upside down)*

Why should this be so? One's first thought is likely to be that the answer lies in a *ray diagram*. But this can't be—for a diagram can be held any way round. So it can not show what is vertical or horizontal. This is the same for a map. A map can't show where north (or west or east, or whatever) is without a compass bearing, because a map can be held any way round. This is just the same for an optical ray diagram: a ray diagram can not explain why a mirror reverses right-left but not up-down because it can be held any way up.

Now let's ask: do plane mirrors *always* switch right and left? Let's try a little experiment—with a match and its box. Hold a match horizontal and parallel to a vertical mirror. What happens? When the head of the match is to the right, its image is also to the right. It is *not* right-left reversed. Now take the match-box and view it in the mirror. Its writing is right-left reversed. So the match and its box behave differently! Why is the match *not* reversed though the match-box writing *is* reversed?

Here is a related puzzle: hold a mug with writing on it to a mirror. What do you see in the mirror? The reflection of the *handle* is unchanged—but the *writing* is right-left reversed. Can a mirror *read?!*

These questions are totally mysterious until one sees the point of 'mirror reversal.' Once one sees it, they are almost trivial.

The problem (if it is problem for the reader) is to see what *kind* of answer may be appropriate. There is a general lesson here. If one asks 'silly' questions, one generally gets back 'silly' answers. This has happened for many philosophers and also scientists reflecting on mirrors. It shows how important it is for science and philosophy to ask the right questions. But of course we can hardly know what are good questions until we know the answer. Isn't asking good questions the art of science?

It is entirely possible that the reader will simply see this answer, in which case he or she will be puzzled that there is general puzzlement. But the strange fact is that very few people can give a coherent explanation, and many books and papers by philosophers and scientists give conflicting answers. Let's look at some answers that have been suggested over the centuries.

Ancient Answers

Plato relates mirror-reversal to his theory that light shoots out of our eyes and enters them, to produce the turmoil of experience. Looking at a mirror, Plato says:[14]

And the principles governing reflections in mirrors and other smooth reflecting surfaces are not difficult to understand. All such appearances are necessary consequences of the combination of the internal and external fire, which forms a unity at the reflecting surface, though distorted in various ways, the fire of the face seen coalescing with that of the eye on the smooth reflecting surface. And the right-hand side appears as the left in the image because reverse parts of the visual stream are in contact with reverse parts of the object as compared with what happens in normal vision.

This is not altogether easy to understand, but Plato seems to think that light behaves very peculiarly in a mirror. Indeed it does, but not in this way.

Several centuries later the Roman poet-scientist-philosopher Lucretius (Titus Lucretius Carus, *c.* 99–55 BC), in his great poem *De Rerum Natura*, thinks of visual perceptions as given by coloured 'skins', or surface 'films', continuously given off by objects. This makes vision somewhat like the sense of smell, from air-borne particles. Lucretius considers mirror reversal:[15]

> And if in the mirror the right side of the body
> Appears on the left, it is because when the image
> Strikes on the mirror's surface it does not rebound
> Without having undergone change: what happens is this,
> It turns inside out, as would happen with a plaster mask
> If, before it was dry, someone slapped it against a pillar
> And it somehow preserved the lines of the features in front
> And was pressed backwards as it received the shock;

It would happen that the right eye became the left
And conversely what had been the left eye would be the right.
It can happen that an image is carried from mirror to mirror
So that there are five or six reflections of one object.
Things which are hiding behind a mirror, or in some
Tortuous recess, however out of the way,
Are all brought out by the repeated reflection;
It is the play of the mirror which brings them to light.
So the image is repeated from mirror to mirror,
What was left in the object becomes first the right
And at the next reflection is true left again.

Perhaps it is not entirely clear what is meant; but Lucretius seems to be saying that light flips over like a pancake when bouncing from a mirror.

Lucretius goes on to consider cylindrical mirrors:

There are concave mirrors which curve to our sides,
These send back the image of our right hand to the right;
That the image comes to us, or else because
On the way to us it makes a turn in the air
In response to the curvature of the mirror it came from.

This seems to be an extension of his optical explanation for plane mirrors, rather than a new principle. But as the cylindrical mirror is not symmetrical, it is extremely different from a plane mirror.

Lucretius comments (curiously for us now) on how mirror images move simultaneously with our movements. This was a problem for his notion of images as 'skins' of objects floating in the air. He sees them as turning over pancake-like when bouncing from a mirror—a process that one would think would take some time. But:

You would think that images step out and put their foot down
At the same time as we do, and imitate our movements.

Doesn't this show how hard it is to think of images? They are still puzzling for us today.

Modern Notions

The looking-glass is optically symmetrical up-down and right-left. But as we have seen, it is *not* symmetrical in-out, and it *does* optically reverse depth. Can this help to explain the right-left/up-down asymmetry? As depth is at right angles to both, how can it?

A mirror gives a virtual image which appears to lie behind the mirror—as far behind as the object is in front—so the scene is reversed in depth. The ray diagram tells us why this is so: the path length of light increases as an object (or part of an object) is further from the mirror. But as this optical reversal is at right angles both to up-down and to right-left, the *ray diagram can not explain the right-left/up-down asymmetry of a mirror image*. In spite of this, many distinguished scientists and philosophers have assumed that right-left mirror-reversal is also an optical effect.[16]

Newton's diagram for the virtual image of a mirror (Figure 4.2) shows that the image is the same way up as the object, and that there is no right-left cross-over of light. Unlike for the pinhole, and the positive lens producing a real image, there are no crossings of light rays with a looking-glass. So, for its virtual image, the top remains top; bottom remains bottom; right remains right; left remains left. Very differently for the real image of the pinhole or the positive lens, there is *both* up-down *and* right-left reversal. Neither for lenses nor mirrors should we expect reversal to be *only* horizontal or *only* vertical.

Intuition of Space Theories

The German philosopher Immanuel Kant (1724–1804) considers mirrors in a famous passage in the *Prolegomena to any Future Metaphysics* (1783). He is discussing the 'intuition' of space, by which he believed we know the world of objects from experience, and which sets limits, according to him, to what we can see and know. In trying to prove that space and time are not actual qualities, inherent in things in themselves, Kant uses the puzzle of mirror reversal as evidence for his doctrine of innate categories of space:

When . . . we have in vain attempted its solution and are free from prejudices at least for a few moments. . . we will suspect that the degradation of space and time to mere forms of our sensuous intuition may perhaps be well founded.

Kant continues:

If two things are equal in all respects . . . it must follow that the one can in all cases and under all circumstances replace the other, and this substitution would not occasion the least perceptible difference . . . .

What can be more similar in every respect and in every part more alike to my hand and to my ear than their images in a mirror? And yet I cannot put such a hand as is seen in the glass in the place of its original; for if this is a right hand, that in the glass is a left one, and the image or reflection of the right ear is a left one, which never can take the place of the other. There are in this case no internal differences which our understanding could determine by thinking alone. Yet the differences are internal as the senses teach, for, notwithstanding their complete equality and similarity, the left hand cannot be enclosed in the same bounds as the right one (they are not congruent, or *enantiomorphs*); the glove of one hand cannot be used for the other. What is the solution? These objects are not representations of things as they are in themselves and as some mere (or 'pure') understanding would know them, but sensuous intuitions, that is appearances whose possibility rests upon the relation of certain things unknown in themselves to something else, namely to our sensibility.

Kant goes on to suggest that this shows that: 'Space is the form of the external intuition of this sensibility, and the internal determination of every space is possible only by the determination of its external relation to the whole of space'. He concludes: 'The part is possible only through the whole'. So Kant sees a lot in the puzzle or 'paradox' of mirror reversal—surely far too much.

Possibly, though I doubt it, Kant is pointing out that *reflection* requires an *extra dimension*. Plane mirrors are two-dimensional; but for an object to be seen reflected it must be separate from the mirror. So an extra dimension from the plane of the mirror is needed. We will look at this later (page 103), but surely this is not what Kant had in mind.

Kant just might have been thinking of *conceptually* deciding which glove is right-handed and which left-handed.[17] This conceptual rotation takes a lot of time. He is talking about vision, which is much too fast for conceptual rotation (see page 96).

Confusion of Language

Is it a matter of confusions of *meanings* of the words 'right' and left'? These are indeed confusing, as William James says in his classic *Principles of Psychology* (1890):[18]

If we take a cube and label one side *top*, another *bottom*, a third *front*, and a fourth *back*, there remains no form of words by which we can describe to another person which of the remaining sides is *right* and which *left*. We can only point and say *here* is right and *there* is left, just as we should say *this* is red and *that* is blue.

Can language so affect visual perception? Such a claim is made by some anthropologists, especially B. L. Whorf, who for example claimed that Eskimos have more words and more visual distinctions than English speakers do for snow.[19] Roger Brown comments on the 'Whorfian hypothesis' in *Words and Things* (1958):

There is evidence to indicate that the speaker of English *can* classify snow as the Eskimo does. If we listen to the talk of small boys it is clear that they pay particular attention to at least two kinds of snow—the *good packing* and the *bad packing*. Whorf himself must have been able to see snow as the Eskimos do since his article describes and pictures the referents for the words.

There may be effects here—perception affecting language and language affecting perception—but these effects are small compared to the dramatic all-culture all-languages experience of mirror reversal. We can be verbally confused by ambiguities of right-left descriptions; but here we are considering systematic universal perceptual experiences which always occur, which is very different.

The British philosopher Jonathan Bennett (1970) holds that confusions of the language of 'right' and 'left' account for mirror-reversal:

Failure to grasp the conventions underlying our use of 'left' and 'right' has generated a mildly famous 'mirror problem': why does a mirror reverse left/right but not up/down? Martin Gardner [see below] presents the only clear account I know of the solution to this: the answer to 'Why does a mirror . . . etc.?' is *It doesn't!* Your image in the normal mirror is a visual representation of an incongruous counterpart of your body, and we conventionally describe this sort of relationship as 'left/right reversal.'

Jonathan Bennett continues:

But this convention does not pick out one dimension as privileged over the other two: it is merely a natural and convenient way of expressing the fact of enantiomorphism in a case where each member of the enantiomorphic pair has—like a human body—a superficial overall bilateral symmetry. (Of course an object which was perfectly and totally bilaterally symmetrical could not have an enantiomorph). If we are to describe what an ordinary mirror does, in a way which really does select one axis of the body in preference to the other two, then we must say this: if you face the mirror, it reverses you back and front; if you stand side-on to it, it reverses you left-right; if you stand on it, it reverses you up/down. These facts, once they are properly described, do not offer a problem. They are explained by routine optics.

So for Bennett it is all a matter of optics—*except* for the crucial asymmetry, which he explains (or explains away) as a convention of language. It is not surprising that linguistic philosophers look to language to clear up puzzles, for we all use the tools that are familiar to us and which we are expert in using. This applies as much to putting up shelves as to philosophy and science. But it is all too easy to use inappropriate tools, or to use tools inappropriately.

Linguistic explanations can take the form of persuading us that there is nothing to explain. In this case it might run: 'Well, it depends what you *mean* by "right" and "left" . . . I call this hand *my* right hand—but I would call it *your* left hand. . . .' So the phenomenon is supposed to disappear.

Mental Rotation Theories

It has been suggested that mirror reversal is a psychological phenomenon: perceptual or imaginative mental rotation. Perhaps the most famous experiment in the whole of experimental psychology is G. M. Stratton's wearing up-down and sideways reversing glasses, for days on end, to see whether his brain would adapt to the optical inversion.[20] The general finding is that after about a week the world starts to look more or less normal, interaction by touch with objects being very important for this perceptual rewriting of reality. Stratton says that at first:

The memory images brought over from normal vision still continue to be the standard and criterion of reality. Things were thus seen in one way and thought of in a far different way. This held true also for my body. For the parts of my body were felt to be where they would have appeared had the instrument [the inverting goggles] been removed; they were seen to be in another position. But the older tactual and visual localisation was still the real localisation.

On the *third* day (of a second experiment):

Walking through the narrow spaces between pieces of furniture required much less care than hitherto. I could watch my hands as they wrote, without hesitating . . . .

On the *fourth* day he found it easier to select the correct hand:

When I looked at my legs and arms, or even when I reinforced my effort of attention on the new visual representation, then what I saw seemed rather upright than inverted.

By the *fifth* day he could walk around the house with ease. When he was moving actively, things seemed almost normal, but when he gave them careful examination they tended to be inverted. Parts of his own body seemed in the wrong place, particularly his shoulders, which of course he could not see. But by the evening of the *seventh* day he enjoyed for the first time the beauty of the scene on his evening walk.

What happened when he removed the inverting goggles at the end of the experiment? He took them off on the *eighth* day and found that:

. . . the scene had a strange familiarity. The visual arrangement was immediately recognised as the old one of pre-experimental days; yet the reversal of everything from the order to which I had grown accustomed during the last week, gave the scene a surprising bewildering air which lasted for several hours. It was hardly the feeling, though, that things were upside down.

Stratton also used mirrors, mounted on a harness, to displace his body in space (see Figure 4.9). After wearing the mirrors for *three* days he reported:

I had the feeling that I was mentally outside my own body. It was, of course, but a passing impression, but it came several times and was vivid while it lasted . . . . But the moment critical interest arose, the simplicity of the state was gone, and my visible actions were accompanied by a kind of wraith of themselves in the older visual terms.

Stratton concluded:

The different sense-impressions, whatever may be the ultimate course of their extension, are organised into one harmonious spatial system. The harmony is found to consist in having our experiences meet our expectations . . . . The essential conditions of the harmony are merely those which are necessary to build up a reliable cross-reference between the two senses. This view, which was first based on the results with the inverting lenses, is now given wider interpretation, since it seems evident from the later experiment that a given tactual position may have its correlated visual place not only in any direction, but also at any distance in the visual field.

Further experiments were undertaken, at Innsbruck, by T. Erismann and I. Kohler, who got their subjects to live active lives while their world was reversed.[21] They found that things do not gradually return to normal, but flip suddenly, rather like reversing Necker cubes (see Figure 8.13). Perhaps adaptation is never

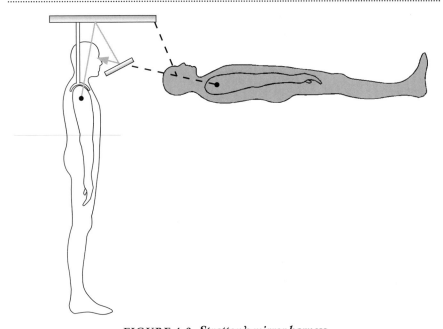

FIGURE 4.9 *Stratton's mirror harness*

Stratton went for country walks with this arrangement of mirrors which made him appear suspended in space.

entirely complete, and it may be limited to the situations that have been explored by touch. This was investigated by James Taylor and Seymour Pappert, in experiments on right-left reversal.[22] Pappert served as subject for experiments with left-right reversal, for half of each day, the rest of the day being normal, with carefully planned specific tasks. The results strongly suggest that adaptation is limited to specific sets (or subsystems) of behavioural skills:

It was soon realised that the adaptation of one subsystem does not guarantee adaptation to other subsystems, despite the fact that retinal stimulation is operative in all of them. . . .

Some of our training procedures were directly inspired by the example of the Innsbruck school. Riding a bicycle is one of the exercises regularly adopted there. Another extremely valuable procedure that we adopted was to draw a curved line in chalk on the floor and get the subject to walk along this line, always keeping it between his feet. This is a very difficult task, not only because the direction of curvature is reversed, but because the foot that is perceived as being the right foot is in reality the left. When the subject tries to move the foot that he perceives as being his right foot, he actually does move the right foot, but the foot that he sees moving appears to be his left foot. What he sees as his right foot remains stationary, and yet he feels his right foot to be in motion. The response is negatively reinforced, and this often has the effect that the subject is unable to move either foot for a time, as if he were rooted to the floor. [This is just what happens when drawing in a mirror (see page 248)].

This exercise illustrates very neatly the principle of the relative independence of the several subsystems all involving retinal stimuli but different motor [voluntary movement] variables.

It was found that learning many small tasks was much more efficient than attempting complex adaptations in one go.

The adaptation is very different from optically reversing a scene:

In the transitional stage of the experiment the subject reported some strange forms of perception, such as seeing two chairs, one on each side of the body, where only one existed. Many comparable experiences have been reported by other investigators. For example, in the [unforgettable] film, *Die Umkehrbrille und das aufrechte Sehen*, made by Erismann and Kohler, the subject was confronted with two faces, one erect and the other inverted; but when the owner of the erect face began to smoke a cigarette, the direction of the smoke was incompatible with the inversion, and it suddenly appeared to be erect. But again there was something odd about the perception. The subject explained it by saying that the face appeared to be both erect and inverted. The erect face appeared to have acquired a beard, as if the crown of the head had failed to jump with the rest and now occupied the space of the chin. To common sense this is completely impossible, but it is not at all impossible if we assume that the new engrams [brain memory traces], with the assistance of the direction of the smoke, were exactly equal in strength to the old ones that were in process of being inhibited.

The emphasis on interactive behaviour for learning to correct for reversal is important, as we will see when we journey through the looking-glass (see Chapter 9).

There is another kind of mental rotation: when you stand on your head, the world does *not* look upside-down. It is remarkable that things remain upright when you are upside-down. This is not well understood; but presumably it is activated by signals from the balance organs of the inner ear, the otoliths. There are rare cases of people who suddenly experience the world turning upside down.[23] Presumably this is due to some upset of the balance mechanism. In any case, this does not produce systematic right-left reversal. Although this is interesting, and needs study, we will not discuss it further here.

Rotation in Imagination Theories

Is it possible to rotate objects in the imagination? This has been investigated experimentally by R. Shepard and J. Metzler.[24] Their technique is to display a flat drawing of a simple three-dimensional shape and, near this, a second drawing showing the object rotated. But—the second drawing may not be of quite the same object. The task is to see whether the objects are the same or not. Pairs of drawings were used, such as those shown in Figure 4.10. It was found that this mental rotation takes several seconds. As the angle of rotation is increased the time required increases approximately linearly. It is faster for some objects, and for some axes of rotation, than others (see Figure 4.11).

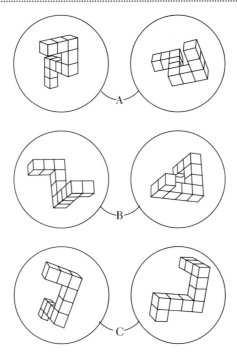

FIGURE 4.10 *Mental rotation shapes*

These shapes were used by Roger Shepard and Jacqueline Metzler (1971) to measure the speed of mental rotation through different angles. The question for the subjects was: is the second drawing, of the same object as the first, rotated; or of a different object? The mental rotation was found to be slow, taking several seconds—increasing roughly linearly with increasing angle. Reprinted from Cognitive Psychology *by kind permission of the MIT Press.*

There is evidence that it is easier to imagine rotation of a familiar object, such as one's hand, and harder to rotate mentally some unlikely or impossible object or manoeuvre.[25] This is also found by Roger Shepard and his colleagues. Shepard inclines to believe that mental rotation is given by brain *analogues* of the perceived or imagined object. Clearly, analogue brain models could not represent all object properties. A green object is certainly not represented by bits of brain turning green. An alternative account would be that the rotation is given by symbolic representations, somewhat like language. Shepard thinks that the linear increase in time required with more 'rotation' could hardly be explained this way; but might be related to the increasing number of eye movements (or internal mental 'eye movements') for comparing the two shapes; however, he prefers rotating brain analogues. At present there is no consensus.

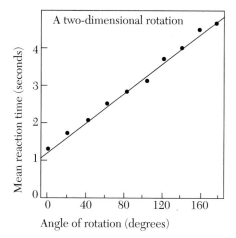

FIGURE 4.11 *Mental rotation data*

Getting subjects to rotate the first figure in their imaginations, to see whether it matches the second figure, Shepard and Metzler found that the process is slow even with a simple figure. The time required increases linearly with the angle of rotation. From Shepard and Metzler (1971) in Cognitive Psychology, *by kind permission of MIT Press.*

The Oxford philosopher D. F. Pears invokes a mental rotation in imagination for mirror reversal:[26]

Imagine that I look into a mirror and then produce a full-length portrait of myself accurately painted over the mirror image. Next suppose that I go round behind the mirror and face the back of it. Suppose also that the mirror is made of some flexible plastic material. Then I put the portrait of my face on my face like a mask, and the portrait of the rest of my body on the rest of my body like a complete suit of clothes. . . But suppose that instead of turning in the vertical axis I turned in the horizontal axis about which we pivot when we turn head over heels: suppose that I stood on my head behind the mirror. It is equally clear that if I got into my portrait in this way, left and right would not be reversed while top and bottom would be reversed. Of course if I got into the portrait in this way it wouldn't fit very well, since I would be putting the 'legs' on my head and vice versa. But this bad fit occurs merely because I am not symmetrical above and below the waist.

Evidently David Pears thinks that what happens to the mirror image depends on what we imagine. Since we can not change the reversal at will, this must be an inflexible unconscious power of mind. But do we really have this visual mental ability, this power of mind to rotate images immediately and completely, for mirrors? It is important to note that mirror-reversal occurs even when there is no clue that a mirror is involved. It is indeed this that makes mirrors so effective for conjuring. The mirror may be an entire wall, with no frame—nothing to trigger mental rotation. And conversely, a frame looking like a mirror does *not* produce reversal. Further, photographs taken in a mirror are mirror-reversed, though cameras are mindless.

Shepard and Meltzer find that mental rotation is slow—though in mirrors whole scenes, however complicated, are *immediately* seen reversed. And we do not have to concentrate: it just happens, whatever our attention; and happens too for a camera. This is very different from mental rotation in imagination. So it hardly seems a plausible candidate for mirror-reversal. Yet, together with verbal ambiguity of 'right' and 'left', it features in what is probably the best known account of mirror-reversal.

The Ambidextrous Universe (1964) is an interesting, very well-known book writ-ten by Martin Gardner, the inventor and presenter of hundreds of puzzles in the *Scientific American* and author of many valuable and delightful books including *The Annotated Alice*. *The Ambidextrous Universe* evokes three principles we have referred to above, but which we have rejected as not being relevant. These are: we *imagine* ourselves in the space behind the mirror and perform a mental rotation of imagination. Martin Gardner supposes that the vertical axis is chosen for this cognitive act; so we turn around on our heels, mentally to face ourselves in the mirror—because as our bodies are nearly right-left symmetrical, the right-left reversal is the easiest mental transformation. He also suggests that how we *speak* of right and left has a part to play. Lastly, he invokes optical *depth-reversal*, as rele-vant to *right-left* reversal.[27]

Curiously, the answer depends on the fact that our bodies, like the bodies of most animals, have only one plane of symmetry. It passes, of course, vertically through the centre of the body, dividing the body into mirror halves. . . . When we look into a mirror we see a dupli-cate of ourself, inside a room that duplicates the room in which we are standing. When we move our right hand, we see our twin move his left. We describe the reversal as a left-right one because it is the most convenient terminology for distinguishing a bilaterally symmet-rical figure from its enantiomorph. In a strict mathematical sense the mirror has not reversed left and right at all, it has reversed front and back! . . .

We can summarise it this way. A mirror, as you face it, shows absolutely no preference for left and right as against up and down. It *does* reverse the structure of a figure, point for point, along the axis perpendicular to the mirror. . . . Because we ourselves are bilaterally symmetrical, we find it convenient to call this a left-right reversal. It is just a manner of speaking, a convention of words.

Let's look at Martin Gardner's claim that our right-left body symmetry selects the vertical axis for mental rotation. Does not a one-armed man see himself as two-armed people do, right-left reversed? Of course he does. And what of, say, a room: why is a room or *any* scene right-left reversed, though it does not have any right-left symmetry? And why on this account should printing or writing (which are not at all left-right symmetrical) appear as mirror-writing? Presumably the notion is that a general cognitive strategy is set up early in life, or innately, from our body structure. Is this plausible? Why should it affect only *mirror* perception? For many reasons this account does not work.

The Answer to the Mirror Puzzle

We may summarise the various accounts of mirror-reversal that have been proposed—together with what are surely rather obvious objections—or 'buts'. These 'principal principles' that have been and still are invoked are true—but are they relevant for answering the question?

Principal Principles—with 'Buts'

- *There is no problem—because the mirror reflects top to top; bottom to bottom; left to left; right to right.*

  BUT: This is symmetrical—though the reversal is asymmetrical. (This violates Pierre Curie's principle that asymmetry cannot be generated from symmetry.)

  SO: There *is* something to explain.

- *Optical ray diagrams show why there is right-left / up-down asymmetry.*

  BUT: A diagram cannot show preference for right-left over up-down—because the *diagram* can always be rotated. It has no absolute orientation. (This is like a map: maps can only show where north is, or east or west or whatever, when they are correctly orientated from a compass. There is no such external reference for optical ray diagrams.)

  SO: This asymmetry cannot be explained by ray diagrams.

- *Plane mirrors produce optical reversal in depth—this produces right-left, though not up-down, reversal.*

  BUT: Indeed there *is* optical depth reversal—as the further from the mirror an object is, the longer the reflected light-path. But depth is related *symmetrically* to right and to left. (It is orthogonal, at right angles, to both the horizontal and the vertical axes of the mirror.)

  SO: Depth reversal cannot explain the asymmetry, or preference, for left-right over up-down reversal.

- *Our eyes are separated horizontally. This asymmetry produces the mirror asymmetry.*

  BUT: Shutting one eye makes no difference. A person blind from birth in one eye sees the usual reversal. Tilting the head (or placing the eyes vertically) makes no difference. And why should this apply *only* to mirrors?

  SO: That our eyes are horizontally separated is not relevant.

- *Ambiguity of the words 'right' and 'left' misleads vision.*

BUT: 'Right' and 'left' can indeed be ambiguous and so confusing; but how could this produce *systematic* visual reversal (violating Curie's Principle)?

SO: Although the words 'right' and 'left' are ambiguous, this cannot cause systematic visual reversal.

- *Mirror-reversal is mental image rotation.*

    BUT: Mental image rotation (as investigated in experimental psychology) is slow and imperfect even for simple objects. Mirror-reversal is immediate and precise, for the most complicated objects or scenes. And it occurs though there is no indication (such as a frame) that a mirror is present. Conversely, false information (a mirror-frame without a mirror) does *not* produce rotation.

    SO: Mirror-reversal is not mental image rotation.

- *Mirror-reversal is horizontal because our bodies are more symmetrical horizontally than vertically.*

    BUT: An object of *any shape* appears horizontally reversed, for example writing. And people who are asymmetrical (having one arm, for example) see the same as symmetrical people.

    SO: Our (roughly) horizontal body symmetry is not relevant.

Scientists seldom give up at the first 'but' that challenges a pet theory, though some philosophers think they should.[28] It is an open and very useful game to counter objections to theories, for often objections turn out to be misplaced; but certainly objections should at least make one pause to think. What is so surprising about the mirror puzzle is that this is just what people generally do not do.

Now let's list what seems both *true* and *relevant*:

- Writing on a *transparent* sheet (such as an overhead transparency) does not show reversal when held before a mirror.

- When writing on a transparent sheet is turned around (so its front and back surfaces are switched over) the image *is* reversed.

- An *opaque* sheet of writing (or a book) must be turned around to face the mirror—then the image is reversed.

- When the transparent sheet is rotated around its *horizontal* axis, it is vertically and not horizontally reversed.

A mirror allows us to see the back of an opaque object though we are in front of it. But to see its front, in a mirror behind it, the object must be rotated. When, say, a book is rotated around its *vertical* axis to face the mirror, its *left and right* switch over. It is this that produces mirror reversal. It is really object reversal.

What happens when a book is turned around its *horizontal* axis to face the mirror? It then appears upside down. Because it *is* upside down and not right-left reversed.

Object-rotation does not produce these effects without a mirror because the front of the object gets hidden, to be replaced by its back as the object is rotated. So the mirror is *necessary*, though it doesn't *cause* the reversal. It is necessary because without it we can't see the front of the rotated object.

When looking behind while driving a car, one looks in the rear-view mirror to avoid turning one's head. When an ambulance is behind the car, by rotating one's head one sees AMBULANCE. In the mirror this appears as:

ƎƆИA⅃UꞖMA

So it is often printed or stencilled reversed—to appear non-reversed in the mirror.

A mirror shows us *ourselves* right-left reversed (reversed from how others see us without the mirror) because we have to turn around to face it. Normally we turn round vertically, keeping our feet on the ground. But we can face the mirror by standing on our head—then, we are upside down in the mirror and *not* left-right reversed. So again the reversal is rotation of the *object*—oneself.

Is this a new explanation? I thought of it at least forty years ago (and, once I had thought of it, I was amazed that my friends were puzzled and that so many books and papers were nonsense). But what seems obvious can be wrong! Others have come to the same conclusion. As reported recently by his biographer James Gleick, the American physicist Richard Feynman (1918–1988) was fascinated by mirror reversal, and even he found it puzzling. According to Gleick (1992):[29]

As early as his MIT fraternity days he [Richard Feynman] had been puzzled over the classic teaser of mirror symmetry: why does a mirror seem to invert right and left but not top and bottom? That is, why are the letters of a book backward but not upside down, and why would Feynman's double behind the mirror appear to have a mole on its right hand? Was it possible, he liked to ask, to give a *symmetrical* explanation of what the mirror does—an explanation that treats up-and-down no differently from left-and-right? Many logicians and scientists debated this conundrum. There were many explanations, some of them correct. Feynman's was a model of clarity.

Imagine yourself standing before the mirror, he suggested, with one hand pointing east and the other west. Wave the east hand. The mirror image waves its east hand. Its head is up. Its west hand lies to the west. Its feet are down. 'Everything's really all right,' Feynman said. The problem is on the axis running *through* the mirror. Your nose and the back of your head are reversed: if your nose points north, your double's nose points south. The problem now is psychological. We think of our image as another person. We cannot image ourselves 'squashed' back to front, so we imagine ourselves turned left and right, as if we had walked around a pane of glass to face the other way. It is in this psychological turnabout that left and right are switched.

Is this *quite* clear? Can we not imagine ourselves 'squashed' back and front? We generally appear squashed rather flat in a photograph, which indeed is why 3D stereo photographs are impressive. Do we really *imagine* ourselves turned left and right—and is there a *psychological* turnabout? This may not be entirely clear; but

what Feynman is then quoted as saying is, in my view, absolutely correct and perfectly clear:

It is the same with a book. If the letters are reversed left and right, it is because we turned
the book about a vertical axis to face the mirror. We could just as easily turn the book from
bottom to top instead, in which case the letters will appear upside down.

Now he had avoided the *imaginary* turning.

The American philosopher N. J. Block is also, in my view, correct[30] in his
cogent if somewhat difficult paper (Block 1974). Ned Block clearly states that
it is physical rotation that produces the mirror rotation. He goes on to discuss
the language of 'right' and 'left' as being more difficult than 'up' and 'down',
because only up and down are set by gravity. As in practice we do not see
very distant objects on Earth, gravity is normally unambiguous for up and down.
This is clearly right, but it doesn't explain reversal. Ned Block is quite right to
draw attention to how hard it is to see these simple matters correctly and clearly.
Experiments can help.

Let's try the match experiment once more (page 80). Hold a match to a mirror,
horizontal and parallel to the glass, with its head to the right. The image looks the
same way round as the object—for both, the match head is to the right. There is
no horizontal reversal. But, of course, one sees the *back* of the match in the mirror.
If you painted one side a different colour, the colour of the mirror image would be
different from the direct view.

Now look at the match box: you have to rotate it to see the writing of its front in
the mirror. Then it is 'mirror writing.' Now try slowly rotating the match, so that
its head comes towards you. In the mirror it goes away. Depth is reversed. Now,
holding the match in one hand and its box in the other hand, move the match
further from you: it looks *nearer* in the mirror. Again, depth is reversed. (And
movement is *not* reversed across the mirror, or vertically, but is reversed for depth.)

Now look at your face in the mirror. Are *you* depth-reversed? Do you look *hollow*? One's own nose sticks out towards the *mirror*—the image nose sticks out
towards one's *face*. When one's nose touches the mirror, it meets its image, end to
end. We see our own face in the mirror as though it were another person looking
at us. Exactly the same is true for a room or any other objects. The mirror gives
optical depth-reversal. This does not produce right-left reversal—but the third
dimension is needed to rotate the object or ourselves to face a mirror.[31]

The bottom line is that mirror-reversal is not a psychological turnabout, or a
problem of description: it depends on the book or whatever being *physically*
turned around. No brain or mind is involved here. If it were due to a *mental* rotation, the phenomenon would be an astounding fact of brain physiology and cognition that should attract urgent research.[32] But it isn't so all we have to do is think
clearly!

It is interesting that the third dimension—depth—is needed for seeing images in looking-glasses and for rotating objects (including ourselves) to give mirror reversal. What would happen if there were no third dimension?

Flatland

The notion of dimensions of space, and how things would appear with restricted dimensions, are elegantly and entertainingly explored in *Flatland*, by A. Square (1926).[33] In this two-dimensional world live beings who can not see and can hardly appreciate the third dimension. This is introduced by considering a coin on a table: for us, when lowering the eye to the plane of the table, the coin becomes a straight line. This is the Flatlanders' view. They learn to see shapes from touch. They see shapes best when fog reveals distance, by gradually obscuring the further features—so there is a depth-gradient of fuzziness.

The Flatlanders try to conceive a third dimension by imagining a sphere emerging out of the plane into the third invisible dimension, as shown in Figure 4.12. But what the Flatlanders see is a circle of changing size. This is how a Flatlander explains it to Mr Mathematician:

You cannot indeed see more than one of my sections, or Circles, at a time; for you have no power to raise your eye out of the plane of Flatland; but you can at least see that, as I rise in Space, so my section becomes smaller. See now, I will rise; and the effect upon your eye will be that my Circle will become smaller and smaller till it dwindles to a point and finally vanishes.

For Mr Mathematician:

There was no 'rising' that I could see; but he diminished and finally vanished. I winked once or twice to make sure that I was not dreaming, . . . But to me, although I saw the facts before me, the causes were as dark as ever. All that I could comprehend was, that the Circle had made himself smaller and vanished, and that he had now reappeared and was now rapidly making himself larger.

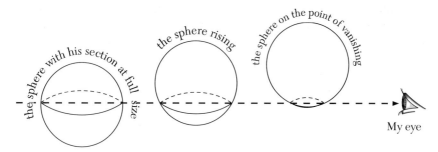

FIGURE 4.12 *Looking for the third dimension*
We can see the sphere moving out of the plane—but the Flatlanders can only see a circle of changing size.[33]

When he had regained his original size, he perceived by my silence that I had altogether failed to comprehend him. And indeed I was now inclining to the belief that he must be no Circle at all, but some extremely clever juggler; or else that the old wives' tales were true, and that after all there were such people as Enchanters and Magicians.

In a dream, Mr Mathematician speaks to the King of Lineland, who can only see points. So the King can't see right and left:[34]

> KING: Exhibit to me, if you please, this motion from left to right.
>
> I: Nay, that I cannot do, unless I step out of your Line altogether.
>
> KING: Out of my Line? Do you mean out of the World? Out of Space?
>
> I: Well, yes. Out of *your* World. Out of *your* Space. For your Space is not the true Space. True Space is a Plane; but your Space is only a Line.
>
> KING: If you cannot indicate this motion from left to right by yourself moving in it, then I beg you to describe it to me in words.
>
> I: If you cannot tell your right side from your left, I fear that no words of mine can make my meaning clear to you.

There is no mention of mirrors in Flatland. Although looking-glasses are flat—so they could exist—their images could never be seen, for they could not be *through* the glass. And object rotation, giving mirror reversal, would not be possible, objects could not be rotated. Flatlanders could never see themselves or anything else reflected—so they would not have puzzles of mirrors.

Notes

1. Plato (427–347 BC) *Timaeus* 45. This osmology was Plato's last work.
2. Aristotle came close to appreciating images as he did see that dapple from trees is given by multiple overlapping images of the Sun from small gaps in the foliage. It is curious that this did not suggest at that time single images as in a pinhole camera.
3. For a full history of the camera obscura, see Hammond (1981).
4. Al-Haytham, Ibn (Al Hazen) (*c.* 1040).
5. della Porta (1658).
6. The development and use of the camera obscura by artists is fully described with superb illustrations by Kemp (1990).
7. This is 'toys' in the obsolete sense of (*OED*): 'A fantastic or trifling speech or piece of writing', as in Shakespeare (*Midsummer Night's Dream* v.i.3): 'I never may believe These anticke fables, nor these Fairy Toyes.'
8. For a general non-technical account see Gleick (1988).
9. I found this effect (or non-effect) while playing with mirrors. It must be known, but I have not seen it mentioned anywhere.
10. Pierre Curie shared a Nobel Prize with his wife Marie Curie for isolating polonium and radium.

11. Gregory and Heard (1979).

12. Stewart and Golubitsky (1992).

13. This does not refer to depth through the mirror. This is optically reversed. The further the object (or any part of it) is in front of the mirror, the further away the image is through it, as the path length increases.

14. Plato (427–347 BC) *Timaeus* 46.

15. Lucretius (*c.* 80 BC) Book 4.

16. For example: 'a single reflection causes a lateral reversal of the image' (Riggs (1965), page 20). A ray diagram is given—but this does not show the supposed asymmetry. This diagram, showing alternate reflections in a series of mirrors, is attributed to McKinley.

17. This was pointed out to me, as a possibility, by Professor Michael Berry.

18. James (1890).

19. Whorf (1956).

20. Stratton (1897). This was suggested two hundred years earlier by Bishop Berkeley, in his *Common Place Book*, where he wonders what would happen if an infant were fitted with 'reversing perspectives' from birth. He does not make a prediction and did not try it.

21. These important experiments are described by Kohler (1931), and also by Taylor (1962). Ewart (1930) performed the converse experiments—reducing the subjects' movements to a minimum.

22. Fully described by Taylor (1962) pages 198–231.

23. John Marshall (1994) personal communication.

24. Shepard and Metzler (1971). This, and other important papers, are available in Shepard and Cooper (1986).

25. Parsons (1987).

26. Pears (1952).

27. Gardner (1964) pages 29–31.

28. Emphasis on refutation, even by a single example, is associated with Sir Karl Popper (1959, 1972). This may apply occasionally in highly structured physics. What looks at first sight a refutation is quite often explained within the accepted theory or paradigm. Hypotheses should indeed be framed to be vulnerable; but it is mistaken to give up a promising idea without fighting to save it, as often the 'refutation' turns out to be wrong.

29. Gleick (1992) page 332.

30. Block (1974).

31. Is this what Kant (1783) was getting at when he said that mirror images 'are not representations of things as they are in themselves and as some mere (or 'pure') understanding would know them, but sensuous intuitions, that is appearances whose possibility rests upon the relation of certain things unknown in themselves to something else, namely to our sensibility'? I doubt it.

32. Strangely, this seems to be tacitly ignored by psychologists who believe it to be a psychological phenomenon. But recently the distinguished perceptual psychologist William Ittleson, with his colleagues Lyn Mowerly and Diane Magid (1991), have carried out experiments on differences of appearances of objects seen in a mirror or through a window. Any empirical approach is to be welcomed; but very curiously they call up the linguistic definition issue to question whether an object rotated horizontally appears simply upside down or also right-left reversed (their page 570). But the same considerations of terminology and definition apply to any object, whether or not seen in a mirror. Evidently Ittleson and his colleagues seek the explanation of mirror reversal directly in perceptual appearances; but, as

generally in science, appearances are not simply related to what is going on behind the scenes. This is, indeed, something of a warning against pushing phenomenalism too far.

33. A. Square was the pseudonym of Edwin A. Abbott (1926).

34. Abbott (1926) page 61.

5

‚àûﬁ

Light on Matter

First he breathed Light upon the Face of Matter or Chaos.
FRANCIS BACON

I N the Old Testament, light was the beginning of everything; and light has generally been associated with knowledge and perfection. In antiquity light and mirrors were an acknowledged part of scientific study. There were several books by highly distinguished thinkers on *catoptrics*, though unfortunately few texts have survived. The Greek scientist, mathematician and inventor Archimedes (*c*. 287–212 BC) wrote a treatise on mirrors which is lost; but the writings of Euclid (*c*. 300 BC) do survive.[1] An interesting account is Hero's *Catoptrics* of the first century AD.[2] The Greek text is lost, but there is a thirteenth century Latin version. For Hero, the study of mirrors, including the puzzle of right-left reversal, is:

Clearly a science worthy of study and at the same time it produces spectacles which excite wonder in the observer. For with the aid of this science mirrors are constructed which show the right side as the right side, and, similarly, the left side as the left side, whereas ordinary mirrors by their nature have the contrary property and show opposite sides. It is also possible with the aid of mirrors to see our own backs, and to see ourselves inverted, standing on our heads, with three eyes, and two noses, and features distorted as in intense grief.

Hero continues with uses including a hint of the occult:

The study of catoptrics, however, is useful not merely in affording diverting spectacles but also for necessary purposes. For who will not deem it very useful that we should be able to observe, on occasion, while remaining inside our own house, how many people there are in the street and what they are doing? And will anyone not consider it remarkable to be able to tell the hour, night or day, with the aid of figures appearing in mirrors? For as many figures appear as there are hours of the day or night, and if a [given] part of the day has passed a [given] figure will appear. Again, who will not be astonished when he sees, in a mirror, neither himself nor another, but whatever we desire that he see?

Greek notions of light were very different from ours. Hero thought of light as shooting *out* of the eyes to touch objects. Plato thought of light as both shooting out and entering eyes. As optics is generally reversible, whether light is regarded as entering or leaving has little effect on the equations of optics; though it changes very greatly how we may think eyes function.

Euclid, who wrote extensively on light and mirrors, also thought of vision as working by rays shooting out of the eyes to touch surrounding objects. For Euclid—as an eye is so small compared to the vastness of the world we can see—eyes could be regarded as mathematical points, with no significant internal structure. (Mathematicians are apt to ignore things to make problems easier, which, though often legitimate and useful, does have dangers.) Euclid must have seemed justified in ignoring the inside of the eye, as he and all writers in antiquity were totally unaware of retinal images.

The Greeks had no conception of the retina at the back of the eye as a screen on which images of objects are projected optically, in geometrical perspective. They had no idea of the lens and cornea as focusing light to form an image. As they had no such technology, they simply did not see the eye as an optical instrument. Nevertheless, one might think it would have been obvious that light enters rather than shoots out of eyes; for how did the Greeks explain why they couldn't see in the dark? They were bothered by why the Sun hurt the eyes, and they were surprised that when the eyes are opened both near and distant objects appear at the same time. Distant objects (especially stars) should appear long after near objects, as light was thought to travel at a finite speed. The fact that a distant coin, fallen upon the ground, is harder to see than a nearby coin was, however, explained: the further coin could fall between the spreading-out rays from the eyes, though a nearby coin would be bound to touch at least one ray. It is interesting that back-to-front ideas can quite often provide convincing explanations.

A very different ancient and medieval view was that objects emanate expanding *simulacra*, or shells of themselves, rather like ripples from a pebble dropped in a pond, but preserving the form of the object, however distant. Both the ancient ray and simulacra notions hint of modern views of light as particles or waves, or both.

The notion that rays shoot out in straight lines from the eyes evidently appealed to Euclid's geometrical sense; it fitted his geometer's notions of lines and points and angles. He explained that light travels in straight lines because of its great speed, by analogy with projectiles or arrows. Strangely, before Galileo (1564–1642) even cannon balls were thought, and evidently were seen, to travel in straight lines, before suddenly coming down to earth.

The Greeks did not think that light travels at an infinite speed, but whether they were right remained controversial until the speed of light was measured—first with astronomical observations, requiring a telescope—by the Danish astronomer Olaus Röemer (1644–1710). Röemer deduced the speed from variations in time of eclipses of the planet Jupiter's four large satellites. The intervals between eclipses got longer, then shorter, in cycles that were associated with the changes of the distance of Jupiter from Earth. He realised that the cycle of eclipse times must be due to the finite speed of light, for he saw the events later whenever Jupiter was more distant. Knowing the changing distances, he could calculate light's speed through space.

This is discussed by Newton in the *Opticks*, where he also explains why he is sure the observations are not due to 'eccentricities' of the satellites. The observation that light takes finite time—so astronomy sees into the past—should have made it clear that vision is never directly related to objects. But this important insight on sight has very generally been resisted by philosophers as making relations with surrounding objects uncomfortably uncertain. This does not however apply to Newton, who immediately accepted Röemer's interpretation, that the observations refer to a property of light and not to the behaviour of the satellites. Proposition XI of the *Opticks* reads:

PROP. XI

Light is propagated from luminous Bodies in time, and spends about seven or eight Minutes of an Hour in passing from the Sun to the Earth.

This was observed first by *Röemer*, and then by others, by means of the Eclipses of the Satellites of *Jupiter*. For these Eclipses, when the Earth is between the Sun and Jupiter, happen about seven or eight Minutes sooner than they ought to do by the Tables, and when the Earth is beyond the Sun they happen about seven or eight Minutes later than they ought to do; the reason being, that the Light of the Satellites has farther to go in the latter case than in the former by the Diameter of the Earth's Orbit. Some inequalities of time may arise from the Eccentricities of the Orbs of the Satellites; but these cannot answer in all the Satellites, and at all times to the Position and Distance of the Earth from the Sun. . . But this inequality [changing speeds of Jupiter's satellites according to the position of the Sun] has no respect to the position of the Earth, and in the three interior Satellites is insensible, as I find by computation from the Theory of Gravity.

This is a delightful example of Newton reasoning from observation to a conclusion, supported by related observations, and then from calculation based on a general model, enabling him to interpret what is going on. So he decides what is truth, and what is illusion.[3]

The speed of light was brought down to earth in 1849 by the French physicist Armand Hyppolyte Fizeau (1819–1896). His method was essentially Galileo's— a theoretically correct but impracticable idea for measuring the speed of light with observers with lanterns and shutters, separated on distant mountains. When the shutter of one lantern was opened, the other would be opened as soon as the light was seen; then the first shutter would be opened again for a brief moment, and so on many times. The interval between opening and closing the shutters should make it possible to compute the speed of light. But as light travels so fast this was not a practical method over earthly distances. It was, however, how Newton successfully measured the speed of *sound* by clapping his hands. Newton clapped his hands while standing at one end of a cloister of his College in Cambridge. As soon as the echo returned, he clapped his hands again, repeating this several times. He counted the number of claps in, say a minute; and knowing the interval between claps and the distance of the sound-reflecting wall, he computed the speed of sound. One might think that there would be a cumulative error, due to delay in responding to the echo, because of neural reaction-time (ten or more milliseconds), but this is not so. For after a few claps Newton could anticipate the returning echo and so respond immediately with no delay at all. Thus this is an interesting experiment both physically and psychologically.

Fizeau realized that a superhumanly fast apparatus is required to apply this method for the speed of light. He looked through slits in a rapidly rotating disc to a distant mirror (see Figure 5.1). If the slit had moved on by the time the light returned, so that the light was cut off by the disc, he could calculate the speed of the light just as Newton did for sound, though without any problem of human response time. The speed of light in a vacuum can now be stated with a high

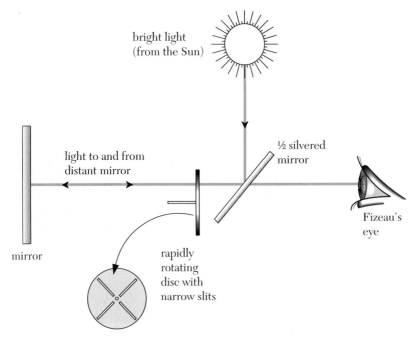

FIGURE 5.1 *How on Earth Fizeau measured the speed of light*

Fizeau looked through the slits of a rapidly rotating disc, to a distant mirror. If the light is delayed sufficiently it will miss the slit and be blocked by the opaque disc. Knowing the path length and the speed of the slits, it was possible to calculate the speed of light on Earth.

degree of accuracy as 299 792 458 m/s.[4] (Technically, since 1984 the speed of light has been fixed and this value now defines the metre in terms of the—independently specified—second. More accurate measurements that may be made in the future will be interpreted as redefinitions of the—now secondary—length unit). As a matter of chance, the speed of light is just a million times the speed of sound: sound in air travels at 670 miles per hour, and light at 670 000 000 miles per hour.

It takes just seven-and-a-half minutes for light to reach us from the Sun; four-and-a-half years for light from the nearest star Proxima Centauri; and about two-and-a-half million years for light from the most distant object visible to the naked eye, the Andromeda galaxy. It follows that we do not see the Sun and the stars—or any objects—directly. We see the Andromeda galaxy as it was at the time of the first human beings on Earth. An eye image of this book sends its signals to the brain several milliseconds after light reaches the retinas (neural signals are far slower than light, and slower than the speed of sound). Signals to the brain are always delayed—from millions of years to a few milliseconds—so perceptions can never be directly related to objects. We see (and hear and touch) the 'present' by anticipating the future from delayed signals from the senses.

An important property of light is that it travels slower in a transparent medium, such as glass or water, than in space. It is because glass slows the speed of light that a lens can focus, and our eyes would not have images if light were not slowed by the fluid in the front of the eyes (the aqueous humour) and by the crystalline lenses.[5] This was totally unknown to the Greeks; but Hero, following Aristotle's incorrect notion that a constant velocity requires a constant force, anticipated the important *principle of least time* (see page 117), saying:

For whatever moves with unchanging velocity moves in a straight line (meaning moving very fast it keeps a straight line). The arrows we see shot from bows may serve as example. For because of the impelling force the object in motion strives to move over the shortest possible distance, since it has not the time for slower motion, that is, for motion over a longer trajectory. The impelling force does not permit such retardation. And so, by reason of its speed, the object tends to move over the shortest path. But the shortest of all lines having the same end points is a straight line.

Hero realised that if light always takes the *shortest path* to travel from A to B via a mirror, the *angle of incidence must equal the angle of reflection* (see Figure 5.2). This is indeed correct geometrically; but it can be puzzling, for how does light 'choose' to strike the mirror at just the right place for its passage, via the mirror, to be the shortest path, or (more precisely) to take the shortest time? This question has only received an answer very recently (see page 147).

The Greeks did not appreciate images, but they did know that light could be brought to a focus by a curved mirror. This was used as a burning glass. The curve formed is still known as a *caustic*. It can be seen very clearly in the reflection of

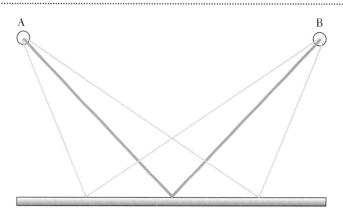

FIGURE 5.2 *Equal angles and the shortest time path*
The thick lines show the path light takes—the shortest path from A to B is when the angle
of incidence equals the angle of reflection. This was recognised by the Greeks as a key to
light and reflection; but it raised a problem that has only recently been resolved: how does
light 'choose' this shortest path?

light by a cup onto the surface of the tea, as shown in Figure 5.3. Figure 5.4 shows how a caustic is created, from light seen as rays.

How did the Greeks think that mirrors reflect? Not unnaturally the early writers drew analogies from familiar, easier-to-understand objects, such as bouncing balls. Hero says:

Now the essential characteristic of polished surfaces is that their surfaces are compact. Thus, before they are polished, mirrors have some porosities upon which the rays fall and so cannot be reflected. But these mirrors are polished by rubbing until the porosities are filled by a fine substance; then the rays incident upon the compact surface are reflected. For just as a stone violently hurled against a compact body, such as a board or wall, rebounds, whereas [for] a stone hurled against a soft body, such as wool or the like . . . the force merely slackens and is separated from the stone.

So in the first century AD Hero invoked porosities, or 'little holes', to explain why some light is reflected from a piece of glass while some goes through. This idea of lots of little holes was used until modern times to explain partial reflection, in water or glass. Partial reflection turns out, however, to require a very different kind of explanation from Hero's 'porosities' (see pages 122–123, 145–148).

We only experience light by its interactions with matter—most intimately with the specialized matter of our eyes, accepting light from surfaces of objects, and signalling their presence to the brain by neural action potentials. But the more perfect the reflecting surface, the less visible the surface becomes. Highly polished mirrors are the extreme case where the surface is invisible. Less perfect reflection reveals the texture of objects. Looking at a polished mahogany table,

FIGURE 5.3 *A caustic reflection in a cup*
After Berry (1995).

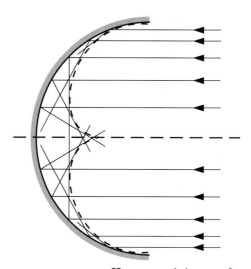

FIGURE 5.4 *How a caustic is created*
After Ronchi (1957), by kind permission of Dover Publishing Co. Inc.

with the sun shining on it, where the light is reflected the dark wood looks white. As it becomes a mirror-surface with polishing, the table's colour and texture become invisible. For we see textures and colours of objects only by diffused light scattered from imperfect surfaces, as shown in Figure 5.5.[6] For the perfect mirror, it is useful to think of a ray of light hitting the surface at some angle, and a single ray leaving it at the same angle the other side of the 'normal', as shown in Figures 5.5 and 5.6.

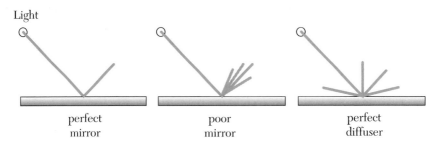

perfect   poor   perfect
mirror   mirror   diffuser

FIGURE 5.5 *The more perfect the surface, as a mirror, the less is it visible*
*For the perfect mirror, when one ray strikes the surface a reflected ray bounces off in a single
direction. For less perfect surfaces, many rays bounce off around this direction. For a
completely diffusing surface rays bounce off in all directions: then we can see the surface's
texture and colour. This is called 'Lambertian reflection', after Johannes Heinrich Lambert
(1728–1777).*

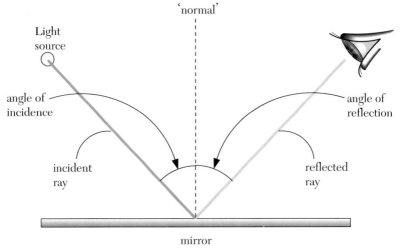

FIGURE 5.6 *Perfect mirror reflection of 'rays'*
The rules are: the angle of incidence *equals the angle of* reflection. *The rays lie in the
same plane.*

Already there are many questions: why do mirrors (especially metal mirrors)
reflect? Why are they invisible? Just how does diffused light reveal surfaces of
objects? What happens to light that is *not* reflected? Are there really *rays* of light?
What is light made of? Such questions have been asked for millennia and receive
ever more bizarre answers as science digs deeper beneath appearances.

That light is bent by water or by glass had been known from the earliest times,
and measured—for example by the Alexandrian astronomer and geographer

Claudius Ptolemy (*c.* 90–168 AD), who made a list of the angles from a beam of light entering water. But how and why the light bends were mysteries, and there were no obvious analogies for *refraction*, like the bouncing balls that could be used to explain *reflection*. Refraction is lawful, but the law was not discovered until the seventeenth century, and it requires the notion of sines of angles (see Figure 5.7). In 1621 the Dutch mathematician Willebrod van Roijen Snell (1591–1626) proposed what is now known as Snell's law: *the sine of the angle of the light entering the denser medium is equal to the sine of the angle of the beam in the denser medium, multiplied by a constant depending on its density*. For water, the constant (the *refractive index*) is 1.333.[7]

How refraction happens is an important question for any theory of light and of matter. It has key importance for the creation of images—focusing—by lenses. A lens may be thought of as a pair of (curved) prisms; in Figure 5.8 the lens could be acting as a burning glass, focusing rays from the Sun. The idea that unifies reflection and refraction, and is the key concept of focusing by mirrors or lenses (as anticipated by Hero two thousand years ago), is that light always takes the *least time* to travel from A to B. A good analogy[8] is an athlete *running* fast and *swimming* more slowly. Running faster than he can swim, he should take a path that reduces the distance through the water. So if the water is not at right angles

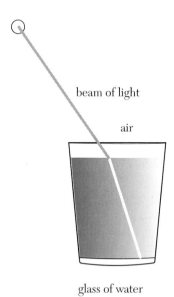

beam of light

air

glass of water

FIGURE 5.7 *Refraction*

A beam of light is bent when it passes from air to a denser medium such as glass or water. The angles were measured by the Greeks, but were not generalised into a law until the 'law of sines' was formulated in the seventeenth century.

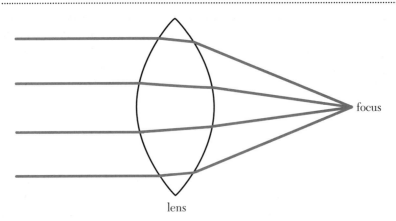

lens

FIGURE 5.8 *Parallel rays brought to a focus by a convex lens*
This a burning glass. When rays from many points of an object come to a focus, an image
is formed. But here we may think of the Sun almost as a 'point source', producing more heat
than light! However much it is concentrated by the lens, the brightness can never exceed the
brightness of the surface of the Sun.

he should not continue in a straight line, but should deviate, to take a shorter path where he has to go more slowly (see Figure 5.9).

If light is directed from the dense to the less dense medium, at angles below a certain value it will be trapped by *total internal reflection* (as shown in Figure 5.10). A dramatic example of this can be seen in diamond. The uniquely brilliant flashes of diamonds depend on the artifice of how they are cut. As found, they are dull pebbles. Cut diamonds sparkle with their brilliant 'fire' of colours because maximum use is made of their high refractive index and large dispersion. For gems they have to be ground and polished to certain shapes, the most spectacular being the brilliant-cut, which is shown in Figure 5.11. Practically all the light is internally reflected at the facets, which produces spectral colours because of the high dispersion of diamond. As all light is reflected towards the front, viewed from the back a well-cut diamond is black.

Recently glass has been made so transparent that trapped light will travel through fine glass fibres for many kilometres with scarcely any loss. This is the basis of modern fibre optics, which is proving very useful for communication systems and for medical endoscopes. This most-efficient-of-all-mirrors, the optical fibre, is revolutionising long-distance data transmission as laser light signals can be switched on and off, or changed in intensity very rapidly, to convey information at unprecedented rates over great distances (see Figure 5.12).

According to the light-is-rays concept, this efficient total internal reflection should take place at the precise boundary of the dense and less dense media. But the reflection is not always total, as can be seen if two dense media—two glass

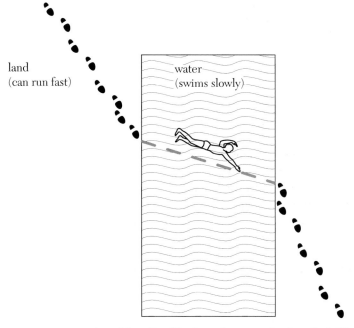

land
(can run fast)

water
(swims slowly)

FIGURE 5.9 *An athlete should take a shorter path where he is likely to be slower*

Light does exactly the same. Light takes the least-time path—for reflection and for refraction. Lenses and mirrors designed to focus to a point bring all the rays (or the wave front) as near as possible to an image-point, by making all the least-time paths the same.

plates for example—are separated by a less dense medium such as air. Some of the light from the first plate will leak across the gap, into the second plate (Figure 5.13). This is evidence that light is not simply rays or particles but *waves*. On the wave account, this leaking should take place over a distance equivalent to several wavelengths—which can be shown by placing a second glass plate close to the first. That the leaking happens is evidence that light is waves; but what does it tell us about reflections? Let's start with rays and particles of light.

Why does Light Reflect?

From antiquity, light has usually been thought of as travelling in straight lines as rays. So Newton's notion of light as streams of tiny particles has ancient origins. It is not surprising that ray diagrams are accepted as useful for conceiving of light and reflections; but gradually it has become clear that, in important ways, light is not like particles, or like the lines of a ray diagram. The classical idea of *lines of*

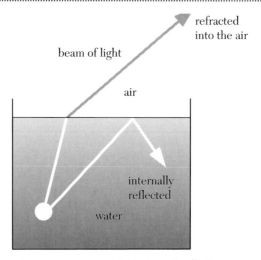

FIGURE 5.10 *Total internal reflection*

At angles below a certain value, light approaching a less dense from a denser transparent medium (here, water), will be trapped—to be reflected back into the denser medium.

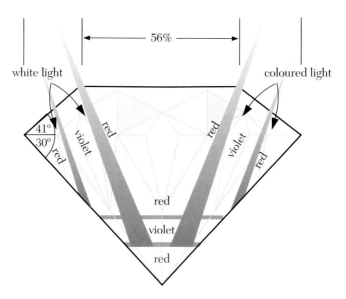

FIGURE 5.11 *A brilliant-cut diamond*

This must be the most sophisticated example of total internal reflection, with extreme dispersion producing brilliant colours.

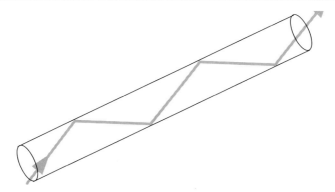

FIGURE 5.12 *Fibre optics*
Light will travel a very long way trapped in a glass fibre.

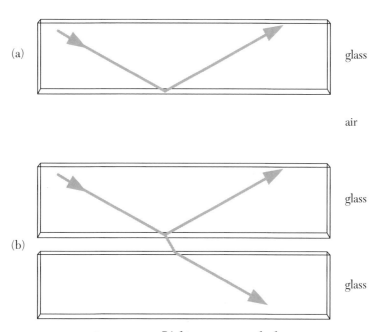

FIGURE 5.13 *Light as waves can leak out*
Part (a) shows internal reflection from a dense medium (glass) to air. In Part (b), placing a second glass close to the first, some light leaks out to the second plate. This can be explained by light-is-waves, though not by light-is-particles.

light is, however, still the basis of many diagrams in books on optics, especially near the beginning. As later the notion of lines of light becomes inadequate, the diagrams change with our notions of what light is. But light turns out to be so odd we cannot quite draw or visualise it.

Hero answered the question 'Why is light reflected from mirrors?' by analogy with the familiar behaviour of balls bouncing off hard surfaces. Of course one might go on to ask why balls bounce, and why rubber bounces so much better than most other substances, such as wood. We would now look for answers at the atomic level. This was conceived by the Greeks before Aristotle—by Democritus and Leucippus—and it was considered later by the Roman poet Lucretius in his great poem *De Rerum Natura* (*Of The Nature of Things*).[9]

> For far beneath the ken of senses lies
> The nature of those ultimates of the world;
> And so, since those themselves thou canst not see,
> Their motion also must they veil from men—
> For mark, indeed, how things we *can* see, oft
> Yet hide their motions when afar from us
> Along the distant landscape.
>
> . . .
>
> But the primordial atoms with their old
> Simple solidity, when forth they travel
> Along the empty void, all undelayed
> By aught outside them there, and they, each one
> Being one unit from nature of its parts,
> Are borne to that one place on which they strive.
>
> . . .
>
> Nor to pursue the atoms one by one
> To see the law whereby each thing goes on.
> But *some* men, ignorant of matter, think,
> Opposing this, not without the gods,
> In such adjustment to our human ways,
> Can nature change the seasons of the years,
> And bring to birth the grains and all of else
> To which divine Delight, the guide of life
> Persuades mortality and leads it on.

The notion that light is particles was accepted by Newton, though he realised that this did not give a complete description of all the phenomena known in his time. Much has emerged since, to show that light is in some ways unlike particles—indeed unlike any familiar touchable matter—but clearly it was right to start from the familiar to explain what may turn out to be beyond belief.

Neither ray diagrams nor Newton's streams of particles explain why light shining through a pin-hole spreads out; why shadows from a small source are blurred; why lights from neighbouring small holes 'interfere' to give patterns of light and dark; why soap films have their glorious colours—or how lasers and holograms work. To think of any of these, we need to conceive of light as waves.

Light as Waves

The important idea that light is waves is due to the Dutch physicist Christiaan Huygens (1629–1695). Huygens supposed that light propagates like ripples in water. This has turned out to be an extremely significant idea, which we need to look at it in some detail to appreciate mirrors. Our understanding here will be mainly limited to 'hand-waving' descriptions of what are given in mathematical terms in textbooks of optics. The idea is based on experiments one can try out in the kitchen. Even for the mathematically minded, such simple 'hands-on' experiments can be very useful, for it is all too easy to learn the equations but miss their significance.

There are two kinds of waves: *transverse* wiggles and *longitudinal* compressions. Both kinds can be defined in terms of their speed, length, amplitude and frequency. The *speed* of travel depends on the medium (sound is faster in steel beams than in air: light is faster in space or air than in glass). The *wavelength* is the distance between adjacent crests, and the amplitude (for *transverse* waves) is half the depth between crest and trough. The *frequency* is the number of waves passing a particular point in one second. Though they are very different, both light and sound involve waves; but sound involves compression *longitudinal* waves, and light involves wiggly *transverse* waves.

There are many examples of waves apart from sound and light. Mechanical waves travel through a physical medium, such as a slinky spring, or water. The matter through which the waves move does not itself travel—tides and currents are quite different, and the moving air of winds is quite different from sound waves. But if it is not matter that is travelling in waves, what is? It is *energy*.

The properties of waves can be seen in a skipping rope and in a slinky spring (see Figure 5.14). The transverse waves of light are like the waves of an oscillating skipping rope. The direction of this oscillation may be horizontal, vertical—or any angle. This is the angle of *polarisation*.

If one end of the rope is tied to something solid, the waves are reflected back. This is most easily seen with a single wave, or pulse. A reflected wave will pass through an oncoming wave. Once they have passed, normally neither wave has been affected by their meeting.

When light shines on glass, most is transmitted and about twenty per cent is reflected. Partial reflection of waves is seen in a thin rope tied to a thicker rope as

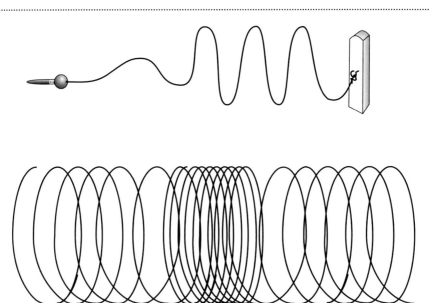

FIGURE 5.14 *Kinds of waves*
*The vibrated skipping rope shows transverse waves running
along it. The slinky spring shows longitudinal compression waves running along the coiled
spring. The rope is like light; the spring is like sound.*

shown in Figure 5.15. When a wave pulse running along the thin rope meets the
thick rope, part is reflected back, and the rest continues along the thick rope. (It
travels faster along the thin rope.) When reflected back from the thick rope, the
wave is inverted; but the continuing wave in the thick rope is not inverted. All this
is also true of light and mirrors.

Sound waves are like the compression *longitudinal* waves in a slinky spring.
These waves can not be polarised. If one end of the spring is fixed to something
solid, the waves are reflected back. Again, this is seen best with a single wiggle or
pulse. This reflected pulse passes through the next oncoming wave. As it passes, it
adds or subtracts; but once passed, neither wave nor pulse has been affected by
the other. This 'superposition' also happens in transverse waves.

When switched on and off at irregular intervals, or modulated in intensity or in
frequency, waves may carry information through time. Many simultaneous
waves, of various amplitudes or frequencies, may represent information, in an
instant, as spatial patterns, as in optical images.

Waves do not always travel: there can be *standing waves* from reflections. This
can happen between two parallel, facing mirrors. Standing waves are given by
reflection from each mirror when the distance between the mirrors is an exact
multiple of the wavelength. These 'mirrors' could also be the attachments at each

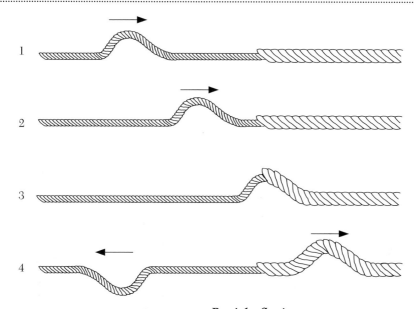

FIGURE 5.15 *Partial reflection*

When a wave pulse running along the thin rope meets the thick rope, part is reflected back, and the rest continues along the thick rope. When reflected back from the thick rope, the wave is inverted.

end of a rope, or at each end of the vibrating string of a musical instrument. Thus for the string of a violin or the column of air in an organ pipe, the waves do not run along: they are standing waves—an apparently still superposition of waves travelling in opposite directions.

Another feature of waves is *resonance*, which is also important in musical instruments. Resonance can be described by analogy to a child's swing. When pushing the swing, only a small force is required to keep it going provided the pushes are timed right. The swing has a 'natural period', and so do vibrating ropes or strings. When energy from a wave is received by a mechanical or electrical system, the system is set into sympathetic vibration when its resonant frequency (or a multiple of it) equals the frequency of the wave. This makes stretched strings or tuning forks 'answer back', and allows radios to be tuned. Mirrors are like many tuning forks, receiving and sending back waves.

Pure waves are simple undulations: they are *sine waves*, named from how they are described mathematically. Sine waves and their harmonics (multiples of the fundamental frequency) form the more complex waves which give musical instruments their timbre. It is a remarkable fact that, however complicated a wave, it can be described, and also created, as a combination of many simple sine waves of various frequencies and amplitudes. This is Fourier analysis and synthesis.[10] This is how an entire orchestra can be heard from the single vibrating cone of a loud speaker.[11] Fourier analysis can also be applied to spatial patterns of images, so it is important for describing optical images and early processes of vision.[12]

Simple experiments on water waves in a ripple tank can show them reflected from straight or curved barriers, and bent by refraction.[13] A flat baking tin with some water in it is fine for a ripple tank. One can make ripples with one's fingers, or with pencils, though it is better to use electrically driven small plungers set to vibrate at a chosen frequency. Straight or curved barriers put into the water show reflections of waves; and lenses and prisms can be made from shapes under the water (not quite reaching the surface). These change the speed of the waves, and show bending and focusing by refraction.

Figure 5.16 shows how waves are reflected from a plane mirror. But light is not quite like bouncing balls or ropy waves. These experiments help—they lead to understanding—but surprises remain.

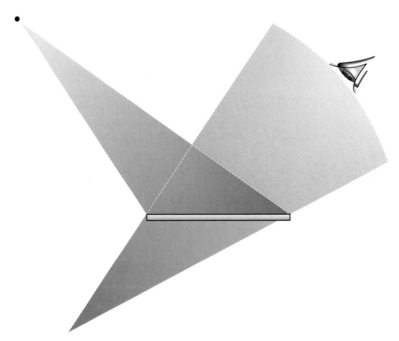

FIGURE 5.16 *Waves reflected from a plane mirror*
From Ronchi (1957), by kind permission of Dover Publishing Co. Inc.

Light in Matter

Light enters a mirror—it is absorbed—before it is reflected. Other surfaces also absorb light, and rather less is reflected back. What happens to absorbed light was utterly mysterious until quite recently. Could light simply disappear? The Scottish physicist Sir David Brewster (1781–1868) wrote in 1831:[14]

Philosophers have not yet ascertained the nature of the power by which bodies absorb light. . . . If the particles of light were *reflected*, or merely turned out of their direction by the action of the particles, it seems to be quite demonstrable that a portion of the most opaque matter, such as charcoal, would, when exposed to a strong beam of light, become actually phosphorescent during its illumination, or would at least appear white; but as all the light which enters is never again visible, we must believe, till we have evidence to the contrary, that the light is actually *stopped* by the particles of the body, and remains within it in the form of imponderable matter.

This is not at all how we see it today, just over one hundred and fifty years later. It is now accepted that the absorbed light vibrates the material's atoms, producing heat. After many adventures, the heat is radiated away as part of the 'heat death' of the Universe.

In transparent substances such as glass, absorbed light undergoes a series of internal emissions and re-emissions which slow it down. It is this slowing that makes prisms and lenses bend light, and eyes produce images by refraction. This, however, can be thought of as *waves* being deviated by the denser medium. In Figure 5.17 the wave fronts are deviated as they are slowed by the denser medium—the glass—to produce an almost perfect point-image. This is also shown with the ripples. The larger the lens—or concave mirror—the smaller the point-image, because it incorporates more waves. Though not easy to 'see', this is a vital principle for designing microscopes and other optical instruments, to give sharp, high-resolution images.

Colours of light are associated with different wavelengths, or frequencies. Surfaces that absorb light appear coloured when some wavelengths are absorbed

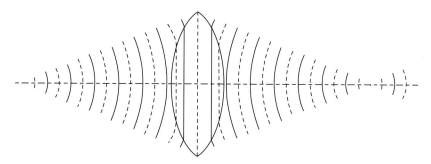

FIGURE 5.17 *Waves focused by a convex lens*

more (reflected less) than others. A red surface appears red because it reflects long-wavelength light, which is red, and absorbs much of the rest.

White light is a mixture of all wavelengths—all colours—of the visible spectrum, with about the same relative energies as the wavelengths in sunlight. But the light we can see is a minute band of the enormous range of the whole spectrum of electromagnetic radiation. Eyes respond to only one octave, between about 400 and 800 million million $(4\times10^{14}-8\times10^{14})$ waves, or cycles, per second.

Specifying wavelength is equivalent to specifying frequency, for (in space) all the radiation travels at the same velocity, c. This is 3×10^8 metres (186 000 miles) per second. The whole range extends from low frequency radio waves, which can be less than a million cycles per second (less than 10^6 Hertz), at which frequency the wavelength is 300 metres. Then comes the infrared heat waves, then the single octave of visible light, then ultraviolet, and beyond that the 'soft' then 'hard' X-rays and gamma rays. The shorter the wavelength, the more energetic the radiation.

Because different wavelengths (or frequencies) are slowed by different amounts when light enters a denser medium, the angles by which the different colours of light bend are also different. This is why a prism splits white light into a spectrum of rainbow colours. The shorter wavelengths—the blue colours—are slowed more, and deviated more, than the longer-wavelength red colours. This phenomenon occurs most dramatically in a rainbow. When sunlight passes through a raindrop it is internally reflected several times, and bent twice by refraction. As in the prism, the angle through which the light is bent is slightly different for each wavelength of the sunlight. The rainbow is a perfect circle (a semi-circle when cut off by the horizon) because the angle of direction from the Sun is precisely the same around the bow for each colour.

The spreading into colours is somewhat different for various transparent substances. Some kinds of glass disperse light more than others, and there can be differences for particular regions of the spectrum—even with reversal for some wavelengths, or colours. It was because Newton did not realise this (it did not fit his particle theory of light) that he made his reflecting telescope.[15] For Newton thought it impossible to avoid the coloured fringing produced when he used lenses, so he used mirrors instead—for mirrors reflect light of all colours at the same angle.

It turned out that Newton was not correct in thinking that lenses inevitably produce coloured fringes. A Swedish mathematician, Samuel Klingenstierna (1698–1765), showed a flaw in Newton's experiments by placing a glass prism within a water prism. The important idea that it is possible to avoid colour fringing by making lenses out of glasses with different dispersions was developed by John Dolland (1706–1761), and described by him in 1759, and then by the inventive genius William Wollaston (1766–1828).[16] This made possible high definition 'achromatic' telescopes, microscopes, and cameras. The English inventor Chester Moor Hall (1703–1771) made the first refracting telescopes with lenses having elements of different kinds of glass.

Interfering Waves

Water waves go through each other. Similarly sound waves pass through each other, and beams of light are generally not affected by other light (see Figure 5.18). If this were not so, vision and hearing would be impossible. But under certain conditions waves can interfere with each other.

It was the English physician-physicist Thomas Young (1773–1829) who showed that when a beam of light is passed through a narrow slit, and then through two close-together slits, a pattern of alternating light and dark bands is seen on a screen (see Figure 5.19).[17] He attributed this to light waves interfering with each other, adding and then cancelling as they come in and out of phase, like the ripples in Figure 5.20. So two lights can produce local darkness. This is so only when the waves are in step—*coherent*—as they are in light that has passed through a small hole or slit (as in Young's experiment), or in laser light, which is much brighter.

If light is like ripples spreading out on a pond, how can light appear as *rays*? Huygen's idea was that light is, like ripples, travelling wave *fronts*; but as wavelengths of light are very short, it appears as rays, at right angles to the wave fronts.[18] One can see this with water waves passing through a pair of slits, as shown in Figure 5.20.

Although they appear very different, electromagnetic waves at all frequencies are regarded as essentially the same. Different wavelengths (or frequencies) have

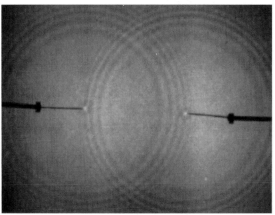

FIGURE 5.18 *Waves pass through each other*
By kind permission of Oxford University Press.

FIGURE 5.19 *Interference pattern from two slits*

If light is waves, one would expect such patterns from light waves adding and cancelling as they come in and out of phase. This should not occur with particles—yet electrons also show interference patterns. So there is much more to light and matter than is generally realised. By kind permission of Addison Wesley Publishing Co. Inc.

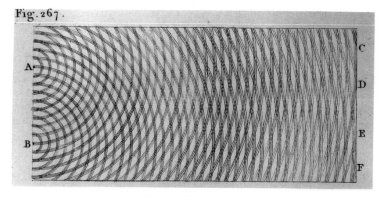

FIGURE 5.20 *Thomas Young's interference patterns*

The water waves emerging in step from the slits at A and B alternately add to and subtract from each other. So they get twice as large, then fall to zero, as they get in and out of phase. (The slits should be about 1 mm wide, and separated by about 50 cm.) Courtesy of the Royal Society, London.

different properties because *they interact with matter differently*. These differences tell us a lot about the nature of matter. In the visible region of the total spectrum, light casts quite sharp shadows, which the much longer radio waves do not; long-wave radio waves go round large obstacles. This tells us about radiation rather than about matter. On the other hand, visible light will not pass through matter transparent to radio waves, which tells us about matter. X-rays, of course, pass through flesh and to a lesser extent through bone; and waves with very short wavelengths are even more penetrating. How radiation is affected on its way through matter, and how it is reflected, can reveal atomic and molecular structures—especially for the repeating patterns of crystals.

Why are eyes sensitive to only one octave? This is because of the absorption by molecules of photopigment in the retina. Why should it be this particular octave? There are several likely reasons, including the available biological materials for eyes and the need for eyes to be small, which means that low frequencies (though safer biologically) could not give high resolution images. The energy of the Sun's spectrum peaks at around the visible region.[19] (The visual-octave of insect vision is displaced into the ultraviolet, by half an octave; this might be because the elements of their compound eyes are very small and so need shorter wavelengths to get adequate resolution or detail.)

Light, Magnetism and Electricity

The history of discoveries leading to the most recent understanding of light are so dramatic it would be sad indeed to ignore them. It seems incredible that the key for unlocking the nature of light was a simple experiment with a magnet and a coil of wire, carried out by Michael Faraday in 1831. Doesn't this show how unpredictable and full of wonderful surprises is the unique adventure of science?

Hans Christian Oersted (1777–1851) found, in 1820, that an electric current exerts a force on a magnetic compass needle. He noticed this accidentally during a lecture-demonstration. Michael Faraday, at the Royal Institution in London, found in 1831 that moving a magnet through a coil of wire produces electricity. More accurately: relative motion between a magnet and conducting wire generates electricity (see Figure 5.21). This extremely important experiment—which anyone can now do in a few minutes—revealed a close connection between electricity and magnetism. By recognising symmetries between electricity and magnetism, Faraday invented the dynamo and the electric motor, and so introduced an entire new industry which changed human life. It was also a conceptual revelation illuminating light itself.

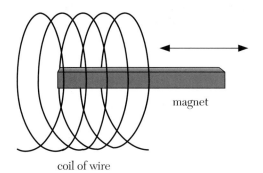

magnet

coil of wire

FIGURE 5.21 *Faraday's magnet and coil experiment (1831)*
Electricity is generated by moving a magnet through a coil of wire. The polarity of the electricity reverses when the magnet changes direction through the coil.

Faraday went on to show that when an electric current is *changing* it can induce changes in matter distant in space. This is *induction*. It is the basis of electric transformers, which work only with changing or alternating electric currents.

Faraday suggested that a magnet produces lines of force in space. The region occupied by these lines—the region where the magnetic force acts—he called the magnetic *field*. When a conductor of electricity, such as a wire, moves through the lines of force, what we now see as its electrons are set into motion.[20] With alternating fields, as the magnet moves back and forth, the electrons move forwards then backwards along the wire. When the wire is joined to form a circuit, current may flow to do useful things, such as heating filaments of lamps to emit visible light. Here, though, we have jumped the gun historically, for Faraday knew nothing of electrons; but his experiments led to their discovery.[21] He could hardly have guessed that it would lead to understanding light—yet he did predict that light would be affected by strong magnetic or electric fields.

If the magnet were moved to and fro through the coil a million times a second, long-wave radio waves would be produced. In fact this is exactly what a radio transmitter does, though the magnet does not physically move in an electronic oscillator. If Faraday's magnet were oscillated at around 10^{15} Hertz it would produce coherent light.

Electrical induction works only for small separations; yet the first claims for radio transmission and reception were dismissed as being no more than Faraday's induction. When the distances were increased from centimetres to metres, and then to many kilometres, it became clear that something else was going on. It was the German physicist Heinrich Hertz (1857–1894) who first demonstrated waves that are like visible light but much longer—an achievement that eventually led to radio communication.

Faraday found that as the magnet is moved faster through the coil, the voltage of the induced electricity increases linearly (the voltage doubling as the relative speed doubles.) So, what happens when electrons are *accelerated*? They generate radiation! This energy does not decrease as much with distance as does induction, so (like visible light) this radiation can be transmitted and detected across the Universe.

In spite of the great differences in how different wavelengths react to various kinds of matter, all electromagnetic radiations are regarded as essentially the same, because they can all be described with the same equations. The crucially important equations were the great achievement of the Scottish physicist James Clerk Maxwell (1831–1879).[22] Starting from Faraday's experiments on electricity and magnetism, Maxwell developed his theory that *light* and *electricity* and *magnetism* are all closely related, and his equations show how they are linked.

A key to Maxwell's theory was Faraday's discovery, in 1845, that a beam of polarised light in glass is rotated by a magnetic field. William Thomson (later Lord Kelvin) (1824–1907) was struck by the fact that the handedness of this rotation depended on the direction of propagation of the light. This is different from the rotation of polarisation through optically active substances such as a sugar solution, for these substances each have a handedness which is the same whichever way light travels through them. This suggested that magnetism is a rotation (in some medium, the 'ether'[23]) which can also convey electricity. Maxwell thought of magnetic fields as vortices in the ether. He devised a mechanism to show how electric and magnetic fields might be related. One problem was how coupled vortices could revolve in the same direction. He separated them with 'idle wheels' like ball bearings (though they had not been invented). The idle wheels were seen as travelling—carrying electricity (see Figure 5.22).[24]

Maxwell started by thinking of mechanical models of the ether as carrying particles which are displaced by an electric field, giving a 'displacement current'. He also considered Faraday's principle:

An electric field is induced in any region of space in which a magnetic field is changing with time. The magnitude of the induced electric field is proportional to the rate at which the magnetic field changes. The direction of the induced electric field is at right angles to the changing magnetic field.

Maxwell's principle is exactly the same—except that *electric* is replaced by *magnetic*. This shows a fundamental symmetry of nature. The final account combined (with some modifications) four laws of electricity and magnetism, to give a coherent theory for which there are no known experimental exceptions. It allowed Maxwell to deduce the speed of light in space from electromagnetic constants, and to predict that there should be radiations of different wavelengths travelling

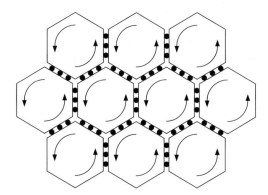

FIGURE 5.22 *Maxwell's model of vortices*

The vortices are rotating lines of magnetic force. The 'idle wheel' particles (like ball bearings) were seen as moving along, carrying electricity. Maxwell used such mechanisms as thinking tools for developing his mathematical models. After Siegal (1991).

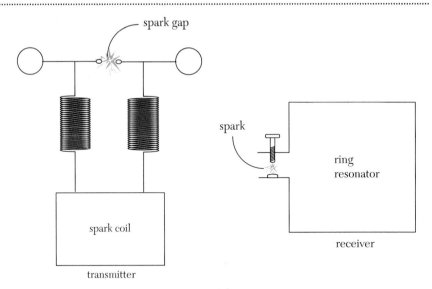

FIGURE 5.23 *Heinrich Hertz's apparatus*
The first demonstration of radio waves (1886–1888).

at the same speed. Sixteen years later this was verified experimentally with Heinrich Hertz's much longer radio waves, using the very simple apparatus shown in Figure 5.23.

A detailed discussion of Maxwell's equations is beyond the scope of this book and beyond its author's competence. Their obvious simplicity, though, is impressive: in a few lines they link the electric field E and the magnetic field B in a scheme that describes radiation from all parts of the electromagnetic spectrum:

$$\nabla \cdot E = \frac{\rho}{\varepsilon_o}$$

$$\nabla \times E = \frac{-\partial B}{\partial t}$$

$$\nabla \cdot B = 0$$

$$c^2 \nabla \times B = \frac{j}{\varepsilon_o} + \frac{\partial E}{\partial t}$$

The equations come from measures of electricity and magnetism changing in time. They gave a value within one per cent of Fizeau's measure of the velocity of light, suggesting and confirming that light is magnetic and electric waves, travelling at right angles and feeding each other by Faraday's induction (see Figure 5.24).

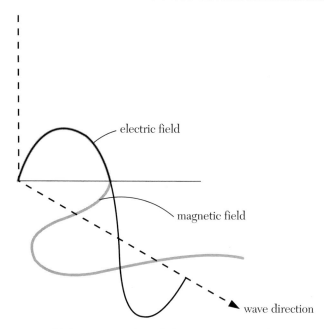

electric field

magnetic field

wave direction

FIGURE 5.24 *Light as magnetic and electric waves at right angles*
The magnetic and electric components of light are transverse waves at right angles to each
other—one increasing as the other decreases, as they are shifted by half a wavelength.

Maxwell's equations say that all electromagnetic radiations, whatever their wavelength, are essentially the same. The radiations appear different because different wavelengths react with matter differently. With beautiful experiments performed in around 1887, Heinrich Hertz demonstrated that what we now call radio waves can be reflected, refracted, and polarised just like visible light, except that the mirrors and prisms and polarisers may need to be made of different materials, and be larger. Metals reflect radio waves well, but Hertz used large prisms made of pitch to demonstrate bending by refraction.

The aluminium parabolic dishes used for reflecting radio waves, especially for producing parallel beams by collimating, and in radio telescopes for focusing radiation from the stars, do not need to be as smooth or as perfectly figured (shaped) as light-mirrors. The shorter the wavelength, the smoother and more precisely figured the surface must be. For a good optical image the surface must be precise to between a quarter and a tenth of a wavelength of light. As radio waves are much longer, cruder mirrors can be used—but they must be correspondingly larger for comparable resolution, so radio telescopes are very large.

Radio receiver aerials act as a kind of mirror. When the radio waves reach a distant aerial, the electrons in the aerial are driven forwards and backwards, copying the motions of the electrons in the transmitter (see Figure 5.25). So a changing voltage is produced that can be converted into speech or music, or whatever.

Thus electromagnetic waves in space or in air interact with electrons, especially in metals. Much the same physics applies to visible light, except that the scale is different. So what is a mirror? It is a bunch of receiving and re-emitting aerials.

Polarised Light

As Newton put it, light may be like *eels* travelling as *transverse* waves, like waves of a vibrating string. A string can vibrate only in one plane at a time, such as up and down, or sideways. But even a very narrow beam of light seems to vibrate in all planes, in all orientations. How is this possible? It does vibrate in only one plane at a time—but the direction of vibration changes millions of times a second. When, in special circumstances, all the waves in a beam vibrate in one plane continuously, the beam is said to be *plane polarised*. It may be made to vibrate, for example, only horizontally, or only vertically, with a polariser.

Polarisation was discovered by Huygens in 1690, while experimenting with Iceland spar (calcite). He found that a ray entering the crystal gets divided into

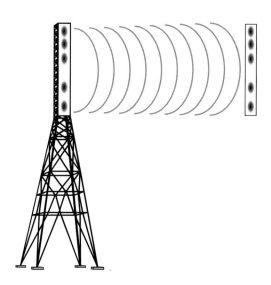

FIGURE 5.25 *Radio aerials*

The electrons moving up and down the transmitting aerial produce radio waves which make electrons in the receiving aerial move similarly. Speech or music is conveyed by modulating the wave, by changing its frequency or amplitude at audio frequencies.

two rays of equal brightness. When one of these rays was passed through a second crystal, what happened depended on the orientation of the crystal. The ray could double again, or come out single, depending on the orientation; so this light from the first crystal could not be symmetrical around its line of travel. This remained unexplained for a hundred years.

In 1801 a French soldier-physicist, Etienne Louis Malus (1775–1812), for some reason looked through a calcite crystal at light reflected from the windows of the Luxembourg Palace. He noticed that the reflections got brighter and then darker as he rotated the crystal. He realised that the glass of the window must have changed the light in a curious way, for when, instead of the crystal, he introduced a second sheet of glass held obliquely—and he rotated it around the axis of the light from a window pane—he found that the light reflected from the glass again got brighter and dimmer as he rotated it. Both sheets of glass had to be held at an oblique angle for this to happen; then the glasses had much the same effect as calcite crystals. Malus had discovered that light can be polarised by reflection from glass (see Figure 5.26).

Malus's experiment is well worth trying. It works best when the backs of the sheets of glass are painted black. It is, however, much easier to look through a Polaroid filter,[25] at light reflected obliquely from a mirror. One can see far better through water with polarised light, as the surface reflection disappears. This is a useful trick for fishermen, using a Polaroid filter.

Try this with a metal reflecting surface. Almost nothing happens when the polariser is rotated, for metals do not appreciably polarise or depolarise light. So a mirror can polarise light, but it matters very much what the mirror is made of. It works for glass—but hardly at all for a metal reflecting surface.

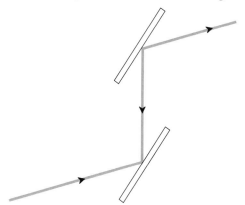

FIGURE 5.26 *Malus's discovery that mirrors can polarise light*
Malus noticed that when the glass sheets are oblique to the light (by about 57°) the light gets dim—bright—dim—bright—as one sheet is rotated. So he discovered that light can be polarised by reflection from glass.

What happens as the angle of the light striking the glass is changed? This was tried by Sir David Brewster, inventor of the stereoscope (see page 168). He found that polarisation is maximum for light reflected from a glass plate at about 57°. He also found that the exact optimal angle depends on the *refractive index* of the reflecting material. This shows that light does not simply bounce off the surface. Depending on the material, it more or less penetrates beneath the surface before reflection. So light 'sees' the atomic structure of matter, and can tell secrets.

As light does not penetrate far into metals it is not greatly polarised by metal mirrors. This is because metals are rich in free electrons. This is also why metals are good conductors of electricity: the lower the electrical resistance, the more reflective the mirror. Thus silver is both a better reflector of light and has lower electrical resistance than, for example, the metal lead. Also, the lower the electrical resistance, the less the polarisation. When light shines on a mirror it causes the electrons of the metal to vibrate. More vibrational energy is lost in lead than in silver, so lead would not make a good mirror. It gets heated, rather than reflecting light efficiently.

As we have said, waves of a string can vibrate only in one direction at a time. Light also can vibrate in only one plane; but the direction changes very rapidly, except when the light is polarised. For normal non-polarised light, the plane of vibration switches in angle randomly about 10^8 times a second. So over a sensible period of time, light is vibrating in all planes, and so is effectively unpolarised. In principle an adequate detector would see light coming through a polariser as *intermittent*, only getting through in bursts when its randomly changing plane of vibration matches the orientation of the polariser. These bursts of light, which are normally at different angles of vibration, are wave-chains of about 30 cm in length. One might think of them as accounting for—or indeed as being—photons, combining characteristics of waves and particles. The light looks continuous to us because the eye can only see flicker up to about 100 Hertz. A time resolution of over a million times greater would be needed to see this intermittency of polarised light.

The traditional polariser is a Nicol prism. This is a large crystal of Iceland spar (calcite) with a clever arrangement for removing the 'ordinary' ray, employing total internal reflection. It is now far easier to use plastic sheets of Polaroid. The molecules have electrons free to move along the long-axis of its molecules—absorbing energy in this orientation. The light that gets through the Polaroid is that which is vibrating at right angles to the light that is lost; so the light that gets through is polarised.

As we have seen, it is an over-simplification to say that light is *a* vibration, for light has two components—the electric and the magnetic vectors. These are always at right angles to each other (see Figure 5.24 above). In plane polarised light they keep a fixed orientation through space. But the vectors can be made to rotate. Then, light travels as a corkscrew. This may be right-handed or left-handed.

One can see what is happening with a bob on a string.[26] If the bob is struck, it will swing in a straight arc. Now strike it at right angles, a quarter of a swing later, and it will swing in a circle. It will also swing in a circle if the second blow is delayed for three-quarters of the swing. Then it swings in the reverse direction. Essentially this happens when polarised light enters a thin doubly refracting crystal. When the crystal is thick the beams separate; but when it is thin the 'ordinary' ray can kick the 'extraordinary' ray so that its vectors rotate. The result may be circular or elliptical polarisation according to the amplitudes and path differences within the crystal, with either direction of rotation. Thin plates of mica have generally been used to show this. Another method is to use a specially cut glass (see Figure 5.27), but nowadays it is far easier, as plastic sheets of circularly polarising filter are available—they are used by photographers and can be obtained from photographic dealers.

Why have I spent so much space and the reader's time on polarised and 'corkscrew' light? Partly because something remarkable happens when circularly polarised light is reflected. In Chapter 9 we will call it 'the Dracula Effect' (see page 251).

Colours

Colours are associated with wavelengths of light. The colours of the rainbow, or the spectrum, are associated with wavelengths of the single octave to which the receptors of our eyes are sensitive. The seven colour names for the spectrum—red, orange, yellow, green, blue, indigo, violet—were introduced by Newton by analogy with the seven basic notes of music. And the number 7 appealed to him as he liked magic. Actually we can distinguish not merely seven but rather hundreds of hues in a spectrum.

There are, however, only *three* kinds of 'cone' receptors in the retina signalling all these hues. What happens is that three somewhat different pigments in the cone receptors absorb energy of different wavelengths. Colours are seen accord-

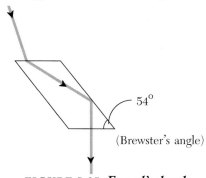

54°

(Brewster's angle)

FIGURE 5.27 *Fresnel's rhomb*
This gives circularly polarised (corkscrew) light.

ing to the relative intensities of the neural signals to the brain from these three kinds of cone receptors. So the number of hues that we can distinguish depends on the ability of the nervous system to distinguish differences in activity of the receptors tuned broadly to red, green and blue light. Yellow is seen by combined stimulation of the red-sensitive and the green-sensitive cones. As they overlap in the yellow region of the spectrum, red and green are stimulated with yellow light, as from a sodium street lamp. So, we can see yellow from two different kinds of lights: single wavelength yellow light; or by two spectrally separated lights, one red and the other green.

What happens when colours are mixed is very important for the artist. Mixing lights and mixing paints give opposite results. Pigments *remove* certain wavelengths of light from white—white light is *all* wavelengths in the visible band. This is the opposite of *adding* lights, as for stage lighting. For mixing paints it is *subtractive*; for combining lights it is *additive*.

The discovery that all spectral colours, and white, can be produced from only three coloured lights was made by Thomas Young in 1801. Adding lights is easily done with slide projectors fitted with colour filters. Three projectors—with red, green and blue filters—give white when their intensities are suitably adjusted. Red and green lights give yellow. Mixing paints is very different, as paints do not add but subtract from whatever light falls upon them. So red, green, and blue *lights* produce white; but red, green, and blue *pigments* produce black. This is illustrated in Plate 12.

Pigments of paints absorb broad bands of the spectrum. The sharpest cut colour filters are thin-film dichroic mirrors—interference filters.[27] They work in the same way as soap films, and oil on water, producing brilliantly coloured reflection or transmission. The colour depends on the separation of closely spaced surfaces, reflection between them producing cancellation or addition of the light, according to the separation of the surfaces and the wavelength. (An interference filter can be made to sweep across a small range of wavelengths, for 'tuning', by tilting it.)

Plate 13 shows reflection from a soap film. As the thickness of a film changes we see a cycle of spectral colours. Single-colour (monochromatic) light gives alternating bright and dim bands of the same colour. This happens as the waves from the front and back surfaces get in and out of phase. When the film is very thin, less than one wavelength, it goes black.[28]

Newton described colours in soap films, and noted that they go black or white when very thin; but he had a hard time explaining these beautiful and highly suggestive phenomena with his theory that light is particles. He spoke of 'fits of easy reflection and transmission.' But it was not clear how the particles would 'know' the distance of the back surface of the film. When light is thought of as waves this difficulty disappears. We can then (with the inner intuitive eye) see that light reflected from the back surface will interfere, adding or subtracting according to phase, with light reflected from the front surface.[29]

A neat experiment is to make a soap film cover a dark cup, or small bowl, and rotate it on a turntable. A beautiful sequence of concentric coloured rings will appear, as the film gets gradually thicker towards the edge. Alternatively, a wedge filter may be made with two microscope slides held together with elastic bands. Place a piece of paper between them at one end. Squeeze them, and the bands of light will run along the glass. Monochromatic yellow light (a sodium flame, or low pressure sodium lamp), gives alternating yellow and black bands. Thin films are added to camera and other lenses (called 'blooming') to prevent reflections between their elements, which would impair the contrast of the image.

Why does the separation between the plates have to be very small (or soap films very thin) to show interference colours? One might expect the cycle of colours to continue to any thickness: window panes should appear as brilliantly coloured as soap films! The reason this is not so is that the spacing between each cycle of colours gets smaller as the separation of the reflecting surfaces increases beyond the wavelengths of the light. When the spacing is so small that the cycles of colours are not resolved by the eye, the colours combine, to merge as white.

Are colours in the light itself, or in the eye and brain? It is important to note that although we speak of 'red' or 'green' or 'yellow' or 'blue', or whatever, light is not itself coloured. Different wavelengths affect the eye differently. Colour depends on eyes and brains. Without eyes and brains there would be wavelengths of light but no colours. Newton was very clear on this point. He speaks of light as 'red-making', 'orange-making' and so on, being clear that it is not the light itself which is coloured. Later in the *Opticks* he simply speaks of red or whatever light; but this is shorthand for what this does to eyes and brains. Actually we do not normally see colours simply according to wavelength, for there is perceptual compensation for the colour of the ambient light, so that surfaces appear almost the same colour over a considerable range of ambient colours. This is 'colour constancy'. It was investigated by the inventive genius Edwin Land, who suggested his 'Retinex' theory of colour vision: that the colours we see depend on relative intensities of what he called the 'long', 'medium', and 'short' wave (cone) receptors—and on the spectral energies of the background or ambient light shining on objects. Recently, the electrophysiologist Semir Zeki, working in London, has identified particular cells in the brain associated with colours as seen.[30] Evidently the brain generates sensations of colour and we now know where this happens.

The New Physics—Born from the Worst-of-all-Possible Mirrors

A looking-glass reflects light so efficiently that it keeps cool, even though intense light is shining on it. What happens to a black mirror? It reflects light so inefficiently that it gets hot. And when it gets hot, like any other hot object, it radiates energy. Even if it receives a single frequency or colour, a black mirror radiates energy at all frequencies. Classical nineteenth-century physics predicted what this energy distribution would be, but this prediction turned out not to fit the facts, and to be impossible. This was shown using a hollow sphere or a box with a small hole, called a cavity. This is a 'worse' mirror than a sheet of the most absorbing material, such as carbon; for with the cavity's multiple reflections it almost completely absorbs the incoming radiation. Something that absorbs radiation this efficiently is called a 'black body' (see Figure 5.28).

Classical physics said that with increasing temperature, the energy will increase without limit (as for the red glow of a lamp filament going more and more towards the blue of the spectrum with higher voltages). But experiments showed that the peak of the energy falls at high frequencies and the peaks of the curves shift towards the shorter wavelengths as temperature increases. (Actually this is not at all simple experimentally because the energy-detecting instrument has its own somewhat non-black-body characteristics). In 1900 the German physicist Max Planck (1858–1947) discovered a formula that fitted the facts.[31] But this introduced an entirely new idea, which at first looked highly suspect. The idea was that energy comes not continuously, but in small chunks or *quanta*. The chunks of light are called *photons*. Planck supposed that both the light entering and the absorbing molecules are *quantized*.

This discovery, made with black-body, worst-of all-possible mirrors, changed science. It created quantum physics which has enabled us to make detailed, highly accurate calculations about the physical world; though it does not give an intuitive sense of understanding. Indeed, in places it looks deeply paradoxical. However, it explains a puzzle which one meets in some kinds of photographic exposure meter. For light to knock electrons out of atoms it is not sufficient for the light to be bright; it must be short-wavelength, high-energy light. It may need to be ultraviolet, or of even shorter wavelength. This is the photoelectric effect.[32]

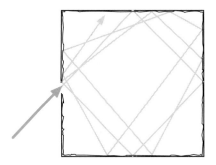

FIGURE 5.28 *Black body cavity*
After many reflections almost all the light energy is absorbed. This worst-of-all-possible mirrors inspired quantum physics.

It was Einstein who first saw the significance of the photoelectric effect. He used the quantum concept in 1905 to explain it—he said that electrons are not 'boiled' off metals according to the strength or brightness of light, but are only removed from the metal by light above a critical frequency (or below the corresponding wavelength). The point is, it is the *energy* in each photon that is crucially important, rather than the *amount* of light, or its brightness. This is like throwing balls at coconuts in a fair: however many balls you throw, and however often you hit a coconut, the balls must be thrown with sufficient energy to have any effect.

Classical physics could not explain these observations: why no electrons are emitted when the light is below a critical frequency; that the *number* of electrons emitted is proportional to light *intensity*; that the *kinetic energy* of the electrons increases with the *light intensity*; that the electrons are emitted almost instantly—before there is time to build up kinetic energy. Quantum theory accounts for these, and much more, but at the cost of making light look highly mysterious.

Einstein thought of light as being rather like packets of waves, as shown in Figure 5.29. Although this idea makes light look like particles, it was not possible to drop the light-is-waves notion because of such phenomena as Thomas Young's light–dark bands observed of light passing through pairs of slits, and the colours of soap bubbles. It was even odder that, as shown by the British physicist Paul Dirac (1902–1984), light has the *dual* properties of waves and particles—but in a given situation light displays *either* wave or particle properties—not both at once. Thus slits show the diffraction pattern of waves, but counters reveal light as particles. Light is seen *both* as waves and as particles. It helps to think of quanta as *packets of waves*, the high frequencies being associated with high energy quanta. But the wave-packets notion is not really adequate, for light does not show wave and quantum properties at the same time. However, a person is not happy and sad at the same time!

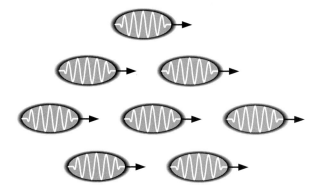

FIGURE 5.29 *Einstein's picture of light*
The packets of waves are photons.

For the eye, the wave character of light is more important than its quantum aspect. The wavelength of visible light sets the eye's limit to resolution—detailed vision—and wavelengths are essentially important for seeing colours. However, the minimum number of photons required for seeing a dim brief flash has been measured, and it turns out to be about three to five quanta reaching a small region of the retina within about a thousandth of a second.[33] This is very close to the most sensitive detector that is possible theoretically. Thus the eye is limited by the fundamental physics of light. Its design here is just about as good as it could possibly be, except that the tissues of the eyes are not as transparent as glass.

Inside the Atom

Crystal structures have revealed structures of molecules and at least hint at the nature of atoms. Their changes in energy, which correspond to the emission and absorption of light, are revealed with the spectroscope. The Danish physicist Niels Bohr (1885–1962)[34] described the pattern of lines in the spectrum of the simplest atom, hydrogen, from a model like the solar system: a central heavy nucleus with much lighter electrons circling in orbits.[35] But if atoms were just like the solar system, the electrons would collapse into the nucleus—because they should be radiating their energy away. The quantum idea suggests that there are discrete possible orbits. Electrons jump into higher energy orbits when the atom receives extra energy, such as when light shines on it, and sooner or later may then collapse back into a smaller lower energy orbit—when the atom gives out light. Thus the phosphor of a TV screen accepts energy from the scanning electron beam and emits visible light. Brighter-than-white soap powders convert ultraviolet light into blue light in this way.

Energy jumps in atoms have been seen for over a hundred years, with prisms or reflecting spectroscopes. The patterns of line-spectra are the fingerprints of atoms and molecules, including those in the most distant stars. The simplest is the hydrogen spectrum, which is shown in Figure 5.30. These lines are produced by passing light through a slit to a prism or to a reflecting grating, which is a mirror with fine rulings producing diffraction. The pattern of the emission lines of hydro-

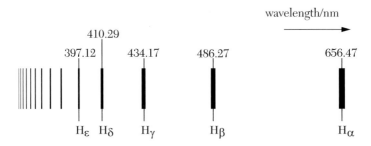

FIGURE 5.30 *The hydrogen spectrum*
The intervals in the Balmer series of lines fit quite a simple equation.

gen forms the Balmer series, discovered in 1885 by a schoolmaster, Johann Balmer (1825–1898). The theory came later. The intervals represent the energies of collapsing orbits of the electron in the hydrogen atom, so we see some quantum effects quite directly.

What is so different from classical physics is that these transformations always take place in jumps of energy. When many atoms are involved, the individual jumps smooth into continuous changes. But to explain many things of vital importance—including the working of the retinal receptors of our eyes[36]—one has to consider the discrete energy steps which are central to quantum physics.

A dramatic example of quantum physics is the laser, which produces *amplified* light. The idea that light can be amplified derives from a theoretical paper published by Einstein in 1917 on the energy equilibrium between matter (atoms) and radiation (photons). This led to the notion that energies of electron states in atoms could be raised, and with the emission of a few photons would simultaneously fall—emitting photons of light in phase at the same single frequency. This was first achieved for radiation lower in frequency than visible light: the result was the maser (*m*icrowave *a*mplification by *s*timulated *e*mission of *r*adiation). In the 1950s the same process was achieved for visible light with the laser (*l*ight *a*mplification by *s*timulated *e*mission of *r*adiation). The first laser consisted of a cylindrical ruby crystal between a pair of parallel mirrors, surrounded by a coiled flash tube (see Figure 5.31).[37] The mirrors were very precisely parallel, and one was slightly transparent so that the laser light could escape at one end. Ruby was chosen because the impurity which gives its red colour (it is a form of chromium) has suitable energy levels. The mirrors bounce the photons backwards and forwards many times along the same direction, to produce an extremely narrow beam of very bright, almost completely monochromatic red light, of almost perfect coherence (Figure 5.32).

Now lasers are useful for optical research, and are vitally important for indus-

coiled flash tube

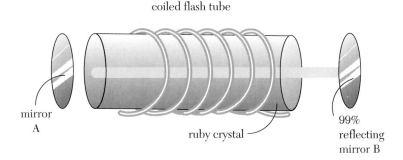

mirror
A

ruby crystal

99%
reflecting
mirror B

FIGURE 5.31 *Ruby laser*

The ruby crystal, with a mirror at each end, is surrounded by a coiled flash tube. The mirror at the right is semi-transparent, so the laser light can emerge as a narrow beam.

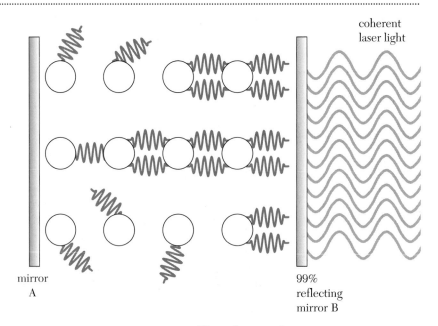

FIGURE 5.32 *How a laser works*

The end mirrors cause the photons to move back and forth, to emerge through the semi-transparent mirror at the right. The photons start off moving in all directions but end up moving in a single direction—to give a narrow intense beam of coherent light.

try: they are used in communications and medical technologies; specialist welding; gun-aiming; and, possibly for the future, energy generation by nuclear fusion. The weakest laser is hundreds of times brighter than the Sun—lasers must never be looked into, even for a fraction of a second.

Uncertainty

A basic concept of quantum physics is the *uncertainty principle* put forward by the German physicist Werner Heisenberg (1901–1976). This states that it is impossible to know both the position and the momentum of a particle with complete accuracy. So at the atomic scale what we can measure is 'granular'. This is related to the smallest possible chunk of energy, which for a particular frequency is the product of that frequency and Planck's constant, h. As it requires energy to detect, or measure or perceive, and as energy is grainy (quantised), knowledge of position and momentum can never be precise.

Consider Thomas Young's double-slit experiment (page 128). One would think that if a light were so dim that only one photon at a time passed through a slit, this would be the same as having only one slit. But this is not so. It is as though a photon 'knows' the other slit is open! For with only one slit, there is no diffraction pattern—yet with single photons when both slits are open, there is a diffraction pattern. This is quite different from the ripple tank, and it is not easy to see from Einstein's wave-packet picture of light (Figure 5.29).

What happens over large separations between the slits? This was the question of the famous Einstein–Podolsky–Rosen (EPR) experiment. The idea is to imagine a single stationary particle split into two equal parts, A and B. The uncertainty principle should prevent us from knowing both the position and the momentum of A or B at the same time. Yet, because of Newton's law of action and reaction (conservation of momentum), a measurement of A's momentum can be used to deduce B's (equal but opposite) momentum. And as (if they are equal) A and B will move the same distance in the same time, at a moment in time after the split a measurement of A's position should give B's position. The point is, because of the symmetry of A and B, an observer on, for example, A could know the momentum or velocity of B, as he or she chooses. But the availability of the choice implies B *has* a definite velocity and momentum. So it must be an objectively 'real' particle. Einstein, in a celebrated debate, used this situation to challenge Niels Bohr, who held that the particles are not 'real' until they are observed. Bohr replied that the other particle is an inseparable part of the quantum system.

But what if the particles are allowed to separate by a *great* distance? How could they still co-operate—though signals cannot travel faster than light? Einstein described this as 'ghostly action at a distance'. It *appears* like this given separate reality for each particle; but for Bohr the reality is that the particles never separate, as our familiar objects would separate, in such a situation. Recently, half a century after it was conceived, this action-at-a-distance (or continuity through separation) has been experimentally established, by the French physicist Alain Aspect, using oppositely polarised photons from a common source.[38]

Such puzzling properties of light can be illustrated with mirrors. Euan Squires (1986) gives the following thought experiment which represents a central puzzle (see Figure 5.33): two mirrors reflect particles to some detectors, and the detectors record a distribution of particles (see Figure 5.34). Now, what happens if a mirror is removed? The distribution of particles with both mirrors is not the same as the distribution with the mirrors separately. This violates common sense.

According to the theory and the experimental results of quantum physics, having two mirrors present is not the same as having one mirror and then the other mirror—and combining the results for each mirror afterwards. What is important is the *possible paths*. The second mirror in place offers more possibilities. So quantum physics is not only of *what is*, but of *what might be*.

QED

Why is glass so transparent that only a small proportion of the light that hits it is reflected—though metals (such as silver) are so reflective that no light gets

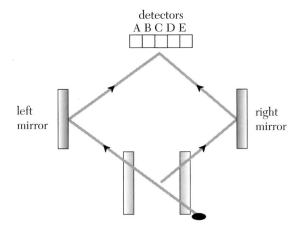

FIGURE 5.33 *Mirror thought experiment*
The mirrors can reflect the particles to the detectors. The 'potential barriers' are part-reflecting mirrors. After Euan Squires (1986).

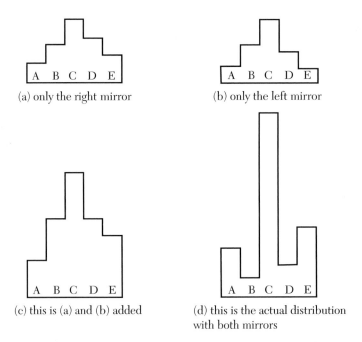

FIGURE 5.34 *Possible distributions of particles in the detectors of Figure 5.33*
After Squires (1986).

through and essentially all is reflected? In short, why is glass transparent, but metals opaque? And why does light travel slower in glass than through space? These are questions of how light interacts with matter. Light does not simply pass through glass as a fish swims through water. In the glass are myriads of electrons set vibrating by the light. The energy of the light is passed hand-to-hand through the glass by the electrons as they absorb and emit energy. The electrons may be thought of as oscillating on springs. Their 'natural' frequency of oscillation is higher than the frequency band of visible light. For glass it is in the ultraviolet range. Glass is generally opaque to frequencies very different from visible light—frequencies which can not vibrate the electrons. Coloured glass absorbs some frequencies more than others: red glass absorbs the higher frequencies, and blue glass the lower frequencies, of visible light.

Electrons are thought of as very small negatively charged particles. When they are in the outer regions of atoms they determine the characteristics of matter, and they are the vehicles of chemical reactions. Electrons can also be freed from atoms, as in the beam of electrons that shoots through the tube of a television to activate its phosphor screen. When the phosphor is hit, its atoms have their energy increased, to collapse back to the original 'ground state'—emitting photons of light. Their wavelength corresponds to the difference between the raised energy and the ground state. So a region of the phosphor of a TV screen struck by the electron beam becomes a source of light, its colour being given by the loss of the electron energy. By using three kinds of phosphors, which have energy collapses corresponding to three appropriate colours of light for our eyes—red and green and blue, as for Young's colour-mixture experiment (page 138)—an almost full-colour picture is produced just from these three colours.

Metal mirrors reflect with so little loss because metals have lots of free electrons. So metals with the lowest electrical resistance are also the most reflective. Metals hardly depolarise light because practically all that the light 'sees' is the free electrons near the surface of the metal.

These ideas, expressed rather loosely here, have been developed into the elegant though difficult theory of *quantum electrodynamics*. The distinguished American physicist Richard Feynman gives the quantum electrodynamics account of reflection from mirrors in his fascinating book *QED* (1985):[39]

When I talk about partial reflection of light by glass, I am going to pretend that the light is reflected only at the *surface* of the glass. In reality, a piece of glass is a terrible monster of complexity—huge numbers of electrons are jiggling about. When a photon comes down, it interacts with electrons *throughout* the glass, not just on the surface.

In this theory, it is necessary to consider every possible step of the dance that the electrons might make. The number of *possibilities* sets the *probabilities* of what will happen. According to Feynman:

In order to calculate the probability of an event, one must be very careful to *define the complete event clearly*—in particular, what the initial conditions and the final conditions of the experiment are. You look at the equipment before and after the experiment, and look for changes.

What happens under various conditions appears to us paradoxical. So much so, that Feynman says: '. . .the more you see how strangely Nature behaves, the harder it is to make a model that explains how even the simplest phenomena actually work. So physics has given up on that.' He has, however, made a significant step in this direction, by representing the probability-dance of the photons graphically—with *Feynman arrows*. He describes what happens in a mirror with his system of arrows of various directions and lengths. This represents a view of mirrors that is different from ray optics, and different from wave optics.

On a ray model, the only part of the mirror that matters is the tiny region struck by a ray that reaches the eye. On a wave model, there must be sufficient area of the mirror to cover several waves. Restriction of aperture in optical instruments is very important: it sets the resolution of a telescope, a microscope, and the eyes. This is related to interference and diffraction of light, as images are made up of diffraction patterns. The startling new QED view is that *all* of even a plane mirror contributes to reflection. This is represented in Figure 5.35. The whole of the mirror contributes, as photons may reach the eye from any part—though the great majority of photons take the least-time path. They have the highest probability of reaching the eye.[40]

The *grand principle* of Feynman's system of arrows representing what is going on in the glass is that the probability of an event is equal to the square of the length of an arrow (the probability amplitude). So, for example, an arrow of length 0.4 represents a probability of 0.16, or 16%. The *general rule* for drawing arrows is that if an event

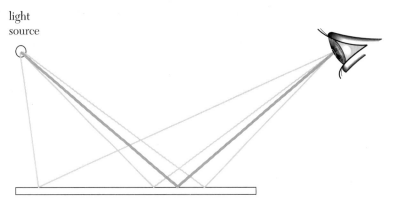

FIGURE 5.35 *QED view of light reflected from glass*
The entire mirror contributes to reflection. The least-time path (the thicker line) is the
great majority path.

can happen in *alternative* ways, an arrow is drawn for each *possible* way. The arrows are combined by hooking them together—the tail of one to the head of the next. The resulting arrow—from the tail of the first to the head of the last—is the one whose square gives the probability of the entire event. Feynman shows that: 'When light reflects from a mirror, the angle of incidence is equal to the angle of reflection; light bends when it goes from air or into water; light goes in straight lines; light can be focused by a lens . . . *every* phenomenon about light that has been observed in detail can be explained by the theory of quantum electro-dynamics. . . .'[41]

We have just said that in the classical *light is rays* view (Figure 5.6) we need only consider the region of the mirror where rays strike, such that the angle of incidence equals the angle of reflection. This not quite so for the *wave theory* of light, as an extremely small mirror would not allow the waves to be reflected without some loss. It is even less true for *quantum theory*, for the entire mirror counts—none of it can be ignored.

What happens if parts of a mirror are removed? This is what is done for *reflecting diffraction gratings*. According to the spacing of the grating lines, they reflect specific colours. Reflecting gratings are extremely useful for producing spectra in laboratories, and for seeing what stars are made of and measuring their velocities.

These ideas are 'beyond sense': they are counter-intuitive. For some physicists this means that the theory is not complete. They would like to get rid of the scaffold and see what is behind it. For other physicists, tools for calculation are the nearest we can come to reality.

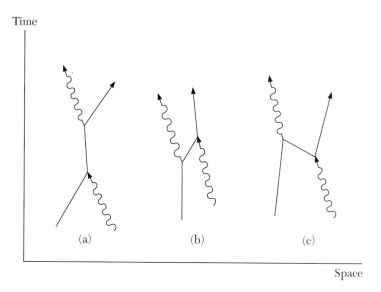

FIGURE 5.36 *Feynman diagram*
This switches the visual brain into a conceptual scheme we have never experienced.

Richard Feynman did not suppose that his arrows actually exist. They are a graphical means to derive correct results without having to go through a lot of tedious calculations (see Figure 5.36). But they give a hint of a conceptual model for perceiving what is happening. Perhaps one might say they are a scaffold for the imagination as well as an aid to calculation. But just what is happening remains hidden from our inner eyes of intuition.

Notes

1. There is some doubt whether the work on mirrors often ascribed to Euclid is by the great geometer. Apparently it may be a later compilation by Theon of Alexandria, at the end of the fourth century AD. But I shall assume it is *the* Euclid.

2. Hero is well known for his books on mechanical and hydraulic gadgets, including his steam engine, though this was little more than an interesting toy. He was both an inventor and a collector of gadgets from several previous centuries.

3. It is also interesting for the philosophy of science that Röemer came to measure the speed of light while he was thinking of quite other matters. This was entirely different from putting up a hypothesis and testing it. However uncomfortable it is for philosophers who are looking for a neat simple story, surely history shows that science works in many ways, and explicit testing of hypotheses to the death is perhaps exceptional. It is striking how separate ideas sometimes come together in a way that is quite unplanned, with entirely surprising and occasionally very important results. It could not have been expected that observations of Jupiter's satellites would provide a measure of the speed of light; or have been imagined that the value, c, of the speed of light would turn out to be one of the most important universal constants.

4. National Physical Laboratory.

5. It is because glass slows light that a prism deviates or bends light; and as various wavelengths are slowed differently—long wavelengths being less affected than short wavelengths—a prism disperses or spreads out light according to wavelength, into the spectral colours.

6. A surface obeying Lambert's Law (1760) is equally bright from any viewing angle. Its brightness is a function of the cosine of the angle of a point source shining on it, and inversely proportional to the square of its distance. Lambert also showed that each layer, of equal thickness, absorbs an equal fraction of the light (Lambert's law of absorption). When there are deep cracks or crevices, Lambert's cosine law does not hold. The Moon reflects more light back towards the Sun than to Earth. The rougher the surface of a sphere the flatter it looks—so Galileo was surprised to find the Moon a sphere, in his telescope. Lambert's Laws are used in computer graphics to generate convincing surfaces. See Oeren and Nayar (1994). I am indebted to Geoff Sullivan for this information.

7. It depends on the relative indexes of refraction of the media. Snell's law is $\sin \theta_i / \sin \theta_t = n_{ti}$.

8. See, for example, Feynman (1970).

9. Lucretius (c. 60 BC).

10. Named after the French mathematician (who accompanied Napoleon to Egypt, and became governor of lower Egypt) Baron de Jean Baptiste Joseph Fourier (1768–1830). In 1807 Fourier showed that almost any repeated wave function is a superposition of a large number of harmonic (sine and cosine) waves, described by assigning values to coefficients for amplitudes and harmonic frequencies. Fourier analysis can be applied to temporal and spatial patterns.

11. It seems amazing that all the instruments of an orchestra can be heard from the vibrations of the single diaphragm of a loud speaker. Indeed it is amazing; but the ear receives all sounds from its single vibrating membrane, the ear drum.

12. For its significance for vision, see Barlow and Mollon (1982).

13. Water waves for illustrating wave properties of light are well described and discussed by Llowarch (1961).

14. Brewster (1831) page 138 (his italics).

15. Newton was not quite the first to think it: the Scottish mathematician David Gregory (1661–1708) had tried to make a 'Gregorian' reflecting telescope a few years earlier, but had failed for technical reasons. His design became very popular in the eighteenth century.

16. It is sometimes said that Wollaston invented achromatic lenses, with earlier 'anticipations'. Credit for an invention or a discovery often goes to the person who makes effective use of it, or sees its significance clearly. There are 'anticipations' of Galileo's astronomical observations, and of some of Newton's classical experiments in the *Opticks*, and of Thomas Young's theory of colour vision. Attributions tend to be drawn to well-known names. So there is a considerable mythology in the history of science. The history of achromatising lenses is given very fully in Hall (1993).

17. Thomas Young was an infant prodigy and an extraordinarily gifted individual, in languages, medicine and science. He made the first useful effort to decipher Egyptian hieroglyphics, and established principles of insurance, blood flow, colour vision, and optics.

18. This is complicated by secondary wavelets, providing energy essentially in radiating lines. It is not easy to see why light appears to travel as rays if it is expanding waves, and Huygens did not quite succeed in explaining it. His notion was developed by the French physicist Augustin Jean Fresnel (1788–1827). Huygen's wave notion was further refined (and related to Maxwell's electromagnetic theory) by the German physicist Gustav Robert Kirchhoff (1824–1887).

19. Barlow (1982).

20. Faraday demonstrated lines of force with iron filings. Beautiful as this is, one must be careful, for the lines one sees are due to the filings lining up, and larger or smaller filings give differently spaced lines. One should not assume that there are lines when there are no iron filings. They may produce rather than reveal the lines.

21. The electron was discovered by J. J. Thomson (1856–1940) from examining cathode rays, in 1897, at the Cavendish Laboratory in Cambridge.

22. James Clerk Maxwell was born in Edinburgh in 1831, and became the first professor of Experimental Physics at Cambridge (1871). His treatise *Electricity and Magnetism* appeared in 1873. His theory, relating electricity, magnetism and light, has been called the greatest insight in physics since Newton. He also carried out interesting colour mixing experiments.

23. Maxwell believed that the ether was the medium which carried electromagnetic waves—an idea which was later abandoned. It was Einstein who demolished the ether conceptually, with experimental support from the famous Michelson–Morley experiment, which showed that there is no change in the speed of light with the Earth's motion through space. Although the ether has been abandoned, light is still thought of as waves—but how can waves travel through nothing? One way of seeing this is to think of light as particles (photons) made of waves (Figure 5.29).

24. The development of Maxwell's ideas is discussed in detail in Siegal (1991).

25. Invented by E. H. Land in 1938, this absorbs waves of unwanted orientations, with long-chain molecules of hydrocarbons, which are oriented by stretching the plastic sheets in which they are embedded.

26. See Wood (1934).

27. For a technical treatment see Heavens (1955, 1991).

28. This and far more is well described by Isenberg (1972, 1992).

29. Robert Hooke used these colours to show the alchemists wrong in thinking of colours in liquids as due to sulphurous, saline, or mercurial elements. Hooke explained these effects, which he observed in thin mica films with his microscope, with his 'pulse' theory, which is not so different from the modern wave theory of light.

30. Zeki (1993).

31. The German physicist Max Karl Ernst Planck (1858–1947) was the founder of quantum physics. Born in Kiel, he studied at Munich under Kirkhoff and in Berlin under Helmholtz.

32. The photoelectric effect was discovered by Heinrich Hertz (1857–1894), who first demonstrated radio waves. Einstein was awarded the Nobel Prize in 1921 for pointing out the immense significance of this effect. His theory of relativity was seen as too controversial for the Prize at that time.

33. Hecht, Schaer and Pirenne (1942); this is very well described in Pirenne (1948).

34. Neils Bohr was born in Copenhagen, and became a professor in Copenhagen after working with J. J.Thomson and Lord Rutherford at Cambridge He was the architect of the intellectual structure of quantum theory—hence the 'Copenhagen Interpretation' of quantum mechanics.

35. The central nucleus is made up of heavy positively charged protons and (except for hydrogen) equally massive neutrons which have no charge. An electron has about 1/2000th the mass of a proton or neutron.

36. Hecht, Schear and Pirrenne (1942) estimated the minimum number of photons required for seeing a dim flash of light. Individual receptors can respond to a single photon, though three or four are needed to ensure it is not 'internal noise'. About half the arriving photons are lost by absorption in the media of the eye.

37. Several people thought of this brilliant move from theory to practical application. The infrared maser was invented by Charles Townes, who with A. L. Schawlow created the laser. For a number of years the laser sat around as an answer to problems that had not been asked, and it seemed almost useless.

38. A way out of this conundrum (see Davies and Brown (1986) pages 8–9; and Feynman (1985)) is to suppose that quantum particles do not have well-defined paths in space. It is sometimes convenient to think of each particle as somehow possessing an infinity of different paths, each of which contributes to its behaviour. These paths, or routes, thread through both holes or slits in the screen and encode information in each. The suggestion is that this is how a particle can keep track of what is happening throughout an extended region of space. The finding, following John Wheeler's suggestion of a 'delayed choice' experiment (that even when the electrons have gone through the apparatus, determining where they have gone destroys the interference pattern), looks like an effect backwards in time. So, even the usual assumption that time must travel forwards is challenged! It is, however, generally stressed that this limited backwards time travel cannot be used to alter the past (see Gribbin (1992)).

39. The quotes on this page are from Feynman (1985) pages 16, 81 and 82.

40. One interpretation is that probability waves, along all possible paths, sum their amplitudes; but only those close to the least-time path are in phase, the others tending to cancel each other out. So the majority contribution is along the least-time path.

41. Feynman (1985) page 37 and Chapter 6.

6

Making and Using Mirrors

Nature is often hidden, sometimes overcome, seldom extinguished
FRANCIS BACON

THE great majority of mirrors are made of metal or of glass; and glass mirrors are 'silvered', though not always with silver. Here we will look first at how mirrors have been and are now made, and then at their various uses: in instruments of various kinds, including telescopes; for navigation, especially sextants; as aids to drawing; for seeing in three dimensions with stereoscopes; in kaleidoscopes for generating symmetrical patterns; as range-finders using parallax, and, conversely, for removing errors of parallax; as optical levers for measuring small rotations; for analysing light; for seeing into eyes; for measuring visual space; and for deceiving and conjuring. Finally we will look at recently discovered mirrors in Nature—mirrors which are not made of metal or glass—which serve for seeing and for avoiding being seen.

Making Mirrors

Metal Mirrors

The earliest Egyptian mirrors were made of un-alloyed copper, cast in flattened circular form. When cool, they were hammered, and fitted with handles usually made of wood. Unlike Greek convex mirrors, Egyptian mirrors were flat. The metal of the earliest copper mirrors had arsenic impurities; tin was added later, which made it less porous and more reflective. Ancient Chinese mirrors had a high proportion of tin, with mercury, alum and deerhorn ash which made them resistant to corrosion.

Glass Mirrors

Naturally occurring glass—volcanic black obsidian—has been used from earliest antiquity. As it is hard and breaks into cutting edges, like flint, it was used for implements and weapons in the Palaeolithic period (3 500 000–500 BC), and although its flakes are far from flat it served as the earliest looking-glass. The image deep within the darkness of the glassy rock looks magical.

Glass is a wonderful material. Made of the cheapest and most common substance—sand—it lacks the glamour of diamond, but glass has many more functional and even aesthetic uses. It is unrivalled for windows, lenses and mirrors.

There is nothing like glass. Although apparently a solid it is classified as a fluid, as it flows, though very slowly. The bottom of an old window pane or mirror is measurably thicker than its top. Telescopes should not be left for long without being moved, or their lenses become distorted as the glass flows. It took thousands of years for craftsmen to appreciate the wonderful properties of glass and how it could be worked in many ways, when heated to be ductile. Its transparency has gradually been increased, taking us from seeing through a glass darkly, to communicating around the world with glass fibres carrying laser light.

Egypt may be the home of the first manufactured glass. The Pharaoh Thotmes established a glass industry at Tel el Amarna in 1370 BC. Beautiful objects were made by pressing hot, still-malleable glass into moulds. The blowpipe does not seem to have been used before the first century BC; but mouth-blown glass vessels are found at Pompeii, buried by the ashes of Vesuvius in August, AD 9, and are represented in pictures of earlier glass objects.

The Roman historian Pliny the Elder (AD 23–79) describes the manufacture of glass in his *Historia Naturalis*, where he draws upon Greek sources. He describes Phoenician sailors camping on the shores of the river Belius (the Naaman in Israel), resting their cauldrons on lumps of soda over a fire on the sandy shore: 'When these became heated and were completely mingled with the sand on the beach, a strange translucent liquid flowed forth in streams; and this, it is said, was the origin of glass.' The Romans used sand mixed with the ash of sea plants (soda glass), and also sand mixed with beechwood, which gave a glass rich in potassium. Examples of soda glass have remained transparent from Roman times. The potassium of beechwood makes this glass less viable over time, but it became more widely used as people came to live in woodlands further from the sea.[1]

Ancient methods of manufacture are preserved, through the ages, in remains of glass workings. A recent find is a first century BC glass-works in Jerusalem's Old City. Glass tubes were found in various stages of manufacture, with blown bulbs. This is evidence that blown glass started from heating glass tubes sealed at one end. The important invention of the metal blowpipe came later.[2] The technology of pipe-blowing led to the making of sheet glass, which was used for windows and later for mirrors. As these were parts of large glass bubbles, they were convex.[3] Convex panes for windows continued for two thousand years, sometimes including the central knob, from where the glass was removed from the blowpipe.

Sheet glass was made even earlier by pouring glass into trays, whose imprint can still be seen on the surface of these generally small pieces of glass. Coloured or stained glass, made by adding metallic oxides, was used, indeed pioneered, in early Christian churches.[4] The art of elaborate beautiful stained glass for windows was developed by the Christian tradition following the book of Genesis. God's first words are: *fiat lux*—'Let there be light'. And then 'God saw the light, that it was good'. Windows were so valued that over the centuries the stone masons worked architectural and engineering miracles to produce huge windows within slender arches.

The huge, glorious glass windows of cathedrals were made up of many small pieces of coloured glass, held together with lead. Large sheets of glass—especially for mirrors—were first produced in Venice, on the tiny island of Murano, where any fires could be contained. The master glass-maker Angelo Beroviero invented a transparent glass known as 'crystall.' This was an extremely valuable invention. With the skill of the Murano glass-makers it soon put the metal mirror-makers out of business. Venice gave special privileges to the mirror-makers—guarding their secrets with special laws, and imposing imprisonment and even sentence of death on the families of those who gave the secrets away to foreigners. The Murano mirrors were made from brown cylinders of glass, split and flattened on a stone, carefully polished, and then 'silvered' with an amalgam of tin and mercury which was pressed on cold, in a process called called 'foiling'. The chief glass-blowers were called 'gaffers', meaning 'learned grandfathers.' The furnace was filled with such wonderful glowing treasures it was called the 'glory hole'. Charles Brosses, a visitor to a Venetian 'glasshouse' in 1739, gives a vivid account:[5]

I have just returned from Murano, where I have been to see the glasshouse. The glass plates are not as large nor as white as ours, but they are more transparent and less faulty. They are not cast on copper tables like ours, but blown like bottles. The work demands extremely large and robust workers, especially to swing in the air those great globes of crystal on the ends of the blow-pipe. The worker takes from the crucible of the furnace a large quantity of molten matter, which is then of a gluey consistency, on the end of his pipe. By blowing he makes a hollow globe, then by swinging it in the air and putting it every now and then into the mouth of the furnace so as to maintain a certain degree of fusion, still turning it very quickly so that the matter does not run more on to one side than another, he succeeds in making a long oval of it. Then another worker with the point of a pair of scissors like sheep-shears (that is to say, they open when the hand is relaxed) pierces the end of the oval. The first worker holding the pipe turns it very quickly, whilst the second gradually opens the scissors. In this way the oval is completely opened up at one end. Then it is detached from the first iron pipe and sealed again at the upper end, on to another specially made pipe. Then it is opened at the other end using the same method I have just described. You have then a long cylinder of glass, of wide diameter. Still being turned, it is put once more into the mouth of the furnace to soften it a little again, and when it comes out, in a trice it has been cut lengthwise with shears and laid out on a copper table. After that, it only has to be heated again in another oven, polished and silvered in the ordinary way.

In the seventeenth and eighteenth centuries great labour was required to make large sheets of glass. Plate glass produced by casting was developed in France in the 1670s (see Plate 14). By 1691 the process—pouring molten glass onto a metal table and spreading it evenly with large metal rollers—was so improved that very large mirrors could be made without undue effort. But the glass had still to be ground and polished, which was tedious and time-consuming. When Dr Samuel Johnson visited Paris in 1775 he visited a glass-works making mirrors:[6]

We went to see the looking-glasses wrought—They came from Normandy in cast plates, perhaps the third of an inch thick—At Paris they are ground upon a marble table, by rubbing one plate upon another with grit between them—The various sands, of which there are said to be five, I could not learn—The handle, by which the upper glass is moved, has the form of a wheel, which may be moved in all directions—The plates are sent up with their surfaces ground, but not polished, and so continue till they are bespoken, lest time should spoil the surface, as we are told—Those that are polished are laid on a table covered with several thick cloths, hard strained, that the resistance may be equal: they are then rubbed with a hand rubber, held down hard by a contrivance which I did not properly understand—The powder which is used last seemed to be iron dissolved in aquafortis; they called it, as Baretti said, *marc de l'eau forte*, which he thought was dregs—mentioned vitriol and saltpetre—The cannon ball swam in the quicksilver—To silver them, a leaf of beaten tin is laid, and rubbed with quicksilver, to which it unites—Then more quicksilver is poured upon it, which by its mutual [attraction] rises very high—Then a paper is laid at the nearest end of the plate, over which the glass is slided till it lies upon the plate, having driven much of the quicksilver before it—It is then, I think, pressed upon the cloth, and then set sloping to drop the superfluous mercury: the slope is daily heightened towards a perpendicular.

The table was raised a few inches at a time, for several days, until vertical. The puzzling contrivance was almost certainly a sprung lever for reducing the weight of the rubber.

Plate Glass

Plate glass making in England was proposed in 1773, when the British Cast Plate Manufacturers was set up in Southwark, in London, and in Ravenhead near St Helens, Lancashire. The Ravenhead casting hall was the largest industrial building in the country.[7]

By the beginning of the nineteenth century there were three ways of making flat sheets of glass. 'Plate glass' was made by pouring molten glass onto frames, on which it was spread evenly with rollers, then ground and polished (strictly speaking, only ground and polished glass is 'plate'). 'Broad glass' was made by blowing a large cylinder, which was cut and opened out, and flattened on a table,[8] and 'crown glass' was the result of blowing a large sphere of glass, and using it to form a bowl which was spun while hot, to form a disc some five feet in diameter.

All three methods became almost entirely obsolete with the invention in the 1950s of *float glass*, by the Pilkington Brothers at St Annes in Lancashire.[9] As for almost all inventions, this one has a history of earlier failures. Attempts to draw a flat sheet of glass directly from a furnace had been tried for at least a century, but had met all kinds of difficulties. The original scheme was to dip a sheet of metal, known as a *bait*, into the molten glass to pull it out. But the sheet of glass would get narrower. This was overcome by forcing it through a narrow slit in a fireclay float, known as the *débiteuse*. This reduced the 'necking', but there were still problems. The Pilkington method involved floating molten glass on molten tin, in an inert gas atmosphere to prevent oxidising. The beauty of this method is that the tin is extremely flat and free of texture. It is a continuous process that avoids tedious grinding, and involves little or no polishing. This invention has created the industry which provides the vast area of modern windows that make our buildings so different from any in the past, and large mirrors affordable by all. Now it is not unusual for whole walls of rooms (especially in parts of Italy and in California) to be huge, perfect mirrors; so one's home is appreciated twice over. With parallel-facing mirrors a small room stretches out into space, seemingly to infinity.

Following these great achievements in glass-making technology, for various reasons metal mirrors were abandoned in favour of glass. The reasons were: less weight, ease of grinding and polishing, and smaller changes of figure with differences of temperature. A low (preferably zero) coefficient of expansion is very important for telescope mirrors. It is also important for glass dishes for cooking in ovens, as they are less liable to crack. Putting these two together produced 'oven proof' Pyrex glass, which is used for collecting light from across the Universe.

Silvering

Silver was not used for mirrors until about 1840, though confusingly the earlier application of an amalgam of a tin and mercury coating to glass was called 'silvering'. This process was difficult and dangerous. As Dr Johnson described it (page 156), a sheet of clean tin foil was laid out, with no creases, and mercury was rubbed over the surface and quickly taken off. Mercury was poured on the 'quickened' tin foil, until there was sufficient to float the glass upon it. Then the glass was slid across the surface, to avoid air bubbles. Weights were placed on it to press most of the mercury out, then the table was tilted to remove superfluous mercury to a gutter. The glass was left for twenty-four hours under weights, then turned over 'silver' side up and left to harden. Although this process worked well, and many mirrors of this type survive almost unblemished, the amalgam was horrifically damaging to the workers. 'Mad as a hatter' refers to the effects of mercury in hat-making; but the same appalling effects of mercury applied equally to the mirror-makers.

The first 'silver-on-glass' process was invented by the German chemist Justus von Leibig (1802–1873). In 1835 he found that by heating aldehyde with an ammoniacal solution of silver nitrate, in a glass vessel, a brilliant silver surface was produced. Although it was later highly successful, when this process was first tried industrially in Germany (at Doos near Nuremberg) it met with failure. This may have been because they failed to 'sensitise' the glass before silvering.[10] Leibig's silvering was later introduced in two ways: the hot and the cold methods. The hot method used steam, and the ammoniacal silver solution was reduced with tartaric acid. The cold process, which was much used for astronomical telescope mirrors, depends on the power of sugar to reduce silver nitrate. The glass dish is mounted on a rocking-table and most carefully cleaned with nitric acid, potash, and finally with distilled water. The reduced solution (which improves on keeping) is made up from two hundred parts of water, twenty of loaf sugar, twenty of alcohol and one of nitric acid (commercial pure). The silver solution is made of two parts of silver nitrate dissolved in twenty parts of water, and strong ammonia is added until the brown solution becomes clear. A solution of one-and-a-half parts of potash (pure by alcohol) in twenty of water is added, and then ammonia until the solution is again clear. A solution of one quarter part of silver nitrate in sixteen of water is added until the liquid is straw-coloured; it is then filtered. Quantities of the solution, such that the sugar equals one half the nitrate, are taken, diluted, mixed, and poured on to the plate, which is gently rocked. The liquid goes muddy-brown, and in three or four minutes it begins to clear, a thick deposit being formed in about five minutes. The solution is poured off, and water run on, the streaks of the precipitate being removed by lightly held cotton wool. The washing is repeated, and is then run off, and the plate is washed several times with alcohol, and then dried by an air fan. The film is now burnished with a chamois leather pad, and finally with the finest jeweller's rouge, the silver surface being the reflecting surface of the mirror.[11] The process gives the silver a yellow tinge, which is avoided by brushing the silvered surface with a dilute solution of cyanide of mercury.

One does wonder how well such complex instructions were optimised. (Isn't this a doubt also for cooking recipes?) How many controlled experiments would it take? Isn't all this like alchemy? Alchemy and craft-science are sometimes hard to distinguish.

Silver nitrate is unstable. When concentrated it can explode. It is used for detonators, as a small mechanical impact will set it off. (As an aside: my father started his career as a professional astronomer just after the First World War at the National Observatory of Egypt, at Helwan. They had trouble with marauders. By accident or design, after silvering a mirror, small pools of silver nitrate were left on the floor. In the middle of the night, stealthy footsteps became small explosions—followed by yells of terror and a rapid exodus. Being extremely superstitious, the miscreants thought the Devil was after them! This is a reminder that silver nitrate should not be left to concentrate in bottles.)

Though essential for astronomy, surface-silvered mirrors were too liable to damage for domestic use. For looking-glasses, the film was deposited on the *back* of the glass, protected first with a thin layer of copper, and then by a thick tough opaque backing behind that. Unfortunately, back-silvered mirrors have double images, as about twenty percent of the light is reflected from the front surface of the glass (see Chapter 5). This hardly matters for domestic use, but for scientific instruments the double image is such a severe disadvantage that back-silvering is almost never used in optical laboratories or observatories.

The surface of front-silvered mirrors is never touched, and needs to be protected. These mirrors are sacred objects in observatories and optics laboratories. Aluminised mirrors have gradually taken over from silvered mirrors, for although it is slightly less reflecting aluminium is more durable and less subject to tarnishing by atmospheric pollution. The aluminium film has to be renewed every few years, in a large vacuum chamber. Astronomers carry out this dangerous operation with due ritual and superstitious precautions.

Mirrors in Instruments

Visual perception is extremely important for survival and for science, but just as the limited powers of our hands are extended with tools (from knives and spoons and forks onwards), so optical instruments have extended the uses of the eyes. One of the most useful of all discoveries is that simple lenses can improve our eyesight, and so extend the working life of craftsmen and scholars—and all of us. It is interesting that their discovery or invention did not come from science, but rather from chance observations by craftsmen. The first spectacles were made by Venetian glass-workers in about 1286, and for a long time were an embarrassment, both because of their lowly origins and because 'weak sight' was associated with a 'weak brain'.

Quite simple instruments allow us to transform space and time to study perception itself. This can be done in various ways: using stereoscopes, the cinema, and ophthalmoscopes, for example. Mirrors play surprisingly important roles in many of these instruments, which may serve truth or illusion. Here notes are offered on some of them. We will look mainly at plane mirrors, after touching on the curved mirrors such as those of astronomical telescopes, though these are, of course, extremely important.

Mirrors have many important uses in science and technology. Originally these were metal mirrors—as in the telescopes of Newton—but the best metal mirror reflects only about forty per cent of the light falling on it, and it suffers from distortions of shape with temperature changes. Glass, silvered in some way, is now almost universally used in optical instruments.

Telescopes

Newton made the first telescope mirror—or *speculum*—in 1670. Newton's mirror telescope was designed to avoid the chromatic aberration (colour fringing) of lenses. A few years earlier, a reflecting telescope had been invented by a Scottish mathematician, James Gregory (1638–1675), but its speculum proved too difficult to make at that time, as it needed to have a central hole which made accurate grinding difficult. Newton's reflecting telescope, the first to be completed, is now in the library of the Royal Society in London (see Figure 6.1). The first mirrors for telescopes were made of a metal alloy containing copper and tin. Newton invented his own alloy: six parts copper, two parts tin and one part arsenic.

Newton's telescope had a simpler design than Gregory's, and it was easier to make, but it had the disadvantages that it had to be viewed from the side and it had an inverted image, which for terrestrial purposes was a serious snag. Small Gregorian telescopes were popular in the eighteenth century. At least, this is the generally accepted history. But the idea of a mirror telescope may have come considerably earlier, from an Italian professor at Bologna, Francesco Bonaventura (1632), who carried out experiments to discover whether Archimedes really could have burned the Roman fleet with a solar mirror. From successful trials, Bonaventura considered reversing his series of mirrors for a telescope.[12] Although he anticipated Newton's design, he considered it too frivolous to try! The important French scientist Marin Mersenne (1588–1648), a friar who defended Cartesian philosophy, also anticipated the Gregorian and other designs while he was thinking about Archimedes's burning glass.[13] Mersenne did not think mirrors would work as well as lenses for a telescope, and also did not try them out.

Unlike Newton, neither Bonaventura nor Mersenne had any compelling reason to believe a mirror would have any advantage. So it is ironic that Newton's reason—that chromatic aberration of lenses would never be overcome—turned out to be incorrect. Newton tried to cancel out the colour fringes using glasses of different dispersion, but gave it up as he thought it would only work for lenses of infinite focal length. As we said in Chapter 5, this was tried by Chester Moor Hall (1703–1771), who made refracting telescopes with lenses having elements of different kinds of glass, of different dispersions. This was developed by John Dolland (1706–1761), and later by William Wollaston (1766–1828) who made a lot of money from his chemical and optical inventions. This use of multiple elements of different glasses made possible high definition optical instruments, especially refracting telescopes and microscopes.[14]

Metal telescope mirrors, following Newton's speculum of 1670, were softer than glass, and were easily damaged by over-enthusiastic polishing. But they avoided the colour-fringing chromatic aberration problem of lenses, which was eventually solved, both in principle and especially well in practice, by the Edinburgh telescope maker, James Short (1710–1768).

Mirrors could be made aspherical ('parabolised') to avoid the loss of image quality due to the slightly different path lengths from the edge and the centre of a spherical mirror which gives 'spherical aberration'. Mirrors also had the advantage that they could be made far larger than lenses—lenses soon get too heavy, too thick, and lose their correct figure (their shape) when the telescope is moved near the horizon or high in the sky. This is not so for mirrors, as they can be supported from the back. And imperfections such as small bubbles do not matter

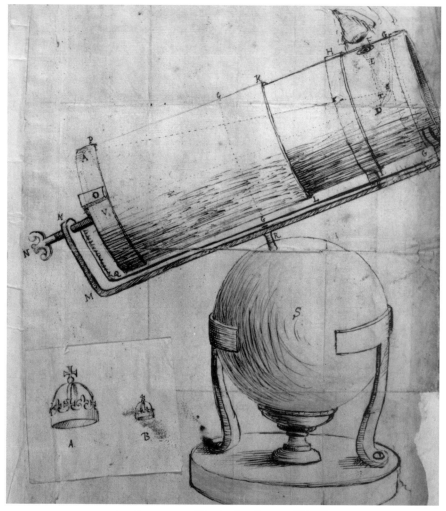

FIGURE 6.1 *Newton's telescope (1670)*
This telescope is now in the library of the Royal Society of London. This drawing is reproduced by courtesy of the Royal Society.

within a mirror, but ruin the performance of a lens. For some reason contrast seems never to be quite so good with a reflecting telescope; so refractors are preferred for planetary observation, where high resolution and contrast are important and maximum light-gathering is not.

The main types of reflecting telescopes are shown in Figure 6.2. Each has advantages and disadvantages. Newton's is simple and easy to make, but one has to look from the side. The Gregorian is hard to make, but one looks straight through and the image is the right way up—so it is good for terrestrial use. The Cassegrain is used for many large instruments. The Schmidt and later developments use a large spherical mirror and a curiously shaped corrector plate to remove the inherent spherical aberration of the primary mirror. It has a wide field of view with great light-gathering power. Schmidt telescopes are used for photographing star fields. Their disadvantage is that the image is inside the telescope, so it is difficult (though not always impossible) to look at it with added external instruments, such as spectroscopes. For capturing the very faint light of distant objects, mirrors are unrivalled. Mirrors of many kinds—including very precise plane mirrors—are essential in astronomy for such instruments as interferometers, and for spectroscopes to analyse light to discover what stars are made of, and to measure their velocities: for the stars are moving away from each other, and from us, in the expanding Universe.

Sir William Herschel (1738–1822) and his son Sir John (1792–1871) made large, very high quality metal mirrors for their telescopes, which transformed observational astronomy. With one of his mirrors Sir William discovered a new planet, Uranus, in 1781. John Herschel mapped the southern sky, and he also improved photography—a vital step towards making permanent high resolution records available for future generations of astronomers.

The third Earl of Rosse (1800–1867) constructed a huge telescope at Birr Castle in Ireland. It was fifty-eight feet long with a four foot diameter speculum mirror. It revealed spiral structures of what turned out to be extra-galactic nebulae (see Figure 6.3). It gave the first intimation that the Milky Way system is an island in space, separated by millions of light years from other galaxies, that light takes 100 000 years to cross. Only one galaxy outside ours is visible to the naked eye, and this only as a dim blur—the Andromeda Nebula 2 000 000 light years distant. Its structure was entirely unknown before this metal mirror was turned to the sky. This has led to pictures of the birth of stars seven billion years ago, from the superb glass mirror of the Hubble Space Telescope, as shown in Plate 15.

In America, the 100-inch Lick and the 200-inch Mount Palomar telescopes revealed unsuspected objects—pulsars and quasars—and measured the expansion of the Universe with the Doppler shift—spectral lines shifted to the red when the source receded. The largest telescope is now the Keck, on Mauna Kea (White Mountain) on a Hawaiian island. At 4200 metres this has the best 'seeing' anywhere in the world. As it is extremely cold, most atmospheric vapour is frozen

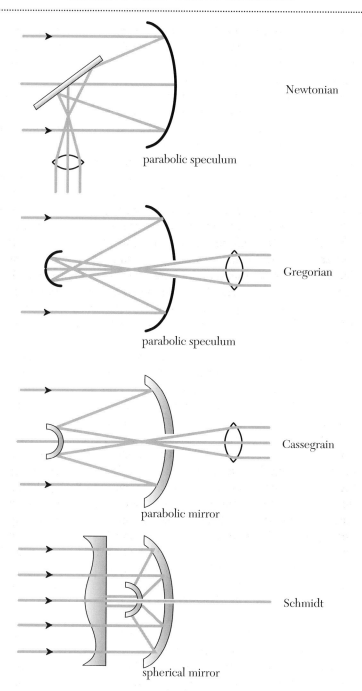

Newtonian

parabolic speculum

Gregorian

parabolic speculum

Cassegrain

parabolic mirror

Schmidt

spherical mirror

FIGURE 6.2 *Kinds of reflecting telescopes*

FIGURE 6.3 *The first drawing of a spiral galaxy (M51)*
This drawing is by the Earl of Rosse: his 42-inch mirror revealed for the first time a spiral galaxy. By kind permission of the Royal Astronomical Society.

out and the air has almost no turbulence. The Keck's mirror has four times the collecting area of the Palomar 200-inch; it can detect fainter and more distant objects than any other instrument. It may reveal planets of stars other than the Sun. Soon Keck II will be built nearby, to be linked as an interferometer to give ten times the resolution of Keck I.

Other types of mirror are also used in astronomy. Large, very light, flexible mirrors can be made from stretched mylar film. The curvature can be adjusted by changing the air pressure behind the mirror.[15] These mirrors may come to be used in orbiting space stations.

The conventional aluminised glass mirror is expensive and it is heavy. An interesting though scarcely used alternative is a spinning dish of mercury.[16] This gives a parabolic curve. The depth of curve, and so the focal length, is given purely by the speed of rotation. So mercury, water or any other liquid will produce a focus at the same distance from the mirror. This sort of mirror always looks upwards; but this could have its astronomical uses.[17] Large spin-cast glass mirrors of high quality are being made by Roger Angel of the University of Arizona. The melting and annealing oven rotates with the glass. The largest is two metres across, and diameters of up to ten metres are planned.

X-rays from space provide useful information, but as X-rays penetrate most materials X-ray mirrors present a problem. The solution (suggested by an article in *Scientific American* on the reflecting eye of lobsters!) is a series of flat metal plates at glancing angles.[18]

Steerable radio telescopes have a very large parabolic mirror with an aerial at the focus. Because the radio wavelength is so much longer than for light, the mirrors do not need to be anything like as accurate (the general rule is that an accuracy of one tenth of the wavelength is adequate).

Disturbance of light by the instability of the atmosphere sets limits to the performance of Earth-based telescopes. There are, however, several very interesting attempts to compensate for atmospheric disturbances by dynamic changes in the form of a flexible mirror. A computer (adaptive neural-net analogue self-learning systems look promising) controls the small dynamic mirror from optical signals of the errors of the wave-front.[19] The most promising method is to beam a very powerful laser through the telescope high up to the stratosphere. This forms a 'virtual star' (from back-scattering), which is disturbed by the atmosphere. This disturbance 'tells' the active optics how to correct the disturbances by putting anti-distortions on to the flexible mirror, dynamically. This may provide very high resolutions, as the mirrors can be extremely large.

Telescopes are placed in space both to avoid the turbulence of the atmosphere, and so that they can detect those parts of the electromagnetic spectrum that the atmosphere would filter out. The Hubble Space Telescope—or rather automatic observatory—has a large, though not on present standards giant, mirror, and several associated instruments. When it was launched there was a small error on the figuring (curvature) of the mirror which gave it spherical aberration. In January 1994 correcting optics were added by astronauts (at a reported cost of half a billion dollars) with a series of dramatic space walks. This great achievement has truly made science fiction fact. The power of the corrected telescope is astonishing, revealing the birth of stars so distant that they are beyond the reach of any other instrument.

Analysing Light

Mirrors are central to interferometers, which have a variety of practical and theoretical uses. They depend on the interference of light waves (as demonstrated by Thomas Young in 1801, see page 128); perhaps the simplest optical arrangement is Lloyd's Mirror (see Figure 6.4). A beam of light reaches the eye (or some other detector) by two slightly different paths: directly, and reflected obliquely

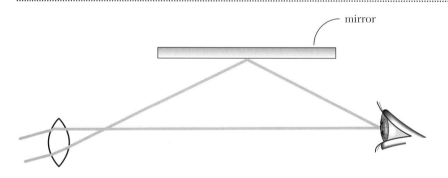

FIGURE 6.4 *Lloyd's mirror (simplified)*

from a mirror. The two paths are of slightly different lengths, so they can produce interference fringes.

A most important kind of instrument depending on the interference of light is the *Michelson interferometer*, which in various forms can increase the resolution of telescopes, even to measuring the diameters of the nearer stars. Its most famous use is in the Michelson–Morley experiment, which gave crucial experimental evidence against the existence of the ether—by showing that the velocity of light is the same whether or not the instrument moves with the Earth's rotation. This was not only evidence against the existence of an ether, but also supported Einstein's theory of relativity (see Figure 6.5).

Periscopes

Most familiar in submarines, periscopes are useful for optically moving the eyes—such as from under the water to above its surface. Although the periscopes in submarines have an elaborate series of lenses, essentially they are just two mirrors, as shown in Figure 6.6.

Stereoscopes

With an arrangement of two mirrors at 45° to the line of sight for each eye, Sir Charles Wheatstone presented slightly different drawings to each eye, giving the first 3D depth from pictures (1832, published 1838) just before the invention of photography (see Figure 6.7). Using a pair of cameras, horizontally separated like eyes, 'stereo-pairs' of photographs gave realistic depth of scenes. Although the mirror-stereoscope is excellent for research, and for war-time photo-reconaissance, it proved too clumsy for domestic use and so was generally replaced by Brewster's 'lenticular' stereoscope using combined prisms and lenses.

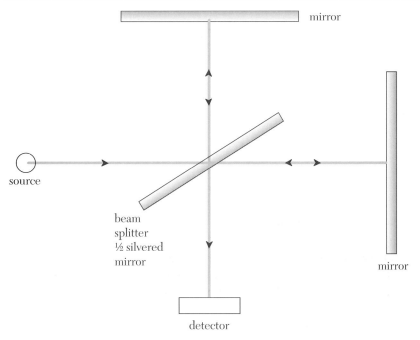

FIGURE 6.5 *The Michelson interferometer (simplified)*

Light from the source is directed to the upper mirror and back through the beam splitter to the detector—which also receives light (reflected from the beam splitter) from the right-hand mirror. A minute change of the path lengths changes the interference pattern observed by the detector. It should also detect a different speed of light when rotated through 90°, if the Earth moves through the ether. No change was found—providing evidence against existence of the ether.

Range-finders

When the position of the eye moves to the right, compared with distant objects near things move to the left. This is worth trying: holding up a finger and move your head slightly from side to side. The relative shift with different distances is called motion parallax). Motion parallax is an important clue to distances of objects, when the observer is moving; and stereo (3D) works in the same way—though without movement as the eyes get slightly different views simultaneously, as they are separated horizontally. (It is likely that stereo vision evolved from very ancient motion parallax, as the eyes became frontal, in, for example, monkeys who needed precise depth information for jumping from branch to branch in trees.) Stereo depth is given both by the eyes converging more when they aim at nearer things, and by the brain's massive parallel-computing of depth by comparing the (horizontal) separations of 'corresponding points' in the retinal images of

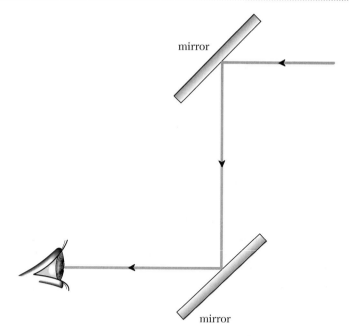

FIGURE 6.6 *Simple mirror periscope*
The eyes are moved optically to the upper mirror.

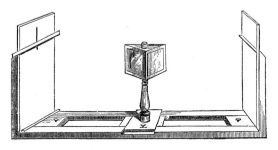

FIGURE 6.7 *Wheatstone's mirror-stereoscope*
See Brewster (1856) and Wade (1983).

the two eyes. Both of these visual strategies are used for two kinds of range-finders. For naval gunnery, where the targets are distant, parallax is increased by using a pair of horizontal periscopes—which effectively increase the separation of the eyes—and so increase the static parallax difference between the eyes (see Figure 6.8).[20]

In the First World War, the German navy used fixed mirrors in the horizontal

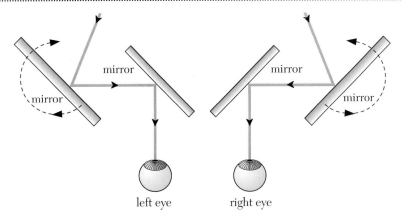

FIGURE 6.8 *Basic range-finder*

The separation of the eyes is increased to the separation of the outer mirrors. This increases the stereo effect (3D depth), and one or more mirrors may be rotated to make the images of an object coincide. This angle of rotation can give distances. These processes correspond to normal stereo and vergence of the eyes—which the instrument enhances and quantifies.

periscopes and introduced a (3D) scale going off into the distance, so that the gun rangers could read off the distances of several ships almost simultaneously. The British navy rotated the end mirrors, to bring each ship into coincidence, as for many camera range-finders. This was slower and probably less accurate.

Anti-parallax

In some situations, such as reading positions of pointers on instruments with scales, parallax and stereo vision are a nuisance; for with head movements, or selecting different eyes, the pointer appears to move against the scale. A neat solution is to place a mirror on the scale, and ensure that the pointer (which is somewhat raised) lines up with its mirror image. Then parallax is avoided.

Optical Levers

When a mirror is rotated, as in Figure 6.9, a beam of light is deviated by twice the angle of rotation of the mirror. This is extremely useful as an 'optical lever' for making sensitive measurements, especially for galvanometers. It was used in this way in 1858 by William Thomson (Lord Kelvin) for signalling across the Atlantic with the first cables—which indeed it saved from destruction, as it worked with a very small applied voltage for the signals. It could be used for Morse code, or for indicating individual letters, as shown in Figure 6.9. Actually it was extremely difficult to read these letter-messages, because the cable's signals changed slowly,

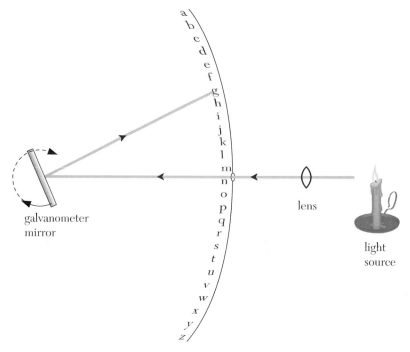

FIGURE 6.9 *Lord Kelvin's 'mirror-speaking' instrument*
A narrow beam of light is reflected on to a scale of letters of the alphabet. When the mirror
tilts the light-beam moves to a different letter.

so where the light landed depended on which letter it had moved from. Only experienced operators could make sense of it.

A rapidly rotating mirror was used by physicist Charles Wheatstone (1802–1875) to see the structure of electric sparks, and to time the passage of electricity through wires. His method has also been used for measuring the speed of light.

Many thousands of tiny rocking mirrors are being used experimentally for large-screen projection television. There is a mirror for each pixel—three for colour projection. The mirrors rock very fast, to allow a beam of light to reach each pixel-place or avoid it. The brightness is given by the time each mirror is allowed to aim light to the screen. This system allows huge bright pictures, up to at least sixteen feet across, to be projected.[21]

A mirror can be rotated very fast—and the reflected beam may be very long—so the end of the beam may move faster than the speed of light. But according to Einstein, nothing can move faster than the speed of light. So does the rotating mirror violate Einstein's theory of relativity? The answer is that nothing is actually moving, and no information can be transmitted in this way, so it does not violate the theory of relativity.

Sextants

The original idea for measuring angles with two mirrors may have come from Newton. It was, and still is, immensely important for navigation. The brass sextant was developed from the English mathematician John Hadley's earlier wooden quadrant; the first was probably Edward Troughton's sextant of 1788. Figure 6.10 shows a brass sextant used for navigation. The upper, fully silvered mirror is mounted on a moveable arm pivoted at the top, and its position is measured on the scale at the bottom of the instrument. The other mirror is half-silvered; so the

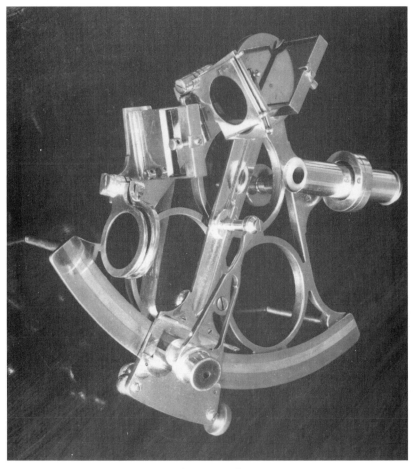

FIGURE 6.10 *Sextant for navigation*

observer looking through the small telescope sees the horizon through the lower half-silvered mirror and the Sun reflected off the pivoted mirror. The scale indicates the angular separation of the Sun and the horizon for calculating longitude. Latitude is of course found in the Northern hemisphere simply from the height of the North Star above the horizon.

Calculations of longitude require both a sextant and a very accurate clock. In 1713 the British government offered a price of £20,000 for the invention of such a clock; and a suitably accurate 'chronometer' was first achieved by John Harrison (1693–1776). Harrison was originally a carpenter, and after a lifetime of labour he was finally awarded the Longitude Prize in 1773.

Sextants can also be used when there is no visible horizon (as when surveying, or hiding or locating buried treasure on an island). In such cases, an 'artificial horizon' is used. This is a horizontal mirror adjusted with bubble levels; or it may be a pool of mercury protected from the wind with a glass cover (see Figure 6.11).

'Cat's Eyes'

Three mirrors fixed at right angles (like the corner of a box; or the walls and ceiling of a corner of a room) have the remarkable property of directing light back to its source. This is the principle of highway 'cat's eyes'. A car's headlights are reflected back very precisely—so for the driver near the headlights they appear very bright, but from another position they are dim or invisible. Looking in a corner mirror, one sees oneself looking at oneself wherever one moves. Corner reflectors were placed on the Moon so that very precise distance measurements could be made with radar.

Camera Lucida

The camera lucida was invented by William Woollaston (1766–1828) as an aid to drawing. It makes a distant scene appear to fall on to a sheet of paper, for an artist

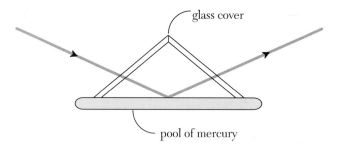

glass cover

pool of mercury

FIGURE 6.11 *Artificial horizon*
A pool of mercury protected from the wind with a glass cover was used with a sextant for determining positions on land when no horizon is visible.

to trace in perspective. This differs from the camera obscura ('dark room') in giving a virtual not a real image. A camera lucida may consist simply of a part-reflecting mirror, held at about 45°, to combine the scene by reflection with the paper by transmission through the glass. But the scene appears inverted. This does not matter, however, for making drawings from a microscope, so this simple form can be useful.

Wollaston's instrument avoids the inversion with a special prism which has four angles: 90°, 135°, and two of 67° 30' (see Figures 6.12 and 6.13). One of the two faces containing the right angle is placed toward the scene. Filters are used to optimise the brightnesses of paper and scene, and there are hinged lenses to bring the scene and the drawing into simultaneous focus. The observing position is critical, as the eye has to be placed so that half the pupil receives the scene through the prism while the other half views the paper directly.

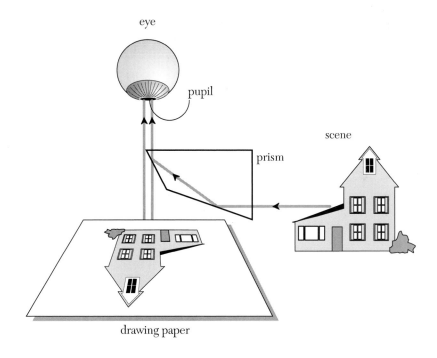

FIGURE 6.12 *Wollaston's prism*

The prism combines the scene with the drawing paper; but it is not easy to use as the position of the eye is critical. For a microscope, where the inversion does not matter, it is better to use a part-reflecting mirror rather than a prism.

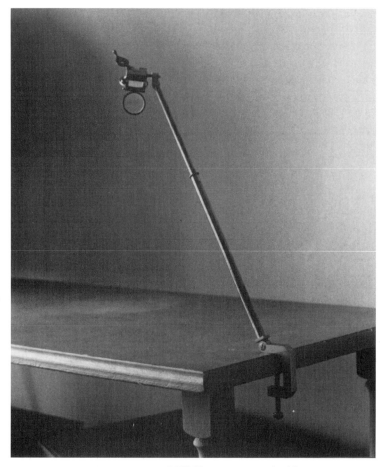

FIGURE 6.13 *A Wollaston camera lucida*
The prism is mounted on a telescopic stalk with a table clamp. From the author's collection.

Memory-Mirrors: Photographs

The first successful photographs were etched by light on mirrors—silver plates treated with mercury vapour to develop the image. This discovery by Louis Jacques Mandé Daguerre (1789–1851), who was an artist in Paris and familiar with the camera obscura, followed earlier though not very successful experiments with paper by Humphry Davy and by Josiah Wedgwood. Much of Daguerre's work was shared with Joseph Niépce (1765–1833), who died before success was achieved. How the discovery came about is a wonderful mix of applied intelligence and luck; for it was not just a simple improvement of the first faint images on silver plates, but depended on a new concept. After many trials Daguerre placed an exposed silver plate, which had little or no image, in a cupboard overnight. The cupboard happened to contain several jars of chemicals. Next morning, he found that the surface of the plate was a miraculously wonderful picture in exquisite detail, though black-white reversed. Realising that the vapour from one of the chemicals must have done the trick, he identified mercury as the active agent by removing one jar at a time. It turned out that mercury vapour 'developed' the 'latent' image on the silver. This was a concept that had not been anticipated.

Daguerrotypes (as they came to be called in spite of the agreement with Niépce to share credit for all their past and future work) were available from 1840. They were highly successful straight away, even though they were expensive. They were mirror-reversed on their silvered copper plates, and, according to the lighting, might appear as 'positives' or 'negatives.' Henry Fox Talbot placed silver on glass (Calotypes, or Talbotypes), which appeared as 'positives' when placed on black velvet.

Talbot succeeded in producing photographic images at the same time as Daguerre. Unaware of Daguerre's experiments, and not himself being an artist, he was led to drawing by light through using a camera lucida to sketch Lake Como. Talbot found drawing by camera lucida to be a difficult skill: he wrote in *The Pencil of Nature* (1844) that 'When the eye was removed from the prism—in which all looked beautiful—I found that the faithless pencil had only left traces on the paper melancholy to behold. I came to the conclusion that the instrument required a previous knowledge of drawing, which unfortunately I did not possess.' This led him to the camera obscura, in which he placed paper to trace the real image directly. But: 'it baffles the skill and patience of the amateur to trace all the minute details on the paper; so that, in fact, he carries away little beyond a mere souvenir of the scene. . . .' So Talbot set out to allow light to be its own pencil. Returning to his home, in 1834, he tried nitrate of silver brushed on paper; but this required immensely long exposures. After many trials he found a great improvement when the paper was previously brushed with a weak salt solution and left to dry. Success finally arrived when he discovered how to fix the pictures with a strong solution of salt. He made pictures of leaves by simply laying them on the paper. Then, following many experiments to increase the sensitivity of the paper with alternate washings of salt and silver, he made superb scenes of his house and estate—Lacock Abbey[22]—taken with small camera obscuras, which he called 'mouse boxes'. These, however, required too long an exposure for photographing people, until he hit on iodine for sensitising the paper. This converged on Daguerre's use of iodine for sensitising his silver plates. Daguerre's results were made public in January 1839. This shattered Talbot's belief that he was the first to draw pictures with light, though his results were announced by Michael Faraday at the Royal Institution in London six months before the details of

Daguerre's method were revealed, with the title: 'Photogenic Drawing'. Fox Talbot's process had the great advantages that positive copies could be made, and it was less costly than Daguerre's superb silver memory mirrors.

Liquid Crystal Displays

The liquid crystal screens of digital watches and portable computers are patterns of thousands of very small mirrors changing according to local electrical charges. This is a remarkable development of Faraday's 1845 discovery that a magnetic field can rotate the plane of vibration of light in glass. It does not have to be glass; some rotation occurs even in air. That this works also for electric fields was discovered by the Scottish physicist John Kerr in 1875. Placed between crossed polarising filters, the Kerr cell and later variants are extremely useful high-speed optical shutters, and can modulate laser light for transmitting information down glass fibres. Liquid crystal displays have helical organic compounds which rotate polarised light much more than, for example, crystals of quartz. These *mesomorphic* liquid crystals can move and change their orientation with changing electric fields. Placed between polarising filters, each becomes a tiny optical shutter, or variable-reflecting mirror. The Kerr cell has been made so fast it has been used to photograph the flight of light itself—it can photograph a dollop of light lasting less than a million millionth of a second from a pulsed laser.[23]

Looking into Eyes

The Ophthalmoscope

How the ophthalmoscope makes it possible to see into the eye is conceptually illuminating. Why does this need a special instrument? Why can't we simply see into each other's eyes—or into our own eyes with a looking-glass?

The reason is that one's own eye and head prevent light reaching the other retina, because they are in focus on the retina, and so the surrounding light fails to reach just where it is needed. As both Helmholtz and the mathematician Charles Babbage (1791–1871) realised at about the same time, the answer is to direct light along the line of sight into the pupil. A part-reflecting mirror works well for this, as shown in Figure 6.14.

Pandora's Box

I devised 'Pandora's box' for plotting the visual space, in three dimensions, of observers looking at pictures (see Figure 6.15). The notion is to use the stereo vision of the two eyes to measure monocular depth seen in pictures.[24] The device uses a part-reflecting mirror at 45° to introduce a movable spot of light which can

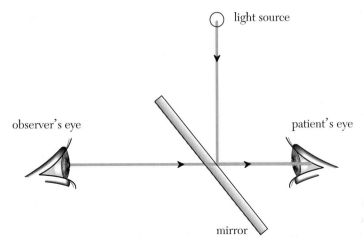

FIGURE 6.14 *Ophthalmoscope (simplified)*

As the observer's eye (and head) is imaged on the patient's retina, surrounding light can not reach where light is needed. So the pupil appears black, though the retina in the patient's eye is pink and reflects plenty of light. The angled part-reflecting mirror sends light into the patient's eye along the observer's line of sight.

be placed optically anywhere in the picture—including in front or through the picture. It is seen by both eyes, but the picture is visible only to one eye, by cross-polarisation. So the stereoscopic vision of the two eyes can be used to measure the apparent depth of any part of the picture, given by monocular cues seen with a single eye. Thus it is possible to plot perceptual space in the eye's mind.

Pandora's box was designed for relating visual depth to illusory distortions of such figures as the Muller–Lyer illusion (page 224). It works best with quite dim back-illuminated transparencies (or a computer screen), which have no surface texture.

Conjuring Mirror-Illusions

Now we turn to the 'dark' side of mirrors: their power to evoke illusion. Illusions are not altogether bad; once recognised and explained, illusions can be warnings of errors and pointers to true perceptions. They have, however, been used through the ages by priest and conjurors, to delude for miracles and to entertain with impossibilities.

Pepper's Ghost

Reflections have been used to produce stage ghosts since large sheets of glass

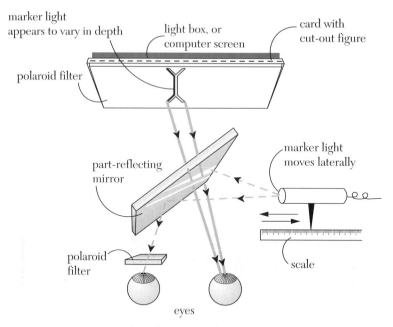

marker light
appears to vary in depth

light box, or
computer screen

card with
cut-out figure

polaroid filter

part-reflecting
mirror

marker light
moves laterally

polaroid
filter

scale

eyes

FIGURE 6.15 *'Pandora's Box' for plotting visual space*

*Both eyes see the movable reference light clearly in depth; but only one eye can see the
picture on the screen, as the picture is cross-polarised to one eye. The light is placed in any
position in three dimensions in the monocularly viewed picture. So the observer's visual
space can be plotted.*

became available in the middle of the nineteenth century. Pepper's Ghost is
named after John Henry Pepper (1821–1900), a professor at the Royal
Polytechnic in London, who invented many scientific demonstrations and wrote
several books on popular science. Pepper's Ghost depends on a large part-trans-
parent mirror (or simply a sheet of glass) which optically combines *reflected* actors
with other actors seen *through* the glass (see Figure 6.16). The intensities of lighting are varied to make them visible or invisible, or combined as transparent
ghosts. It is likely that Lewis Carroll's disappearing grin of the Cheshire Cat was
inspired by Pepper's Ghost (see page 233). This optical effect is the same as in a
one-way mirror. It is commonly seen in one's windows at dusk: the room gradually appears as though it lies outside in the semi-darkness.

This is much more common *optically* than is noticed *perceptually*, for we tend to
ignore irrelevant reflections and after-images of the eyes. This is part of perception's power to edit, and create, our personal realities. The Pepper's Ghost principle is used for many truth-gaining instruments, such as the sextant (page 171); the
camera lucida (page 174); and 'Pandora's box' (page 178).

FIGURE 6.16 *Pepper's Ghost*

A large part-reflecting mirror allows actors to disappear, or become transparent ghosts.
From Pepper (c.1877).

The Kaleidoscope

Starting with questions purely of science, Sir David Brewster was drawn by the beauty of visual phenomena to develop the kaleidoscope as an instrument for the curious and for practical arts. As it is rare for the origin and development of an invention to be recorded, I shall present Brewster's account in detail:[25]

The first idea of this instrument presented itself to me in the year 1814, in the course of a series of experiments on the polarisation of light by successive reflections between plates of glass. . . . In these experiments, the reflecting plates were necessarily inclined to each other, during the operation of placing their surfaces in parallel planes; and I was therefore led to remark the circular arrangement of the images of a candle round the centre, and the multiplication of the sectors found by the extremities of the plates of glass. In consequence, however, of the distance of the candles, &c., from the ends of the reflectors, their arrangement was so destitute of symmetry, that I was not induced to give any further attention to the matter.

In a letter to his French friend and colleague Jean Baptiste Biot, Brewster explains how he saw aesthetic beauty in this science, and developed an instrument spanning science and art:

When the angle of incidence (on the plates of silver) was about 85° or 86°, and the plates almost in contact, and inclined at a very small angle, the two series of reflected images appeared at once in the form of two curves; and that the succession of splendid colours formed a phenomenon which I had no doubt would be considered, by every person who saw it to advantage, as one of the most beautiful in optics.

But this was before he observed symmetry:

Although I had thus combined two plane mirrors, so as to produce highly pleasing effects, from the multiplication and circular arrangement of the images of objects . . . yet I had scarcely made a step towards the invention of the Kaleidoscope. The effects, however, which I had observed, were sufficient to prepare me for taking advantage of any suggestion which experiment might afterwards throw in the way. . . .

At first these were 'wholly destitute of symmetry,' but noticing from his initial experiment that symmetry could occur, Brewster set out the necessary conditions.[26]

1. That the reflectors should be placed at an angle, which was an *even* or an *odd* aliquot part of a circle, when the object was regular, and similarly situated with respect to both the mirrors; or the even aliquot part of a circle when the object was irregular, and had any position whatever. [An *aliquot* is a division without remainder. So mirrors inclined at 30° give $(30 \times 12 = 360)$ 12 sectors, or copies of an object, without overlaps or gaps].

2. That out of an infinite number of positions for the object, both within and without the reflectors, there was only one where perfect symmetry could be obtained, namely, when the object was placed in contact with the ends of the reflectors. This was precisely the position of the cement in the preceding experiment with the triangular trough.

3. That out of an infinite number of positions for the eye, there was *only one* where the symmetry was perfect, namely, as near as possible to the angular point, so that the circular field could be distinctly seen; and that this point was the *only one* out of an infinite number at which the uniformity of the light of the circular field was a maximum, and from which the direct and the reflected images had the same form and the same magnitude, in consequence of being placed when looking through the fluid with which the glass trough was partially filled.

Brewster continues:

Upon these principles I constructed an instrument, in which I fixed permanently, across the ends of the reflectors, pieces of coloured glass, and other irregular objects; and I showed the instrument in this state to some members of the Royal Society of Edinburgh, who were much struck with the beauty of its effects. . . . The great step, however, towards the completion of the instrument remained yet to be made; and it was not till some time afterwards that the idea occurred to me [Brewster's italics]*of giving motion to objects, such as pieces of coloured glass, &c., which were either fixed or placed loosely in a cell at the end of the instrument.* When this idea was carried into execution, and the reflectors placed in a tube, and fitted up on the preceding principle, the Kaleidoscope, in its simple form, was completed.

But Brewster decided that:

In this form, however, the Kaleidoscope could not be considered as a general philosophical instrument of universal application. The least deviation of the object from the position of symmetry at the end of the reflectors, produced a deviation from beauty and symmetry in the figure . . . the use of the instrument was therefore limited to objects, or groups of objects, whose magnitudes were less than its triangular aperture.

The next, and by far the most important step of the invention, was to remove this limitation, and to extend indefinitely the use and application of the instrument. This effect was obtained by employing a draw tube, containing a convex glass of such focal length, that the images of objects, of all magnitudes and at all distances, might be distinctly formed at the end of the reflectors, and introduced into the pictures created by the instrument in the same manner as if they had been reduced in size, and placed in the true position in which alone symmetry could be obtained.

Brewster concluded that: 'When the Kaleidoscope was brought to this degree of perfection, it was impossible not to perceive that it would prove of the highest service in all the ornamental arts, and would, at the same time, become a popular instrument for the purposes of rational amusement.'

Peter Roget (1779–1869), Fullerian Professor of Physiology at the Royal Institution and inventor of the Thesaurus, describes the reception of the Kaleidoscope in the *Encyclopaedia Britannica* :

The sensation it excited in London throughout all ranks of people was astonishing. It afforded delight to the poor as well as the rich; to the old as well as the young. Large cargoes of them were sent abroad, particularly to the East Indies. They very soon became

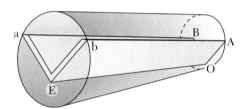

FIGURE 6.17 *Simple kaleidoscope*
After Brewster (1819).

known throughout Europe, and have met with travellers even in the most obscure and retired villages in Switzerland.

Brewster applied for a patent, but as he had demonstrated the principle in public it was refused. The instrument was pirated, and some 200 000 were sold in London and Paris within three months; though but few were designed on correct principles, and Brewster did not receive a penny.

Although it is so simple—just a couple of mirrors—the Kaleidoscope is not an easy instrument to understand. In its basic and most used form, it is a pair of long narrow mirrors, inclined at 30° giving 12 repetitions, or at 45° giving 8 repetitions (see Figures 6.17 and 6.18). The position of the eye is quite critical, and the objects must be close to the ends of the mirrors. What one sees is a polygon of repeated patterns of alternately reversed objects.

Figure 6.19 uses matches to show how a Kaleidoscope works. The small match facing the centre *appears* unreversed because of its symmetry. (If one side is painted a different colour one sees that it is alternately reversed.) The big match at right angles is clearly alternately reversed. A match at an intermediate angle gives the pattern shown in (b).

We have seen why a virtual image is alternately reversed in multiple reflections (page 81). It remains to see why the number of images changes—up to four—with the angle of the mirrors. It is an interesting experiment (see page 82) to hinge a pair of small mirrors and place objects such as matches or coins between them.[27] Instead of looking *along* the mirrors one looks *into* them (Figure 4.6, page 83). As the angle of the mirrors is changed, the number of images will change thus:[28]

The polygon formed by the reflections has as many sides as the number of times the angle of the mirrors is contained in 360°.

As Sir Ernst Gombrich points out, the individualities of the objects are almost lost in the power of the pattern.[29]

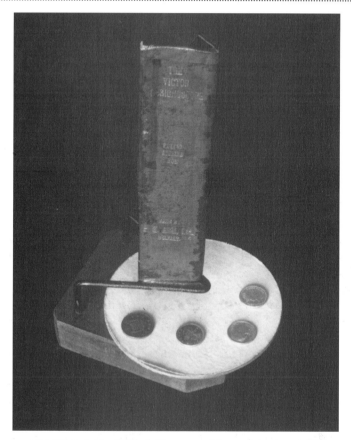

FIGURE 6.18 *45° kaleidoscope with revolving turntable*
*The Victor Designoscope, made by P. K. Arm Ltd, Belfast, 1916. From the author's
collection.*

The Stroboscope

Changing apparent speed, or even reversing direction in time, was first achieved
by Michael Faraday. It had been suggested by an observation made by the engineer Isambard Kingdom Brunel (1806–1859), in the workings of the Thames
Tunnel. There were two large gear wheels rotating in opposite directions, and
Brunel noticed that when he looked at the further wheel through the moving teeth
of the nearer wheel, the teeth appeared stationary. Showing this to Faraday,
Brunel made a series of moving models, including a disc with equally spaced
slots, through which he viewed the back of the rotating disc from a distant mirror.
The spinning disc appeared stationary. Roget pasted a series of slightly different
pictures on the back of the disc, and they seemed to move. These were the first
'moving' pictures: the beginning of the cinema.

(a) How it appears

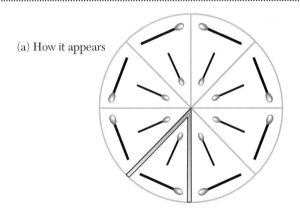

The pair of mirrors, with a small match facing the centre and a large match at right angles.

(b)

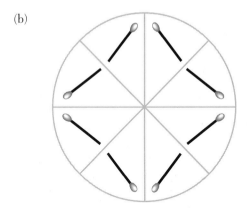

FIGURE 6.19 *Seeing how a kaleidoscope works with matches*
(a) The small match facing the centre appears *unreversed because of its symmetry. (If one side is painted a different colour one sees that it is alternately reversed.) The big match at right angles is clearly alternately reversed. A match at an intermediate angle gives the pattern shown in (b).*

The Praxinoscope

The praxinoscope uses an ingenious arrangement of mirrors to make a series of different pictures appear to move (see Figure 6.20 and Plate 16). It was invented by Emile Reynaud, and was an improvement on the earlier zootrope which had slots in a drum, which was invented by William George Horner in Bristol in 1834.

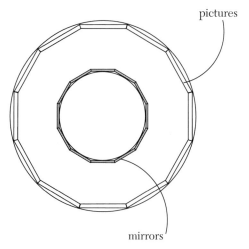

pictures

mirrors

FIGURE 6.20 *The praxinoscope*

Fun-fair (Anamorphic) Mirrors

Bizarre distortions of the human form are very familiar in fun-fair mirrors (see Figure 6.21). It is interesting to draw the distorted shape, and then use the mirror-distortion to reverse the distortions of the image. This can make the shape of an object meaningless, and then restores the meaning. If a shiny metal cylinder is placed upon a sheet of paper it is quite easy to produce a secret drawing. The method is to draw an object on the paper while looking into the mirror-cylinder. The object will appear wildly distorted in the shiny cylinder. The drawing will be similarly distorted and may be unrecognisable. But the cylinder's reflection of the distorted drawing is undistorted, and the drawing becomes recognisable—as shown in Figure 6.22.

The Magic Cabinet

Mirrors are often used in conjuring. One very effective trick—the Magic Cabinet—involves two vertical mirrors hinged at the two back corners of the cabinet, meeting in the middle at right angles. Thus they are at 45° to the sides, and to the back. The audience sees the two sides in the mirrors and mistakes them for the

FIGURE 6.21 *Distorted images*
One's friends and oneself become weird cartoons in distorting mirrors. These have been popuar from the ancient Greeks onwards.

FIGURE 6.22 *Anamorphic drawing*
Shapes more complicated than cylinders may be used.

back. Performers can be concealed behind the mirrors so that the cabinet appears to be empty. If one of them raises his head above the mirror, the head appears suspended in mid-air, with no body.

There are many variations of such mirror-conjuring. For example, a large and handsome box is wheeled on to the stage, so the audience can see under, over and all around it. Being open, it appears to be well lit from the top and perfectly empty. The assistant enters the box, the door is closed and locked. After a few minutes it is opened, and a skeleton appears to be standing in the place of the assistant. Again the door is closed, and next time it is opened the skeleton has vanished and the assistant walks out of the box with a carpet bag rattling with bones. The conjuror, explaining the apparatus, goes in and sounds the walls with his knuckles. While doing this the door is suddenly closed, and being as quickly opened, he is found to have disappeared, to appear when the door is once more closed and opened. This trick is explained in Figure 6.23.

Mirror miracles have served the gods for many millenia, as shown in Figure 6.24.

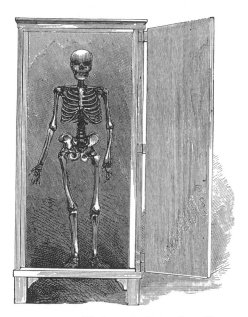

FIGURE 6.23 *'Skeleton in the cupboard'*

The doors have glass mirrors on the sides, and a design at the upper part of the cupboard suitable for the illusion. There is a door of clear thick glass, and an external door. A lamp is hung at the top of the post to light the inside. This was invented by the Davenport Brothers, whose descendents continue to conjure, with or without mirrors.

FIGURE 6.24 *Phantasm of the gods*
*This trick was probably done with a large curved mirror, so that the head is seen suspended
in front, in nothingness.*

Phantom Limbs

People who have lost a limb in an accident may experience the missing arm or leg
as though it is still present. Worse, they may experience pain, which may be
excruciating, in the missing limb. Recently V. S. Ramachandran, with his wife
Diane and S. Cobb, found that for ten out of ten cases of losses of arms, the phantom limb and the pain disappeared when the patient could see a normal hand
'superimposed' with a mirror. Trying this for fifteen minutes a day over three
weeks could make the feeling and pain of the phantom limb shrink and
(so far) disappear for good. This remarkable discovery should be important
medically.

Mirrors in Nature

Hundreds of millions of years before we existed, evolution produced reflecting
devices that we are only now beginning to understand. Nature uses mirrors of
many kinds much as we do—for capturing information, misleading the enemy,
and casting the spell of invisibility.

Cat's Eyes

There are no metal mirrors in nature. The eyes of cats and other animals of the night shine brilliantly when light enters (as often seen when driving at night) because the light is reflected back from a mirror situated behind the retina. This *tapetum* of cats and other nocturnal animals serves to increase the light absorbed by the receptors, as incoming light is reflected back into the photo-pigment of the retinal receptors (rods), giving a second chance of capturing photons.

The tapetum works by what we can now see as highly sophisticated diffraction optics. It is a series of quarter-wave plates, consisting of very thin layers of chitin. Like soap films, they reflect certain wavelengths, according to the separation of their surfaces. The tapetum is a more efficient reflector than a soap film because there are many layers.

Mirror Eyes

Until recently it has been thought that all imaging eyes, except the pin-hole eye of *Nautilus*, work with lenses. Recently, however, Michael Land has discovered eyes in nature which work essentially like reflecting telescopes (see Figure 6.25). Scallops have between sixty and one hundred mirror eyes, around the mantle, looking out from between the tentacles. Michael Land describes how he found that the previous assumption that they were normal lens eyes was wrong:[30]

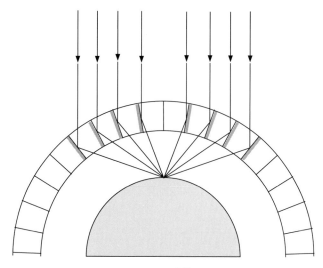

FIGURE 6.25 *Mirror eye*
After Land (1984).

The observation that changed this view was that it is possible to see an inverted image of oneself *in the eye* when looking into it with a dissecting microscope. . . . If these were actually lens eyes no such image could be seen, because an object imaged onto the retina would be re-imaged at infinity by the lens, and as with a human eye one would need a telescope (or ophthalmoscope) and not a microscope to see it. The solution had to be that the image visible in the eye was not formed by the lens, but by reflection from the nearly hemispherical highly reflecting tapetum (or argentea) that lines the back of the eye.

There is also a lens in these eyes, but it is far too feeble to focus the image. The mirror is made of alternating layers of square quanine crystals and cytoplasm.[31] Such dichroic mirrors have only recently become available for manufactured optical instruments.

The Mirror-Scales of Fish

Reflection phenomena are found in the scales of many fishes. Viewed in natural conditions from the side they are wonderful mirrors, making the fish almost invisible. What is so remarkable, since they work by optical interference, is that they are not coloured. They are like many soap films, each of a slightly different thickness, so that although each film reflects one colour, the colours combine to give a colour-free mirror. How this has come about in fish is quite a challenge for evolutionary theory. It is so effective that some shoaling fish have small black spots to make them visible to their companions so that they can keep in shoals, for safety in numbers.

Notes

1. Described in his *Harmonie Universelle* of 1630. See Goldberg (1985).
2. Israeli (1991).
3. A fine later example of a convex wall mirror is pictured in van Eyck's *Marriage of Arnolfini* (1434), now in the National Gallery, London. See Plate 3.
4. See Brown (1992).
5. Charles Brosses, *Letters on Italy*. Letter to M. de Blancey, 29 August 1739, quoted in Roche (1956).
6. Boswell's *Life of Johnson*, Monday 23 October 1775.
7. This was absorbed in 1901 by the renowned firm Pilkington Brothers, founded in 1828, as the St Helens Crown Glass Works.
8. The Chance brothers of Birmingham started production of broad glass in 1832. With the help of French workers using the mechanised cylinder process, they made the glass for the Crystal Palace for the Great Exhibition of 1851. This huge conservatory was completed in three months.
9. The development of this process in the 1950s cost £$\frac{1}{2}$ million: now the method is licensed for use all over the world and it is an immense success.
10. Schweig (1973).
11. Eleventh edition of *Encyclopaedia Britannica*, Vol. XVII.
12. His use of conic sections for the burning mirror, and for a possible telescope, is described in his *Spechio Usterio* (Burning Mirror) of 1632.

13. Described in his *Harmonie Universelle* of 1630. See Goldberg (1985).

14. The history of achromatic lenses is given by Daumas (1972).

15. This has been developed by Peter Waddell, of Strathclyde University in Edinburgh.

16. First attempted by R. W. Wood in 1908; see King (1955). More recently Ermanno F. Borra has built a 1.6 metre spin-mercury telescope, using air bearings to avoid vibration problems. See *Sky and Telescope* (1984) and Manly (1991).

17. We tried spinning plaster of Paris, which is cheap, then when it had set, adding a thin layer of expensive epoxy resin—while spinning at the same rate. It worked fairly though not very well.

18. Grazing incidence optics is discussed in *Sky and Telescope* (1969).

19. I devised, and with the superb engineer Stephen Salter built and tested, a sampling system which rejected disturbed images, building up an image from many accepted exposures. The moments of best 'seeing' were selected from an auto-correlation signal derived from matching the fluctuating images with an internal stored long-exposure master image. The principal problem was getting adequate tracking of the telescope, as an offset ruined the auto-correlation. Unfortunately it never worked as well on the telescope as it did in the laboratory simulator. Such problems involving science and engineering always need more than one bite of the cherry. Stephen Salter, who worked with me for some ten years at Cambridge and then Edinburgh, went on to invent the Salter Duck to get electricity from wave power, and much else. He is now a Professor of Engineering at the University of Edinburgh. See Gregory (1974).

20. Howard and Rogers (1995).

21. The DMD (digital microprocessor device) invented by Larry J. Hornbeck, of Texas Instruments, is a chip 2.3cm^2 covered with almost 500 000 tiny rocking mirrors. Each is controlled individually by electrostatic forces from the chip. See Younse (1993).

22. Lacock, in Wiltshire, now has a museum devoted to the history of photography.

23. Achieved at the Bell Telephone Laboratories, in New Jersey, by Duguay. See Darius (1984).

24. This was invented by the author: it is described in Gregory (1970).

25. Brewster (1856).

26. Brewster (1858).

27. This goes back to the Italian physicist and philosopher who first described the camera obscura: Giovanni Battista della Porta (1543–1615), in his compendium *Magiae Naturalis* (1589).

28. As the angle is decreased this is what happens:

Angle of inclination of pair of mirrors	Number of coins seen
180°	1
120°	2 *
90°	4 (including the direct view of the object)
72°	5 *
60°	6
51$\frac{3}{7}$°	7
45°	8
40°	9 *
36°	10

$32\frac{8}{11}°$ 11*

30°   12

There is no symmetry for the angles marked with an asterisk.

29. Gombrich (1995).

30. Michael Land is at the University of Sussex, near Brighton in England. The quotation and other details come from Land (1984).

31. Land (1966) and (1972).

7

Handed

Most people are . . . 'left brained', that is, all their delicate and specialized movements are handed over to the charge of the left hemisphere
WILLIAM JAMES

IN *The Plattner Story* by H. G. Wells, a young schoolmaster called Gottfried Plattner was blown up by a greenish powder of mysterious provenance. He disappeared. When he reappeared nine days later, all the organs of his body were reversed. In the story a surgeon found that:

The right lobe of his liver is on the left side, the left on his right; while his lungs, too, are similarly contraposed. What is still more singular, unless Gottfried is a consummate actor we must believe that his right hand has become his left. . . Since this occurrence he has found the utmost difficulty in writing except from right to left across the paper with his left hand.

This is fiction. But most of fiction is true to experience or we wouldn't understand it. Here Wells says truly that a three-dimensional object—such as Gottfried Plattner—cannot be reversed by a rotation in three-dimensional space; for an extra dimension is needed for rotation:

There is no way of taking a man and moving him about in space, as ordinary people understand space, that will result in our changing his sides. Whatever you do, his right is still his right, his left his left. You can do that with a perfectly thin thing, of course. If you were to cut a figure out of paper, any figure with a right and left side, you could change its sides simply by lifting it up and turning it over. But with a solid it is different. Mathematical theorists tell us that the only way in which the right and left sides of a solid body can be changed is by taking that body clear out of space as we know it—taking it out of ordinary existence, that is, and turning it somewhere outside space. This is a little abstruse, no doubt, but anyone with a slight knowledge of mathematical theory will assure the reader of its truth. To put the thing in technical language, the curious inversion of Plattner's right and left sides is proof that he has moved out of our space into what is called the Fourth Dimension, and that he has returned again to our world. Unless we choose to consider ourselves the victims of an elaborate and motiveless fabrication, we are almost bound to believe that this has occurred.

So far as we know, this is impossible. But what *is* possible, and occasionally happens, is that someone is born with the organs of the body reversed: this is called *situs inversus*, and occurs in about one birth in 100 000. Very recently it has been discovered that *situs inversus* mice can be produced by changing a single gene. We will look at this briefly later (page 202).

The point that Wells makes, that a three-dimensional body cannot be reversed in structure by moving it through space, is why *handedness* is such a useful term. It is because you can't turn one of your hands into the other hand (and one hand is always attached to your right side and the other to your left side) that hands very conveniently denote right and left.

To put this a little differently: just as one cannot put a left glove on a right hand, so our hands are not substitutable. They are essentially different. So *handedness* is useful for identifying inherent asymmetries, apart from what happens to be to one side or the other. To see how confusing this can be, think of how left and right are reversed for actors and audience in the theatre. There is no such problem for up and down, for we share gravitational attraction. Or at least there is no such problem when we are fairly close together on the surface of the Earth. There is, however, just the same kind of problem for up-down as there is for left-right when we are widely separated or on opposite sides of the Earth. Then our distant feet meet from different directions even though all are 'down'. Normally, up and down do not cause the same bother as left and right, because we very seldom need to describe the situation of people opposed on either side of the Earth. Although we all know now that the world is round, we continue to talk as though it is flat.[1]

Up and down is more of a problem in space where there is no local gravity. Astronauts generally accept that their own feet are 'down', but this is not simple. An experimenter on spatial orientation in weightlessness, J. R. Lackner, says:[2]

Illusions of body inversion and vehicle inversion can be evoked by exposure to weightlessness. . . . Such illusions can involve all possible combinations of self-inversion and vehicle inversion. In the absence of any patterns of external stimulation, individuals may lose all sense of body orientation to their surroundings. . . . Touch and pressure cues provide a perceptual 'down' in the absence of visual input. When vision is allowed, apparent orientation is influenced by a variety of factors including the direction of gaze, the architectural layout of the vehicle, and sight of the body.

It is bad manners in space to float over to someone from behind, while the other way up, for the sudden conflict of up-down can produce nausea.

What happens to mirrors in space? They appear as they do on Earth. Changes of reference do not switch mirror-images any more than they switch objects.

Handedness of Letters

As for most languages, English is handed: it is written and read from left to right. Most of the letters are asymmetrical right-left and up-down. For the lower case, a, b, d, f, g, h, j, k, l, p, q, r, s, y, z are asymmetrical both horizontally and vertically. m, n, u, v and w have (nearly) horizontal though not vertical symmetry. They look (almost) the same in mirror-writing. And so, of course, do the completely symmetrical letters: o and x. Two letters, C and E, look the same upside down though different in a mirror. Seventeen of the twenty-six letters look different when reversed in a mirror. Two pairs, b and d, and p and q, change into each other. These letters are a particular problem for children learning to read and for sufferers of dyslexia.

Letters are unusual objects, and present a special problem for perception, for almost all other objects remain *the same object*, and are just as recognisable, when horizontally reversed. Thus a face looks essentially the same whether facing left or right. The purely conventional asymmetries of many letters makes reading more difficult than it need be.

Handedness of Perception

Up-down reversal makes many objects—especially faces—difficult to recognise. A smile is characterized by the *upward* turn of the lips, which is easily misread in an upside-down face. This becomes truly frightening if the mouth or eyes of a portrait are cut out and replaced upside down as shown in Figure 7.1. Compare how

FIGURE 7.1 *The topsy-turvy face effect*

this looks when the whole figure is rotated to be upside down. Then the separately reversed eyes and mouth appear almost normal. It shows that these features of faces are processed somewhat separately from the face as a whole. (There are unlikely to be such dramatic effects for right-left reversal.)

Objects and pictures can look very different when turned upside down. The American artist Rex Whistler's *OHO!* faces are striking examples.[3] They turn into different faces when rotated (Figure 7.2). This is because normally the eyes are to be found above the mouth, a beard below the chin, and so on. Somewhat ambiguous shapes are 'read' according to what their various features are likely to be—which is affected by their positions and orientations. The sixteenth century Italian artist Arcimboldo could switch faces with quite other objects such as books or bowls of fruit (see Figure 7.3). And interesting effects can be achieved

FIGURE 7.2 *An OHO! face*
When upside down, it turns into a different face.

FIGURE 7.3 *One of Arcimboldo's pictures*
By kind permission of Skokloster's Castle, Bälsta, Sweden.

with lettering, especially in the hands of the Californian type designer Scott Kim.[4] Some years ago Scott did my name for the delightful Californian custom of personal presents for a party. Figure 7.4 is the result.

Left-handedness

Throughout history left-handedness has had a poor press. Right-handers are characters of *rectitude*: left-handers are *gauche*. Our word 'left' comes from the Anglo-Saxon *left* meaning weak or broken. 'Right' means correct. The Devil, witches and, regrettably, females are traditionally associated with the left as evil. Walking around a church against the motion of the Sun is associated with black

FIGURE 7.4 *An upright name*
Try rotating the book.

magic: 'widdershins'. Right-handed, with the Sun, is 'deasil'. The bad are *sinister*—the Latin for 'left'; the good are *right*eous.

Right-left asymmetry of handedness is unique to humans. Individual cats, for example, may have a paw preference but there is no overall right or left pawedness in cats. The assumption is that language is the key to human lopsidedness, as the dominance of the left hemisphere of the cerebral cortex is associated with specifically human language brain activities. The two major areas of the brain responsible for speech production are found on the left: Broca's Area is in the frontal region of the left cortex, and Wernicke's Area lies further back in the left hemisphere. These make the human brain right-left asymmetrical. But what of left-handers? Are their brains mirror-images of right-handers' brains? The surprising answer is: this is not usually so. Most left-handers also have their speech areas in the left hemisphere, though some have speech areas on both sides. This doubling never occurs in right-handers. The dual speech areas, with richer associations across the hemispheres, may with luck confer advantages. For although there are more speech problems, such as stutter, associated with left-handedness, there are also more left-handed geniuses.

In his book *Left Hander*, the Canadian psychologist Stanley Coran prefers to speak of left or right *sidedness* rather than handedness, for the feet and the eyes can have different preferences.[5] Coran summarizes the statistical pattern of human sidednesses neatly:

- 9 out of 10 people are right-handed
- 8 out of 10 people are right-footed
- 7 out of 10 people are right-eyed
- 6 out of 10 people are right-eared

This includes men and women together. Slightly more women are right-handed, and still more right-footed and right-eared. But more women than men are left-eyed. There are fewer left-handed old people than young people: according to Stanley Coran, this is because the accident rate is so much higher for left-handers.

Handedness in Nature

In the inorganic world of physics there are few inherent asymmetries, except for such contingent matters as the rotation of the Earth. It is this, of course, that sets the convention of 'clockwise' and 'anti-clockwise' from the Sun, and the moving shadows of ancient sundials preserved in the hands of mechanical clocks. In spite of the clockwise motion of the Sun, many plants are free to twine left or right.[6]

The rotation of the Earth is, for clear physical reasons, responsible for the directions of cyclones and anti-cyclones of the atmosphere. There are many examples of this kind where one asymmetry generates others. What is extremely rare is inherent non-parity—right- or left-handedness—in basic physics. Until recently it was thought that all the fundamental particles are even-handed. It came as a great surprise when two Chinese physicists, working in America, Tsung Dao Lee (1926–) and Chen Ning Yang (1922–) suggested that one fundamental particle—the massless or almost massless neutrino—is left-handed. That is, no mirror image 'right-handed' neutrinos had been found. When the physicist Wolfgang Pauli heard that experiments were going on to test for this handedness of a fundamental particle, he said: 'I do not believe that God is a weak left-hander.' But the experiments of Chien Shiung Wu and her collaborators at Columbia University in New York showed that Pauli was wrong. Lee and Yang received the Nobel Prize in 1957.[7]

This exception from the general parity in non-organic physics remains entirely mysterious. Almost as mysterious is the fact of biology that many organic molecules are handed. Called *right-handed* or *left-handed*, they have otherwise identical structures, but the 'right' and 'left' forms can have very different properties. For example, the limonene molecules giving the tastes to oranges and to lemons are exactly the same, except that one is right-handed and the other left-handed. It is this mirror-asymmetry that makes oranges and lemons taste and smell differently.

The discovery of handedness of biological molecules was made by Louis Pasteur (1822–1895), in a brilliantly simple experiment showing that biologically occurring tartaric acid has only left-handed molecules.[8] With a pair of tweezers and a microscope, Pasteur separated slightly different-looking inorganic crystals, and ended up with two solutions: one right-handed, and the other left-handed, tartaric acid. For Pasteur, this specifically *organic* difference was a clue to the special nature of life—a difference of a cosmic kind. When he found that this asymmetry could be lost, or even reversed, with changes of temperature he came to doubt its cosmic significance, and decided instead that chance had a great part to play. Why only biological molecules are handed seems to be a tantalising key to the origin of life.

There is no definitely known reason why one handedness should be preferred to the other in biology, or what determines preferences for right or left. It is clear that handednesses were set billions of years ago. Was each handedness a matter of chance at the start of life on earth? However this may be, there is clearly something very special here about organic molecules. Proteins, including enzymes, are constructed only from left-handed ('L' for levorotatory) amino acids. DNA and RNA nucleic acids are only right-handed ('D' for dextrorotatory) sugars.

The identical molecules—that is, identical except that one is right-handed and the other is left-handed—that give the very different tastes of oranges and lemons, can do this because the sense-detectors of the nose and the tongue are specifically handed. This is like right- and left-threaded nuts and bolts. A right-handed nut will not fit onto a left-threaded bolt. And, of course, turning the nut around does not help; it remains the same right- or left-handed thread whichever side is presented to the bolt. Right and left threads are essentially different—as right and left gloves are essentially different—and the same is so for levorotatory and dextrorotatory molecules of life.

The biological acceptability of only half of potentially available molecules has practical significance. If both forms could be digested, there would be twice as much food available in the world. Sugar occurs in two handed forms: only one is accepted for digestion, though both taste sweet. Unfortunately it is expensive to isolate the non-fattening sugar. But research is proceeding apace on handed molecules: it is important for synthesising drugs. Until recently artificially created drugs contained equal numbers of both forms (called isomers). So the patient ingested twice as many molecules as needed, and the 'wrong' molecules might have unfortunate, even disastrous side-effects. The pharmaceutical industry now makes 'handed' molecules, to cut down on drug doses and reduce unwanted side-effects, as well as, perhaps, saving money. How can this be done? One way is to start with a few biological 'seed' handed molecules. In some cases, when stirred in solution, handed 'seeds' convert other molecules to their way of being.[9] Another method is to remove the unwanted isomers with a handed enzyme.

The tragic effect of the sedative thalidomide, given to pregnant women to alleviate morning sickness, was due to only one of its handed molecules. This was in 1961: now, the differently handed molecules of thalidomide can be separated. One is used for treating leprosy; the other (when the female patients are beyond child-bearing) is used for ameliorating arthritis.[10]

There are some clues to why there are biological preferences for right- or left-handed molecules.[11] Pasteur tried to explain them from other asymmetries, such as circularly polarised light affecting proto-biological molecules.[12] It could be just a matter of chance. Pasteur pointed out that the solar system is itself *dissymmetrical*: it would not fit its own mirror image. Is this just chance?

There are indications of very slight physical differences between left- and right-handed molecules, attributable to extremely small asymmetries at the fundamental-particle level of physics—very small differences in the electronic ground states of atoms. Of this, Stephen Mason says:[13]

The natural forces assumed to conserve parity included the newly discovered strong and weak nuclear forces responsbile for alpha and beta radioactivity, respectively. It was found observationally that the strong force conforms to the parity conservation principle but, from 1928, a few experiments involving the weak force gave puzzling results. Ultimately the accumulation of anomalies led Lee and Yang (1956) to conclude that parity is not conserved in the weak nuclear interaction. They designed tests for parity violation and its occurrence was soon confirmed. The experiments establishing parity violation in the weak interaction showed that the fundamental particles have an intrinsic handedness or helicity. The electrons emitted in radioactive beta decay are inherently left-handed . . . whereas the corresponding anti-particles, beta positrons, are right-handed.

It turns out that when time is included parity is conserved—but the asymmetry of time may be introducing the non-parity of these reactions. It is a curious thought that time might reverse—from time to time—maintaining ultimate parity in the Universe!

It turns out that there is a very small difference of energy in the handed forms of amino acids: there is an excess of 10^6 molecules of the stable form in a total of 10^{23}. It was suggested in 1953 by the physicist Sir Charles Frank that in an evolving biological system this might be crucially important, even though the difference of one part in 10^{17} is too small to measure in a physical experiment.[14] The notion is that such a tiny difference may become amplified, over millions or even billions of years, by natural selection. This might occur in isolated lakes over immense time. Such a local origin makes it possible that different handedness occurs in different regions of the world. This has not been found, but presumably such systems would not be entirely isolated.

Handed molecules do not necessarily combine into structures of the same handedness. Francis Crick has suggested that two right-handed α-helices of DNA would twist together to form a left-handed double helix.[15] Nothing here is simple!

We should be just a little cautious here with these terms 'right' and 'left', for we could equally well speak of 'up' and 'down' molecules. It is by reference to the different forms of our hands—which happen to be attached (via the arms) to our sides—that makes 'left-handed' and 'right-handed' convenient, though sometimes misleading, terms. If one of our hands was attached to our head and the other to our feet, no doubt we would speak of 'head' and 'foot' molecules to indicate their 'handedness' (see Figure 7.5). Clearly it is no accident that we are more symmetrical horizontally than vertically. Gravity dictates that almost all earth-based objects of fair size have to be stable; so animals, furniture, houses, have different requirements for their bases and their tops. Fish are far more symmetrical

FIGURE 7.5 *Head-hand, foot-hand*
Would she speak of 'up/down' handedness?

up-down than are land animals. Yet both fish and land animals are asymmetrical fore-and-aft, presumably because it is economical to have specialised organs such as eyes sensing forward movement, and because jointed limbs are specialised for motion in one direction. Trees, which are immobile, do not have such asymmetry; though flowers do, as they seek the Sun. As molecules are essentially unaffected by gravity they do not have up-down asymmetry dictated. Lateral 'handedness' is no more than a conventional term for chemists.

Gravity does not much apply to objects such as organs of the body, and would not prevent the *situs inversus* of Wells' *The Plattner Story*. But our body-plan is quite different sideways and up-down. In *situs inversus* asymmetrical organs, such as the heart and the spleen, are reversed horizontally and are on the 'wrong' sides of the body. These reversed people often have heart problems, because of occasional failed connections, though some reversed people are healthy and otherwise apparently normal.

Right-left mutations can occur in mice. Until recently these gave reversal in fifty per cent of the mice embryos; but very recently a gene has been identified which changes laterality for all the embryos. The reversed mice did not generally fare as well as normal.[16]

This identification of a gene is surely an important step towards solving the great puzzle of developmental biology: what determines right and left in developing embryos? Why, indeed, are most of us right-handed? Why is human *situs inversus* so rare? Now that this gene has been discovered, we may get to know the answers.

Handed Forces

Forces in physics are usually pushes and pulls. It was Michael Faraday who discovered that a wire carrying a current across a magnetic field is pushed *sideways*. As this is quite different from the usual pushes and pulls in physics, its discovery was extremely surprising; though now it is the basis of the millions of electric motors in everyday use. Faraday made the very first current electric motor in 1821, at the Royal Institution in London. This simple, beautiful experiment, showing that electricity flowing in a magnetic field is *handed*, is well worth doing now.

Figure 7.6 shows Faraday's electric motor. The freely suspended wire is in a cup of mercury. When current flows through the wire, the wire rotates around the central magnet. The direction of the rotation depends on the direction of current flow and on the polarity of the magnet. So the force is at right angles. This is a handed force. In which direction does the wire move? For describing and remembering this, the human hand provides a rule-of-thumb: take the thumb and first two fingers of the left hand, held at right angles to each other, with the **F**irst finger pointing along the **F**ield and the se**C**ond finger pointing along the **C**urrent—then the thumb points along the direction of **M**otion, or force (see Figure 7.7). This is Fleming's left-hand rule. It works because of the difference between our right and

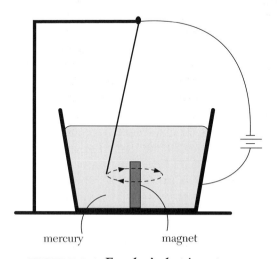

FIGURE 7.6 *Faraday's electric motor*

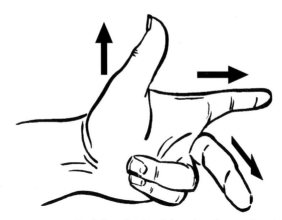

FIGURE 7.7 *Left-hand rule of thumb—for an electric motor*

left hands. It works because we can't put a left glove on a right hand. There is also a right-hand rule (see Figure 7.8): it describes the direction of a magnetic field around a wire carrying a current. The sticking up thumb indicates the current, and the curved fingers show the direction of the field.

'Right' and 'left' refer to the different forms of our right and left hands. They are unambiguous descriptions because our hands are named right and left independently of whether they happen to be to our right or left, as when our arms are crossed. We speak of someone's 'right hand' whether we are in front of or behind her, though the hand is to our left when we face her, and to our right when we stand behind her. This is, of course, why we shake hands diagonally.

There is another way of indicating which way things go with electric currents flowing in magnetic fields. This uses the conventional forms of two letters—N and S—and is shown in Figure 7.9. This depends on the chance conventional forms of the letters N and S. Chance favours intelligence!

There is also the mechanical handedness of tops and gyroscopes. If a vertical spinning wheel, such as the front wheel of a bicycle, is *turned* as if going round a corner, it will tend to *tilt* at right angles to the turn. For when the wheel is turned, say, to the right, those molecules (point masses) which are forced to change direction will resist this change, by their inertia (according to Newton's first law of motion). So the point-masses around the top and the bottom of the wheel will exert a force at right angles to the turn of the wheel. So a turn produces a tilt. And similarly a tilt produces a turn.

From this mental model one can see which ways the wheel 'precesses'. When the top of the wheel is moving away from you and it is *turned* to the right, the wheel will *tilt* to the left. Reverse the direction of spin, and the wheel will tilt to the right. From this 'mental model' of inertia of imaginary point masses of the wheel (or its atoms), we understand tops and gyroscopes without mathematics.

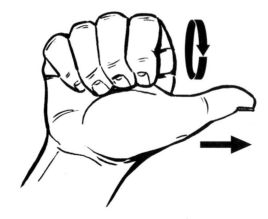

FIGURE 7.8 *Right-hand rule of thumb*

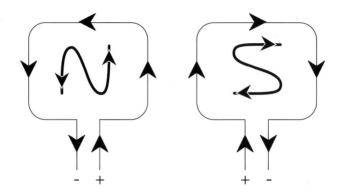

FIGURE 7.9 *Magnetic poles shown by letters N and S*
This mnemonic works from conventional letters N and S, for noting which end of a coil is the north or south pole.

Like Faraday's motor, spinning wheels are surprising. As one comes to appreciate such explanations the immediate surprise of a phenomenon may be lost; but gyroscopes still look magical. The same is so for mirrors—and surely for all of science—for with increased understanding, wonder extends to new deeper questions, as seeing principles giving answers adds infinite delight to our mental reflections.

Notes
1. Block (1974).
2. Lackner (1992).
3. Whistler (1946).

4. Scott Kim's book *Inversions* (1981) has all manner of wonderful examples.

5. Stanley Coran's informative *Left-Hander* (1992).

6. Charles Darwin describes this wonderfully in *The Movements and Habits of Climbing Plants* (1888).

7. See Pagels (1982) and Lee and Yang (1956).

8. This followed from the earlier observation of Jean Baptist Biot (1774–1862) that 'natural' tartaric acid rotated the plane of polarisation of light in the opposite direction from artificially produced para-tartaric acid, though no other difference could be found.

9. Kondepudi *et al.* (1990).

10. The thalidomide molecule is made of atoms of carbon hydrogen, bromine, chlorine, and fluorine. The formula (for both handnesses) is: $C_{13}H_{10}N_2O_4$.

11. This is discussed by Stephen F. Mason (1991) and J.W. Galloway (1991) and others, in the important CIBA Foundation Symposium *Biological Asymmetry and Handedness*, edited by Lewis Wolpert.

12. The Sun's light is only weakly polarised, by scattering from dust, and this reverses at dawn and sunset, so there is little if any overall asymmetry.

13. Mason (1991).

14. Frank (1953).

15. Crick (1953).

16. Yokoyama *et al.* (1993).

8

᎐Ꭶ

Mirror of Perception

What is truth? said jesting Pilate;
And would not stay for an answer
FRANCIS BACON

IT is sometimes said that perception 'mirrors' reality. But the more we learn of how eyes and brains and the other senses work, the more it becomes apparent that perception could hardly be more different from a looking-glass. Yet, like perception, mirror images can be faithful or have distortions and errors of various kinds—they can be *ambiguous* or *distorted* or *paradoxical* or *fictional*. Perceptions are active creative brain-descriptions: mirrors are purely passive. But there is a deep reason for this sharing of illusions.

The reason is this: these illusions of mirrors are in *us* rather than in the mirror. An image is perceptually ambiguous only if the observer fails to 'read' it in one way. What is paradoxical depends on seeing conflicts. What is fictional depends on going beyond, or flouting, or creating, evidence. Distortions are more problematical; for a mirror can have optical distortions which will disturb the input to any conceivable eye, or to a passive camera. But when the mirror is a plane surface, and the perception is distorted, its image must be evoking distortion in the observer.

There is an analogy here to Newton's warning about 'coloured' light. Strictly speaking, it is not light that is coloured; for from wavelengths of light the perception of colour is created by the brain. This can happen in the absence of light, as by pressing the eye, or from a blow to the head. Without perceiving brains, there would be no colours, or sounds, or tickles. Language is a trap here, but we are not misled if we realise (as Newton did so clearly for colour) that it is a shorthand to say that 'light is coloured'—or that 'a mirror is paradoxical'. The paradox, for example, of seeing oneself *through* the mirror while knowing one is in *front* of it (and knowing that one is but one person though we experience two) is not in the mirror or in light—it is in our perception. If we were either more or less stupid, such paradoxes might change, or disappear, or become even richer.

The same is so for illusions of distortion (with a plane mirror) and of ambiguity and fiction. Perhaps most remarkable is perceiving transparency. For here we see two or more objects lying in the same place (though at different distances), from the same region of the retina.

An implication of all this is that to understand seeing (and mis-seeing) in mirrors, we should consider seeing itself. We should consider the nature of perception and of illusion. As this is a fascinating topic it is no hardship; but an immediate snag is that there is not just one accepted way of seeing perception and explaining illusions. There is, indeed, a fundamental dichotomy between those who think of perception as the *passive* pick-up of information from the world of objects, and those who think of perception as *creating* an internal account of external objects, from available sensory cues (or clues) and a great deal of knowledge derived from the past. I take the second view—that perception is an active, creative process. The best known proponent of a passive account is the late J. J. Gibson, whose experimental work is of great importance.[1]

We will continue to speak of mirrors as being 'ambiguous', 'paradoxical' and so on—meaning that they give rise to ambiguous or paradoxical, or whatever, perceptions. An explanation needs to consider both the mirror and the observer; but to avoid tediousness, we may refer explicitly only to the mirror, or sometimes only to the observer. At the end of this chapter we will attempt to disentangle something of this, by attempting a classification of perceptual phenomena of illusions. Meanwhile it might be interesting to compare mirrors with pictures—paintings and photographs. Let's start with their curious ambiguities. But note: the ambiguities are in us.

Visual Ambiguities

Meanings of words often need a context. The same is true of ambiguities of perception. Ambiguity is seeded right at the start by representing three-dimensional space on the two dimensions of the surfaces of pictures. This was appreciated by the discoverer of retinal images, the German astronomer Johannes Kepler (1571–1630). Ambiguities of depth start in the eye itself, for any retinal image might be given by any of an infinity of shapes of objects (see Figure 8.1).

Kepler realised that all optical images and pictures are potentially ambiguous even though most appear reliably stable and fixed. It is sometimes suggested that sufficiently detailed pictures are not potentially ambiguous. This is false. The fact that houses, people, landscapes and so on can be seen as three-dimensional objects in a two-dimensional picture depends on the brain's ability to select particular interpretations from the multi-possibilities of what objects there may be out there. It is this that makes paintings work—and the cinema and television and flight simulators—and retinal images. Kepler was quite right to be puzzled over

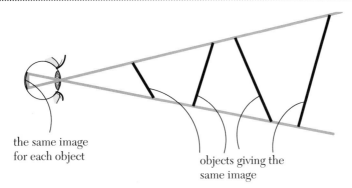

the same image
for each object

objects giving the
same image

FIGURE 8.1 *The ambiguity of retinal images*

The bars represent larger objects at greater distances, giving the same image to the eye, even when the bars are tilted differently. (Actually they would have to be wedges to give the same shaped images). The situation is inherently ambiguous—so the brain has to make up its mind. This ambiguity of retinal images, even though perceptions are usually stable, puzzled Kepler four hundred years ago and is not fully understood today. Why should just one out of an infinity of possibilities be selected for perception?

how three dimensions are extracted, usually fairly accurately, from but two. He suggested a simple solution which, however, turned out to be wrong. Now we know that there is not one simple answer.

Seeing three dimensions from the two of images and pictures involves optics and physiology and subtle cognitive processes of vision, calling upon stored knowledge guided by general rules. It is the fact that perception is not infallible that makes art interesting and scientific observation difficult. There are many instruments for extending and checking the senses, but ultimately their messages depend on context and all manner of assumptions, and they are phenomenally ambiguous according to what we attempt, albeit unconsciously, to read from them.

Kepler was also puzzled that the eyes' images, though not perceptions, are reversed up-down and sideways. He was led to the eyes' images and their powers and limitations through the camera obscura, and by observing optical images in animal eyes when the outer covering (the choriod) was removed. It was immediately clear that the images are upside down and right-left reversed. So—quite apart from mirrors—why do we normally see things *not* reversed though our eyes' images *are* optically reversed? Kepler found this extremely puzzling. He said:

Therefore vision occurs through a picture of the visible thing on the white, concave surface of the retina. And that which is to the left on the outside is portrayed on the right; that which is above is portrayed below; and that which is below is portrayed above. . . . Therefore, if it were possible for that picture on the retina to remain after being taken outside into the light, by removing the anterior portions [of the eye], and if there were a man whose vision was sufficiently sharp, he would perceive the very shape of the hemisphere upon the extremely narrow [surface] of the retina.[2]

Kepler says that he 'dutifully tortured' himself to try to show that the rays cross again to give a non-inverted image. Thus he tried to avoid the problem by invoking a fictitious second optical reversal in the eyes, as Leonardo had previously suggested and for the same reason. Kepler finally rejected the second reversal, accepting that retinal images are inverted. But he remained puzzled, and so were others at the time, that normally things look upright and not right-left reversed.[3] Kepler realized that light does not pass through the optic nerves into the brain, but he did not pursue vision beyond the retina, seeing this as physicians' concern.

The why-don't-things-look-inverted puzzle remained while it was assumed that the image in the eye is seen *as a picture* by the brain. This long-maintained notion has several snags. If there were an internal 'eye' looking at the picture in the eye, this 'internal eye' should have a picture—requiring another eye to see it—then another eye, another picture—an infinite set of eyes looking at pictures. Such a regress gets nowhere. What changed this situation was the important notion that the brain *describes* images in the eyes. It is this description that is perception.

Current brain research is deeply involved in looking for which features of images are used for brain-descriptions. It turns out that particular neurons in the primary visual region of the brain (the striate cortex) respond to lines of certain orientations. So to simplify, one might imagine the letter A being signalled by just three neurons; one for the left oblique, another for the right oblique, the third for the horizontal bar (see Figure 8.2). The firing of these three cells could in principle represent the letter A. The point is, the *picture* is no longer present in the brain, nor is it needed once it is *described* by the presence and absence of specific features. These include orientation, movement, colour and much more, signalled by separate neural channels, and processed in specialized brain modules. The initial discovery of 'feature detectors' for orientation and movement was made by two American physiologists working together: David Hubel and Torsten Wiesel.[4]

On this notion that the brain *describes*, there is no problem about the inversion and sideways reversal of the optical image in the eyes—as there is no eye behind the eye looking at the image, as at a picture. What does matter are positions of features of retinal images compared to experience of objects by touch. These relations have to be learned. But the baby does not have to learn to adjust for the upside down and sideways reversed image. This is not a special problem; but the baby does have to learn what the eyes' signals mean in terms of characteristics of objects. This is so difficult and complicated it is beyond our current computing technology.

Where does the third dimension—depth—come from, in a flat image or picture? Here Kepler could have learned a lot from painters, as artists had known for

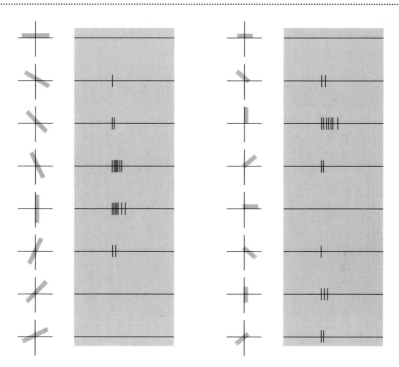

FIGURE 8.2 *Brain-descriptions: Hubel and Wiesel's classical experiment*
Simple features of the world are selected at the early stages of visual processing.

a very long time that depth can be represented with various cues (or clues), such as nearer objects partly hiding more distant objects, and shading and shadows.[5] But Kepler looked for an unambiguous signal for depth from a single eye. This became known as Kepler's cones. His idea is illustrated in Figure 8.3. There is an optical cone from each point of an external object to the pupil of the eye. There is a corresponding cone from the pupil to the points of the retinal image. So the *angle* of the rays striking the retina, at each point, corresponds to object *distance*. Though this is formally correct, it does not work. The retina can not signal the angle of these rays, and the effect is far too small to serve as a range-finder. So Kepler did not succeed in showing that retinal images are not depth-ambiguous. They *are* ambiguous, although accommodation (focusing) does provide some distance information for a single eye from objects lying in three dimensions—though not from pictures.

Although Kepler's suggestion for avoiding depth-ambiguity for a single eye is not in practice correct, there is some information from the state of accommodation (focus) of the eye. This is a minor clue for depth; but somewhat paradoxically, it is sufficient to produce strain and headache with 3D films and virtual reality.

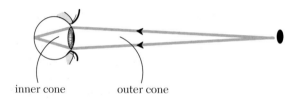

inner cone   outer cone

FIGURE 8.3 *Kepler's cones*
*Kepler was worried by the depth ambiguity of images. He thought the angles of light striking
the retina indicated distance. Unfortunately, this is not so!*

This is because there is retinal disparity—slightly different images—between the
eyes for stereoscopic depth; but the eyes must be focused on the plane of the
screen for a sharp image, producing uncomfortable conflict.

As retinal images are always ambiguous, the brain has to guess what they
mean. Is it a *large distant object*—or something *nearer* and *smaller*? The possibilities
are infinite; yet a single perception is usually selected. This is a major puzzle for
understanding perception. It is surprising that phenomena of ambiguity are relatively quite rare, though of great importance for understanding the nature of perception. Most famous are the Ames Demonstrations (see Chapter 2). These are
objects with built-in perspective shapes. Simpler are well-known figures such as
the Necker cube and the Duck-Rabbit, that flip from one orientation or one object
to another, which may be very different (see Figure 8.4).

For perception we do not respond to moment-to-moment *stimuli* from the
senses, but rather to a running *guess* of what is about to happen. It is this (never
certain) prediction that allows us to hit a ping-pong ball, even though there is considerable delay in transmission of the signals from the eyes and commands to the
muscles of the arms and hands. To avoid neural reaction-time we hit at a *guess* of
where the ball will be and when the bat should arrive.[6] We may say that perceptions are *hypotheses* of what is out there. And for various reasons, hypotheses may
be wrong.

Perceptions as Hypotheses

In my view perceptions are very similar to predictive hypotheses of science.[7] Both
are richer than available data. Both are predictive. And both can reach surprising
conclusions—by following rules, which may or may not be appropriate. This
applies not only to vision but also to all the other senses: none gives direct
knowledge which is free of interpretation and assumptions.

Prediction is very clear for sound. It was Newton's perceptual prediction
which allowed him to measure the speed of sound by clapping his hands to
echoes. By counting the number of echoes in, say, a minute, and knowing the dis-

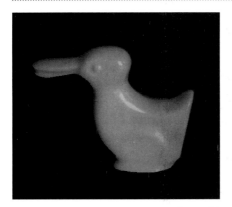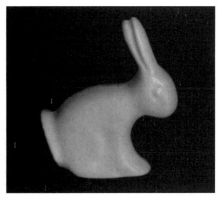

FIGURE 8.4 *An ambiguous figure: the duck-rabbit*

tance of the reflecting wall, Newton was able to measure the speed of sound by clapping his hands to the *prediction* of the echoes—so avoiding his reaction-time (see page 110). A similar experiment would be to get friends (or an audience at a class or lecture) to clap their hands to your regular hand-claps, while your hands are hidden. For the first few claps they will lag behind. Very soon they will become exactly synchronised with *no* delay—though there is neural delay to their brains and to their hands. When you stop, they will go on clapping, once or twice. Their prediction has failed: they are responding to *expected* claps, which don't always happen.

So perceptions do not come immediately or directly from sensory data (such as sounds or images in the eye), and they are far richer than the available data. A great deal of learning is needed, essentially from interacting with objects, for discovering that wood is hard, that water is wet, that ripe fruit is good to eat, that metals make good mirrors. This hard-earned object-knowledge gives meaning to touch, and to the eye's images. This knowledge from object-experience transfers to pictures and to images of mirrors—so they are seen as though they are more or less normal objects, though they are not.

'Eye-deas' and 'I-deas'

Given that *perceptions* are brain-descriptions, and *conceptions* are also brain-descriptions though more general and abstract, it would seem that perceiving and conceiving are not altogether different. We might call them, if not too seriously: 'Eye-deas' and 'I-deas'. The first obviously uses eyes; the second is often supposed (since René Descartes' 'I think, therefore I am') to require an 'I' for thinking. In any case, we may say that both perceiving and conceiving produce *intelligent hypotheses*.[8]

The intelligences of perception and conception can come up with different answers. Perception has to work very fast, within a fraction of a second, to be useful; but conceptions may take days or months, and they can be far more general and abstract than perceptions. Thus we *see* particular triangles, but we can *conceive* of abstract triangularity. How far mental images are involved is a controversial issue.[9]

The fact that Eye-deas and I-deas may disagree shows that mind is not unitary. The visual brain is organized with many specialized modules, undertaking different tasks. How it all comes together, though sometimes with disagreements, is not yet known. It is disturbing that conceptual understanding often does not correct mis-perceptions—or perceptions correct conceptual misunderstandings. Thus understanding the optics of why objects appear through mirrors does not affect how they are *seen*. So mirrors separate Eye-deas from I-deas. This is indeed so for all illusions, when we are fooled and yet know why we are perceiving wrongly.

As we are fooled by illusions that we understand, it might be supposed that vision does not require knowledge. This, however, would not be correct. Knowledge is essential for seeing objects—but the brain's perceptual knowledge-base is not the same as its conceptual knowledge-base. There are, indeed, dangerous gaps between perceptual and conceptual knowledge. These gaps between perception and conception give art much of its creative tension of ambiguities and paradoxes, and demand precautions for science.

There are aesthetics of perceptions and conceptions. It is often said that visual symmetries are beautiful, as in the appeal of the kaleidoscope (page 180), and conceptual symmetries in equations of physics and mathematics are beautiful. It is often said that beauty is a guide to truth, but this is fallible. Beguiled by beauty, Johannes Kepler was for years seduced away from his great discovery that the planets move in ellipses. Kepler spent years of arduous calculation to escape from the unaesthetic—yet true—picture of the Sun occupying one focus of an ellipse, for the orbit of Mars, with nothing in the other focus. This is like drawing an ellipse with only one pin instead of the usual two! Kepler was driven for aesthetic reasons to consider egg-shaped orbits before finally being convinced, by Tycho Brahe's observations and his own calculations, that the unaesthetic had to be accepted. We are now so used to this model of the solar system that it feels right and proper. This is so for new shapes in technology. Aerodynamic forms looked strange and ugly at first, but now they have beauty and 'rightness.' It would be hard to argue that aircraft designers initially were guided by aesthetics: what now seems right and beautiful was inspired by surprising results from wind tunnel tests of ever weirder and at first ugly models.

Visual perception is a complex of active processes for making sense of the world, quickly, from limited information. The eyes only receive light, yet (it seems miraculously) vision allows us to behave appropriately to *non*-visual characteristics of things. This shows immediately that knowledge is essential for see-ing. The two meanings of 'see' (as in 'I see a clock', and 'I see how it works') are related, though by no means identical. Although Plato was unaware of optical images in eyes, he was not entirely incorrect when he thought of vision as work-ing by light shooting out of the eyes, and returning to mingle in an internal fire—for light enters the eyes to form optical images, which are *projected psychologically* out into the external world, as hypotheses of what might be out there.[10] Sometimes, this projection creates fictions. Touch may confirm what we see, but touch is not infallible. Of course not everything is touchable: most objects are too distant for the hands. Very often what we see can not be confirmed by the other senses, and *they* are themselves also not altogether reliable. So we have to trust the psychological projection of the eyes' images into outer space—which *is* visual perception.

The psychological projection from the eyes to the world of objects is seen most dramatically in after-images. They are like photographs stuck on the retinas; but they appear not in the eyes, but in the outside world of objects. Try looking at a camera flash. Then turn your eyes to a wall, or to the palm of your hand. You will see a patch of light (or dark) on the wall or on your hand. You see it out there though it is stuck on your retinas. It moves as you move your eyes. It will look *larger* the more *distant* the screen it is 'projected' on. Try moving your hand nearer and further away: the patch gets bigger as you move your hand further away. (This works also in the dark, when your hand can't be seen, but its distance is signalled proprioceptively[11]). This is 'Emmert's law': an after-image perceived at twice the distance looks twice as large. This is related to size constancy scaling (see page 219).

Vision is highly active—searching for what might be out there. One can see one's own vision searching for sense and order in a regular pattern such as the one shown in Figure 8.5. The circles seem to form rows and lines and squares, and all manner of subtle patterns. Here one see something of the activity of one's own vision.

The start of perception, from neural signals from the eyes, is usually called 'bottom-up' signals to the brain. Then, very differently, there is knowledge of objects—'top-down' knowledge—which is essential for giving meaning to signals from the eyes and the other senses. There are, also, general operating rules. These we might call (by rough analogy with putting floppy disks into a computer) 'side-ways' rules or algorithms.

Perceptual rules include the Gestalt laws of organisation.[12] Similar features tend to be grouped together. Features that move together (such as leaves on a tree, moved by wind) tend to be seen as one object. Features forming closed shapes tend to be accepted as parts of a single object. These are general rules for object perception. They are usually appropriate as most objects do have repeated pat-terns, and parts that move together, and have closed simple outlines, and so on.

```
O O O O O O O O O O O O O O O O O O O O
O O O O O O O O O O O O O O O O O O O O
O O O O O O O O O O O O O O O O O O O O
O O O O O O O O O O O O O O O O O O O O
O O O O O O O O O O O O O O O O O O O O
O O O O O O O O O O O O O O O O O O O O
O O O O O O O O O O O O O O O O O O O O
O O O O O O O O O O O O O O O O O O O O
O O O O O O O O O O O O O O O O O O O O
O O O O O O O O O O O O O O O O O O O O
O O O O O O O O O O O O O O O O O O O O
O O O O O O O O O O O O O O O O O O O O
```

FIGURE 8.5 *Dynamic organisation of vision*

```
O X O X O X O X O X
O X O X O X O X O X
O X O X O X O X O X
O X O X O X O X O X
O X O X O X O X O X
O X O X O X O X O X
O X O X O X O X O X
O X O X O X O X O X
O X O X O X O X O X
```

FIGURE 8.6 *Organisation by similarity*

Early this century the Gestalt psychologists thought that these rules (or 'Gestalt laws') are innate, and so do not have to be learned. This is possible as they are very general and must have been useful for a long time—millions of years before humankind. But almost all object knowledge must be learned. There can not be innate knowledge of bicycles or telephones!

We see perceptual organisation for similar and different shapes in a pattern such as the one shown in Figure 8.6. Here we tend to see vertical rows of 'O's and 'X's. But the creative activity of visual perception can produce other organisations. Various laws can be pitted against each other, to see which wins. This is illustrated by Figure 8.7. In the left column the dots form pairs, and the nearer dots 'belong together'. This shows the Gestalt law of contiguity. But this law is broken by two dots at the centre of the right-hand part of the figure. These two dots do not 'belong together': one belongs to the longer and the other to the

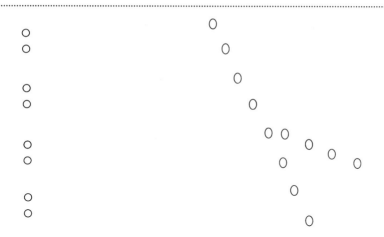

FIGURE 8.7 *Conflicts and hierarchies*

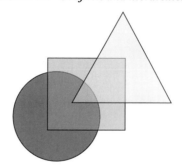

FIGURE 8.8 *Transparency*

Transparency is seen by several visual rules, discovered by Metelli, including brightness ratios. It is also seen, as pointed out by Irvin Rock (1985), by the number of coincidental features making a second object probable.

shorter row of dots. The laws can thus be pitted against each other, to find which is the stronger. Possibly which wins can depend on the task the perceiver is trying to complete at the time; but this is not really known.

There are visual rules for seeing transparency—which is useful for artists—which were discovered through recent experiments by the Italian psychologist Fabio Metelli at Trieste.[13] It is remarkable that we can see several objects from one region of the retina—in a painting or by reflection from glass or water (see Figure 8.8). Reflections evoke two or even more Perceptual Hypotheses.

An important set of rules that give perception of depth from a single eye depends on the optical fact that retinal images get smaller with increasing object distance (see Figure 8.9). So parallel lines converge with distance—giving *linear perspective*—and texture gets more and more dense with distance. It is odd that

FIGURE 8.9 *Depth texture—a gradient of letter sizes*

*This looks like a surface going into the distance. The general rule is that an image shrinks to
half its linear size with each doubling of distance. As this is true of retinal
images, so it can be a rule for the brain to infer distances—and for artists to portray
distances in pictures. Since Brunelleschi's discovery of perspective (see page 29), artists have
used explicitly what the brain discovered implicitly millions of years ago.*

these basic facts of vision were not appreciated much earlier than the fifteenth
century. They are of course very important for artists (see page 29).

Distortions

Visual distortions can have many causes. By discovering these we can learn a lot
about how we see. For example, converging lines enable us to see depth (see
Figure 8.10). They may be 'read' as parallel lines going into the distance by perspective convergence: as images normally shrink with distance, so receding parallel lines converge at the retina. Artists use these ancient brain-tricks for seeing

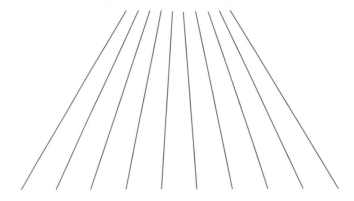

FIGURE 8.10 *Clues of convergence for seeing depth*

three dimensions in a two-dimensional picture, though only quite recently have they been discovered conceptually.

Although images shrink to half their size with each doubling of object distance, this is not how they are seen. Objects appear much the same size over a range of distances. When very far away, however, they do shrink to toys. Size scaling is perceptual compensation for shrinking of images with distance— giving size and shape constancy. It is useful because it is the actual size of *objects* that matter for behaviour. The sizes and shapes of the eye's *image* is not important: what matters is whether it is a cat or a tiger, a half-pint or a pint. It is hardly surprising if such processes, depending on assumptions and rules that do not always apply, sometimes produce distortion illusions.[14]

The theory of such distortion illusions is that they occur when constancy scaling is set inappropriately to the surface of the picture. This is the 'inappropriate constancy scaling' theory.[15] The rule for these distortion illusions is that anything signalled as more *distant* is *expanded* (see Figure 8.11). This is the opposite of the optical shrinking of images in the eyes—for constancy scaling is a *compensation* for distant objects giving smaller images. This perceptual process evidently works early in visual processing, and is not in consciousness.

It is striking that distortion occurs when depth is *assumed* even though there is *no* explicit perspective or other (bottom-up) depth cues. Figure 8.12 is an example of this. The effect is seen even more convincingly in a depth-ambiguous wire cube. The fact that normally a skeleton cube looks like a cube—the back and front

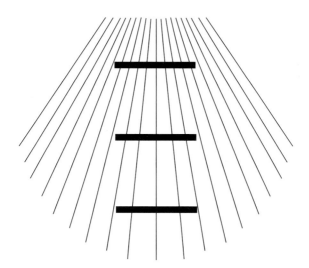

FIGURE 8.11 *Distortion from perspective (bottom-up) mis-scaling*
The three horizontal bars are exactly the same length. But those signalled by perspective convergence as further away, appear longer.

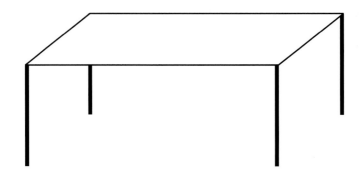

FIGURE 8.12 *Distortion from assumed depth (top-down) mis-scaling*
The upper—apparently further—edge of the rectangle looks longer than the lower, nearer-looking edge. The sides do not look parallel—but they are. This is evidently due to top-down scaling, from the assumed depth of the table. Note that there is no persepctive in the drawing and no bottom-up scaling.

faces looking the same size, and the opposite sides looking parallel—shows that constancy scaling is operating normally, giving appropriate size and shape constancy. But when the cube flips in depth, it *changes shape*. When flipped, the now apparently *back* face looks too *large*, and the sides are not parallel (see Figure 8.13). The scaling has gone into reverse. It has switched with the flip of apparent depth. This must be top-down scaling, from the reversed 'hypothesis' of the cube.

This is worth an experiment: a wire cube is one of the most revealing experimental objects for discovering these processes of vision. Its size is unimportant. Stiff wire is best, but a cube can be made by gluing together long matches or straws. Place the cube so that all the sides can be seen. Soon, it will 'flip' in depth. When the truly near face appears as the back, three remarkable effects are seen.

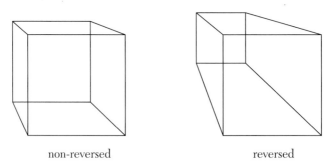

non-reversed   reversed

FIGURE 8.13 *Appearance and reality of a flipping cube*
When flipped in depth it changes shape. While seen correctly (front face seen as near), both faces appear the same size. Reversed, the now apparently back face—but actually the nearer—appears too large. So when reversed it looks like a truncated pyramid.

(At first it may be easier to view with one eye.) According to how it is placed, when it flips, it will stand up on a corner. Secondly, with each movement of the observer it will apparently rotate—in the same direction—following every movement. This is because although the physical motion parallax is unchanged, it is wrongly tagged to what is near and far. The third effect, though less dramatic, is highly informative. The cube changes shape. Its true front (now apparently the back face) looks too large. The cube becomes a truncated pyramid. The closer it is viewed the greater the distortion. This is like Emmert's law for after-images; but it is a 'purer' observation, as there is no change in the bottom-up input from the eyes. (Evidently the size-shape changes are due to 'top-down' scaling. As there is no change in the stimulus input, this must be purely top-down, brain-induced.)

A flat drawing of a cube (a Necker cube) also flips in depth; but a *drawing* will not rotate with the observer's movement It will scarcely change shape when depth-reversed, as top-down scaling hardly occurs for the paradoxical depth of the drawing. (Drawn in luminous ink and viewed in the dark there is a marked size change, much as for a truly three-dimensional cube.[16])

Categories of Illusions

Phenomena of illusions can tell us a lot about the ins-and-outs of perception. It is possible to tease out pathways or neural 'channels', and discover limitations and properties of the brain's information processors. Effects of memory, attention, fatigue and more can be investigated through illusions. This could take us too far away from our theme of mirrors in mind, but it might be useful to put mirror-illusions into the broad context of other illusions. So let's try to classify phenomena of illusion, in terms of appearances and causes.

The first kind of *cause* of visual illusion can be anything that disturbs light between the object and the retinas of the eyes. These I shall call *physical* illusions. Mirrors are in this category. The second stage of vision is the *physiology* of the neural pathway to the brain, and physiological processes in the brain itself. Errors of neural signals we may call *physiological* illusions. The third stage is *cognitive* processes, by which we generally make sense of neural signals.[17] Misreading them causes illusions through no fault of the physiology. The snag may be something wrong with the *knowledge* or with the *rules*. A *knowledge* snag gives a 'top-down' cognitive error. A *rules* snag, we may say, gives a 'sideways' cognitive error (see Figures 8.13 and 8.14).

It is interesting, and important, that vision and touch are intimately related. Especially suggestive is the Size-Weight Illusion. This is very easy to try with kitchen equipment. Get two tins (or cans), one large, the other small. Fill them partially, for example with sugar, until they are the same scale weight. So we have large and small objects of the same weight. Do they feel the same weight? Try lifting them, one in each hand, or one after the other with the same hand.

Their weights feel different: the *smaller* object feels considerably *heavier*. This is because we set our muscles to the *expected* weight—and larger objects are usually heavier than smaller objects. Although this predictive perceptual hypothesis is usually appropriate, here it is not—and we have a very suggestive shared cognitive illusion. It is cognitive, because it depends on knowledge or assumption,

FIGURE 8.14 *The hollow face*

Though hollow, the nose sticks out, not in. The refusal to look hollow is simply because faces are familiar and hollow faces are extremely unlikely.

which is not however, appropriate here. It is this that explains the effect, not the physiology, although of course plenty of physiology is involved.

The eye is easily fooled by situations which are *almost* typical but not quite. The face in Figure 8.14 is hollow—but it looks like a normal face. When rotated, it looks bizarre. It is the typical features of eyes, nose and mouth that select the face hypothesis, which assumes the usual sticking-out nose. This shows the power of top-down knowledge. Looking at the actual three-dimensional mask, the (bottom-up) stereoscopic and other sensory information is overruled by the (top-down) knowledge of faces. As we have said more than once, although we know the reason for a visual illusion we can still be fooled—which is strong evidence for separation of perceptual and conceptual knowledge in the brain.[18]

We have four essentially different causes of perceptual illusions: the *physical*; the *physiological*; and two kinds of *cognitive* illusion—top-down knowledge and sideways rules, which are misleading when they are not appropriate. And it seems there are four strikingly different kinds of illusion for each of these categories.

It may be suggestive that these correspond to the major kinds of errors of language: ambiguities; distortions; paradoxes; and fictions. The link to language may be no accident, for it is possible that language-structure derives from ancient pre-human perceptual classification of objects and actions.[19] This would help to explain how human language has developed so fast, in biological time, if it is a take-over from a far more ancient perceptual classification.[20] For example:

Ambiguity	John is looking funny
Distortion	He is miles taller than mother
Paradox	She is a dark-haired blond
Fiction	Her sister lives in a mirror

It is striking that visual illusions fall neatly into these language categories. Here are examples of well-known phenomena of visual illusion put, sometimes tentatively, into these categories.[21]

Physical

Ambiguities	All 2D images of 3D space, mist, shadows
Distortions	Of space: a stick-in-water
	Of velocity: stroboscopic effects
Paradoxes	Mirrors—seeing oneself double, in a wrong place
Fictions	Rainbows, Moiré patterns

Physiological

Ambiguities	Size–distance signals, from a single eye
Distortions	Adaptations to length, tilt or curvature; the 'Café Wall'

Paradoxes	When visual channels disagree—the after-effect of motion: moving, yet not changing position or size
Fictions	After-images, autokinetic effect, migraine patterns

Knowledge

Ambiguities	Necker cube, Duck-Rabbit, vase-faces
Distortions	Size-Weight
Paradoxes	Penrose Impossible Triangle, Escher's pictures
Fictions	Faces-in-the-fire, Man-in-the-Moon

Rules

Ambiguities	Figure–ground (objects or space between objects)
Distortions	Muller-Lyer, Ponzo (when scaling is set inappropriately), the Moon Illusion
Paradoxes	Impossible Triangle
Fictions	Kanizsa Triangle (illusory surface and triangles), filling in the blind spot and scotomas[22]

Mirrors produce visual paradoxes even though they are not themselves, as objects, paradoxical. One *sees* oneself through a looking-glass yet one *knows* one is in front of it. We accept *two selves* though we know we are one self, with only one body, though here we experience two. One's own face is doubled in the mirror, in a wrong place. What could be more paradoxical? But ultimately the paradox is in us, not the mirror.

Ins and Outs of Vision

Let's picture what seems to be going on as Ins and Outs of vision. Figure 8.15 illustrates the simplest hypothetical scheme. It comprises bottom-up signals from the eyes; top-down object knowledge; and sideways general rules, such as giving depth from perspective.

There are two knowledge bases: *conceptual knowledge* and *perceptual knowledge*. When we experience an illusion and yet know that, and even why, we are being fooled, we learn that conceptual understanding feeds but fitfully and slowly into perception. And the converse is also true.

Let's develop this a little further. Figure 8.16 shows a more developed hypothetical scheme, which indicates: bottom-up signals from the eyes; top-down object knowledge; sideways general rules; feedback for learning by interacting with objects; the intended task setting needs from knowledge and rules; and—the most mysterious—consciousness.

What children see affects only slowly what they understand, and affects it hardly at all without interactive feedback from the world of objects. Later, with

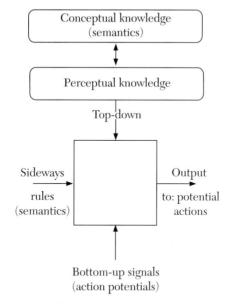

FIGURE 8.15 *Flat box: the simplest hypothetical scheme*

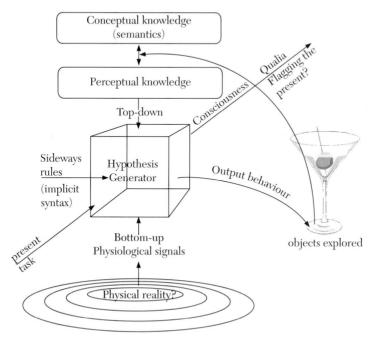

FIGURE 8.16 *Black box of vision: a hypothetical design for the visual mind*

more knowledge, we can learn a lot from passive observing, especially of disturbances.[23] Lewis Carroll saw this when he got Alice to *shake* the kitten. This not only woke the kitten, but it also woke Alice to its existence and much more. By *shaking* we learn the *solidity* of things; we learn about hardness, softness, inertia, and much else. But images have none of these: they are not objects to be appreciated hands-on. Rotations of mirror-images are not experienced, as are rotations of mugs and toys, through the hands. And objects that can be handled can be shared, for competition and games, and for co-operative discovery through more or less purposeful play and experiments. As we can't handle mirror images, their peculiarities are scarcely fed into our knowledge. So it is not surprising if mirrors are puzzling and hard to think about.

Conceptual Illusions

We have seen that perceptual illusions can occur through *misleading analogies* from past experience. Thus the hollow mask is seen as a normal face (Figure 8.14) because the usual face hypothesis, based on seeing millions of faces all with sticking-out noses, is so powerful that it rejects bottom-up data that this particular face is hollow. There are comparable *conceptual* illusions leading to errors of thinking. This has been studied by Daniel Kahneman and Amos Tversky.[24]

Is it obvious how balances and see-saws, for example, work—even though they are familiar objects? Figure 8.17 shows ordinary scales. When a weight is moved towards the end of a beam, that end of the beam moves down. We all know this. The Enigma scales (Figure 8.18) look similar but are crucially different.[25] This has a central parallelogram, with bearings, which keeps the end arms horizontal as they move up and down. Here the weights are at equal distances

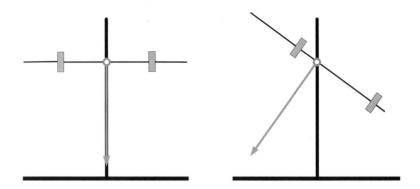

FIGURE 8.17 *Ordinary scales*
This tilts when a weight is moved in or out.

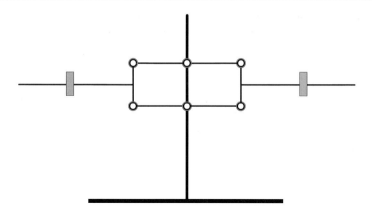

FIGURE 8.18 *Enigma scales—balanced*
This is level—just like ordinary scales.

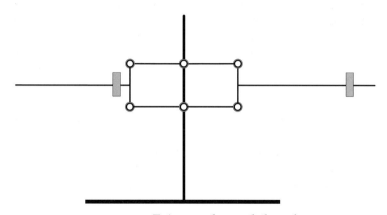

FIGURE 8.19 *Enigma scales—unbalanced*
This remains level when a weight is moved in or out—unlike ordinary scales.

from the centre. When the weights are moved, does it behave like a normal balance or see-saw? What happens when one of the weights is moved in, and the other out (Figure 8.19)? Nothing happens! The Enigma scales remain balanced. Would children appreciate a see-saw like this, which they couldn't balance by moving in or out?

Hands-on experience of the Enigma scales gives one a shock of surprise. This makes one check one's understanding of scales and see-saws and levers. It is surprising, because we see it by surface analogy to visually similar, though deeply different, balances and see-saws. One has to *see* the functional difference to understand what is going on. Then we appreciate ordinary balances and see-saws differently and more clearly.

FIGURE 8.20 *Glass and string conceptual illusion*

We understand the Enigma scales by appreciating that however far out the weights are, they move through the same vertical distance. So the work done is the same wherever the weights are along their beams. If the weights are equal they remain balanced wherever they are. However, a heavier weight on one side will pull the beam down, just as for a normal balance, or see-saw, for then the work done is different.

Figure 8.20 shows another conceptual illusion: of a wineglass and string. Try wrapping a length of string once around the base of a glass. Then unwrap the string, hold one end at the base of the glass and see how far it reaches up the glass. What would you expect? The answer is surprising: it goes much further up than expected—though this should be obvious from one's knowledge of pi. This suggests that although we could easily work it out we do not use our mathematical knowledge to judge it correctly. Mathematicians may be different. Perhaps most of us have not *played* enough with mathematics in mind.[26]

The importance of *playing* is discussed in the next chapter, 'Hands-On Through the Looking-glass'. There is physical hands-on playing and mental exploratory play. They are keys to getting our skills developed and our ideas straight. Playing is the source of effective creativity. Surely the leisure to play creatively, all through life, is the great benefit of civilisation, and makes civilisation possible. But this is a later reflection.

Notes

1. J. J. Gibson was at Cornell University for many years. His *Perception of the Visual World* (1950) and *The Senses Considered as Perceptual Systems* (1966) are classics still read by all students and discussed by experts. Some of my objections to such a passive account are set out in Gregory (1974).

2. Kepler's *Paraligomena*, page 185. See Lindberg (1976) page 200.

3. For example, Kepler's friend Johann Brengger, after reading the *Paralipomena*, wrote: 'The means of vision you explain skilfully and elegantly. I had always convinced myself that vision was accomplished by the reception of the species of visible things on the retina. I was put in some doubt, however, since everything would be received there inverted, whereas vision occurs uprightly.' See Lindberg (1976) page 203.

4. Hubel and Wiesel shared the 1981 Nobel Prize for physiology and medicine with Roger Sperry. See Hubel and Wiesel (1962) and, for a simple account, Gregory (1966).

5. See Gombrich (1995).

6. This was first measured by Helmholtz in 1850.

7. Gregory (1970, 1980). But almost all philosophers think very differently, that perception is passive, with no problem solving involved. This is why, although his writings are of great interest, Berkeley (1713) got into such a tangle. See also Russell (1946).

8. Hence the title of my book *The Intelligent Eye* (1970).

9. See Miller (1987), and a vast if not altogether satisfactory psychological literature on imagery.

10. I accept that vision is highly active—creating hypotheses of the external world. This is very much the account of Hermann von Helmholtz, the founder of modern studies of perception, over a hundred years ago, though he did not quite think of perceptions as hypotheses. Some authorities think, very differently, that vision is passive acceptance of what is out there. I defend active hypothesis-generation in Gregory (1968, 1970, 1974a, 1975, 1980, 1981). This applies to perception, but not to responding to stimuli. Thus blinking to a sudden noise is not perceptual, in that we do not identify or assume the source of the stimulus and react to this 'hypothesis'.

11. Technically this is important, for it shows that Emmert's law is not simply due to more background being covered by the after-images, when the background is more distant. With other evidence, it shows that size scaling is an active process, set by depth cues. See Gregory, Wallace and Campbell (1959).

12. The Gestalt psychologists early this century supposed that there are electrical fields in the brain the same shapes as shapes of seen objects: a circular object giving a circular brain trace and so on. The traces were supposed to organise into simple forms, rather like soap bubbles. This is no longer accepted, but the Gestsalt laws of organisation are regarded as valid and important. The classical papers are translated into English in Ellis (1938).

13. Metelli (1974); for interesting and important accounts of this and related issues in perception see Rock (1983).

14. See Chapter 2: Mirrors in Art. The Ames Demonstrations, such as the Trapezoid Window and the Distorted Room, depend on the observer accepting the rules of perspective—though in these cases they are not appropriate. See Ittelson and Kilpatrick (1951), and for Ames's intellectual relations, Gregory (1994).

15. Gregory (1963, 1980). There are also entirely other kinds of visual distortions, such as the 'Café Wall' illusion: see Gregory and Heard (l979).

16. When a flat pictures is seen in convincing depth, it will rotate with the observer as he or she moves. This is opposite to the direction of motion parallax. One is seeing one's own compensation to the (physical) motion parallax of a three-dimensional object. This reversed apparent motion is a wonderful visual phenomenon, that takes us through the eyes to inner workings of the brain.

17. Cognitive processes can no more be 'reduced' to physiology, than software can be reduced to, or described by, computer hardware. They are essentially different. This dualism is dif-

ferent from Descarte's brain–mind dualism, and does not have the same philosophical problems, for it does not suppose two substances. It might be called 'aspect dualism.' This notion is very familiar in the hardware–software distinction for computing machines.

18. This is developed in my *The Intelligent Eye* (1970), and in other books and papers.

19. This merely touches upon extremely interesting issues of relations between language and thought and perception. Chomsky's notion of deep structure and the idea that there is a universal 'brain language' are brilliantly discussed by Steven Pinker (1994).

20. See Gregory (1974b).

21. This classification I presented at a Discourse lecture at the Royal Institution: see Gregory (1993).

22. Ramachandran and Gregory (1991).

23. A dramatic example is Jupiter bombarded by fragments of the comet Shoemaker-Levy, in July 1994. After centuries of telescopic observation, at last something of the dynamics of Jupiter was revealed.

24. See Kahneman, Slovic and Tversky (1982); Johnson-Laird and Wason (1977); and Piattelli-Palmarina (1994).

25. This can easily be made in Meccano. The secret is: the weights move the same vertical distance, whether in or out. So when lifted, the work done against gravity is the same, wherever they are along the beam. This is essentially different from a see-saw, though it looks similar. One has to appreciate the underlying principle, that the work done is the same wherever the weights are, to see through the paradox.

26. For a couple of other examples of misplaced mental models: a microscope salesman was demonstrating a low power and then a higher power lens of a projection microscope. With the higher power, the picture was dimmer. Reason given: 'The glass of the lens is thicker, so it wastes light'. This lens is thicker, but the significant reason is quite different: the image fills a larger screen area.

Here is another example: while considering demonstrating gear wheels in a Science Centre, a physics graduate said: 'I would like to have two gears the same size with different numbers of teeth—to show one wheel going round faster than the other, according to ratio of numbers of teeth.' This is impossible! It is convenient to think of the ratios of teeth, but what actually matters is not their numbers but the circumferences of the wheels. That different numbers of teeth on the same size wheels won't mesh is so obvious to anyone brought up on Meccano that it is literally a joke. A moment of hands-on experience would have corrected the handle-turning error. But such conceptual illusions are common for all of us. See Chapter 9.

9

Hands-on Through the Looking-glass

In another moment Alice was through the glass, and had
jumped lightly down into the Looking-glass room
LEWIS CARROLL

NOW let's ask how we may see through appearance. This is the individual journey through our eyes to our brains and minds, and it is the shared journey of civilisation through myth to science. This is, however, too simple; for myths are not entirely discarded, and it may be that something is lost at each stage of any journey. Myths can touch our lives where science has nothing to say. Some people see explanations as violating the beauty and wonder of appearances, so no doubt would prefer *unexplained* mirrors to the various accounts we have looked at. This is a personal choice. The prevailing trend is to move beyond naiveté to seeing wonder and beauty in explanations. Mysteries can still have their own fascination, and may inspire further questions, which might be answered in a variety of ways. It is hard to believe that science does not enrich our mental and physical lives. Present questions and available answers are even more intriguing now than in the last century, when Alice explored her world through the looking-glass. They are far richer than for Plato over two millennia ago, when he saw reality as casting ambiguous shadows on the wall of a cave.

Plato's famous Allegory of the Cave, in his *Republic*, had prehistoric origins. It was 'probably taken from the mysteries held in caves or dark chambers representing the underworld, through which the candidates for initiation were led to the revelation of sacred objects in a blaze of light. The idea that the body is a prison-house, to which the soul is condemned for past misdeeds, is attributed by Plato to the Orphics.'[1] Let's enter Plato's cave:[2]

Next, said I, here is a parable to illustrate the degrees in which our nature may be enlightened or unenlightened. Imagine the condition of men living in a sort of cavernous chamber underground, with an entrance open to the light and a long passage all down the cave.

Here they have been from childhood, chained by the leg and also by the neck, so they cannot move and can see only what is in front of them, because the chains will not let them turn their heads. At some distance higher up is the light of a fire burning behind them; and between the prisoners and the fire is a track with a parapet built along it, like a screen at a puppet-show, which hides the performers while they show their puppets over the top.

I see, said he.

Now behind this parapet imagine persons carrying along various artificial objects, including figures of men and animals in wood or stone or other materials, which project above the parapet. Naturally, some of these persons will be talking, others silent.

It is a strange picture, he said, and strange sort of prisoners.

Like ourselves, I replied; for in the first place prisoners so confined would have seen nothing of themselves or one another, except their shadows thrown by the fire-light on the wall of the Cave facing them, would they?

Not if all their lives they had been prevented from moving their heads.

And they would have seen as little of the objects carried past.

Of course.

Now, if they could talk to one another, would they not suppose that their words referred only to those passing shadows which they saw?

Necessarily.

And suppose their prison had an echo from the wall facing them? When one of the people crossing behind them spoke, they could only suppose that the sound came from the shadow passing before their eyes.

No doubt.

In every way, then, such prisoners would recognise as reality nothing but the shadows of those artificial objects.

Plato's shadows in the cave are, like images in a mirror, untouchable. The problem is how to interpret or 'read' them in terms of the world of objects. Although Plato did not quite appreciate this, *our eyes are caves*, with shadow-images of objects of the outside world. Just like Plato's shadows, the images in eyes can but incompletely represent objects. So, just as for shadows, brains must read objects from knowledge, which may not be appropriate, and from assumptions which may not be correct.

Alice

The author of *Alice in Wonderland* (1865) and *Alice Through the Looking-glass* (1872)—Charles Lutwidge Dodgson (1832–1898)—was a logician, a creator of mathematical puzzles, an expert photographer, and a conjuror with simple apparatus, including mirrors.[3] He spent his days protected from normal reality, as a

Fellow of Christ Church College in the University of Oxford. Lewis Carroll was, of course, his pseudonym. A particular friend was John Henry Pepper, who invented 'Pepper's Ghost'—a large part-reflecting mirror, that allowed actors on stage to appear and disappear and become transparent (see page 178). This very likely inspired the disappearing grin of the Cheshire Cat:[4]

This time it vanished quite slowly, beginning with the end of the tail, and ending with the grin, which remained some time after the rest of it had gone.

There were two Alices. The Alice in *Wonderland* was the second daughter of a distinguished Oxford don, Henry George Liddell. The Alice who ventured through the looking-glass was a distant cousin, Alice Raikes. Six years after *Wonderland*, it was a chance encounter with Alice Raikes that suggested *Through the Looking-glass*.[5] Staying in London, Lewis Carroll happened to overhear children playing in one of the Kensington squares and heard them call a little girl, "Alice!" He called her over and told her he liked Alices. He invited her indoors, then put an orange into her hand and asked which hand she was holding it in:

"In my right hand", she told him.
"Now go and look at the little girl in the glass over there," he said, "and tell me which hand she is holding the orange in."
Alice went to the mirror and stood before it thoughtfully.
"She is holding it in her left hand."

Carroll asked if she could explain that to him, and she hesitated before replying:

"Supposing I was on the other side of the glass, wouldn't the orange still be in my right hand?"

He was delighted with her answer, and that decided him. The make-believe world for his new book should be that on the other side of the looking-glass (see Figure 9.1).[6] At the start of *Through the Looking-glass*, this was the result:

"Now if you'll only attend, Kitty, and not talk so much, I'll tell you all my ideas about Looking-glass House. First, there's the room you can see through the glass—that's just the same as our drawing room, only the things go the other way. I can see all of it when I get upon a chair—all but the bit just behind the fireplace. Oh! I do so wish I could see *that* bit! I want so much to know whether they've got a fire in the winter: you never *can* tell, you know, unless our fire smokes, and the smoke comes into that room too—but that may be pretence, just to make it look as if they had a fire. Well then, the books are something like our books, only the words go the wrong way. I know that because I've held up one of our books to the glass and then they hold up one in the other room."

When Alice jumped lightly through the mirror above the fireplace, to the Looking-glass room, she was: 'quite pleased to find that there was a real [fire], blazing away as brightly as the one she had left behind'. Then she noticed that the clock on the chimney piece had got the face of a little old man, which grinned at

FIGURE 9.1 *Alice through the mirror*
From Alice Through the Looking-Glass.

her. This was surprising, for as Alice said: "You can only see the back of it in the Looking-glass." When Alice, with her kitten, returned (by *re-turning*, and so *reversed*!) from Looking-glass Land, she mused:

"It is a very inconvenient habit of kittens . . . that whatever you say to them, they *always* purr. If they would only purr 'yes', and mew for 'no', or any rule of that sort . . . one could keep up a conversation!

But how *can* you talk with a person if they always say the same thing?"

On this occasion the kitten only purred: it was impossible to guess whether it meant 'yes' or 'no'.

Then Alice considers confronting the normal with the mirror world, by trying to get the kitten to look at the Red Queen:

So Alice . . . put the kitten and the Queen to look at each other. "Now, Kitty!" she cried, clapping her hands triumphantly. "Confess that was what you turned into!"

"But it wouldn't look at it," she said, when she was explaining the thing afterwards to her sister: "it turned away its head and pretended not to see it, but it looked a *little* ashamed of itself, so I think it *must* have been the Red Queen."

So just looking wasn't quite adequate. How did Alice, at the end of the dream, turn the Red Queen into the white kitten? By *shaking* her: "I'll shake you into a kitten, that I will!" Lewis Carroll describes what happened in vivid detail:

She took her off the table as she spoke and shook her backwards and forwards with all her might.

The Red Queen made no resistance whatever: only her face grew very small, and her eyes got large and green: and still, as Alice went on shaking her, she kept growing shorter—and fatter—and softer—and rounder—and—and it really *was* a kitten after all.

If we could pick up and shake *images* as we can *objects* we would not be bemused by mirrors.

Looking Back to the Mirror

What have mirrors told us, or made us question? The first question they raise is: why are images so confusing, so hard to think about? And in particular: why is the right-left inversion 'mirror puzzle' so hard for most of us to see?

Once one sees the point it is embarrassingly obvious—even trivial. The difficulty is deciding what kind of explanation might provide insight. When a problem has many seductively tempting paths to follow, it may come to look impossible. The essential here is to reject many temptations: optical, physiological, semantic, metaphysical, psychological. Any of these may, and for many people do, look plausible—though all mislead. As we have seen (pages 99–100), they can all provide explanations based on genuine phenomena. It is this that makes each of them a plausible path to follow for an explanation of mirror-reversal.

Just as for driving on motorways or freeways, a mistaken choice at the outset leads one far astray. The particular question here is why *rotation of the object* is so far down the list of candidates. Let's recapitulate this explanation with a hopefully helpful diagram (Figure 9.2). Consider a book reflected in a looking-glass. The book must be rotated to face the glass. It may either be rotated around its *vertical* axis, as shown in the upper part of the diagram, or it may be rotated around its *horizontal* axis, to face the mirror, as shown in the lower part. Its reflection is as though the book were in contact with the mirror. But as it has been rotated with respect to a direct view without the mirror, the image is reversed. It is reversed *right-left* from rotation around the *vertical* axis. It is reversed *upside down* from rotation around the *horizontal* axis.

Exactly the same happens with a rubber stamp, or with type in a printing press.

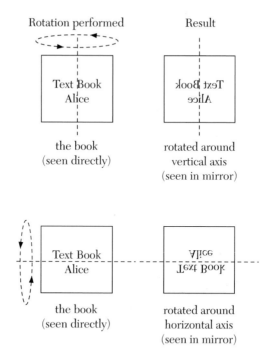

FIGURE 9.2 *What happens for reversal, diagrammatically*

Type has to be made reversed, to prevent 'mirror writing' when the paper is rotated as it is taken from the press. A transparency viewed in a mirror is *not* reversed when it is *not* rotated. (The opaque book *has* to be rotated, for the page to be visible in the mirror.) The same applies when looking at *oneself* in a mirror, as one rotates to face it. Normally this is a rotation around one's vertical axis, because of gravity. But if one stands on one's head, the image is upside down and not horizontally reversed.

There are two confusing, potentially misleading complications. First: *depth* is *optically reversed*, because the light path increases as the object or parts of the object (or oneself) is further from the mirror. Second: when *standing on one's head*, there is a perceptual compensation—so the world (and the mirror image) does not *look* upside down (though your mirror image will look upside down to a friend standing beside you). No doubt the first is a confusing complication—that depth-reversal is entirely different from lateral reversal—but this cannot justify Kant's conclusion that it impossible for the human mind to understand mirror-reversal.[7] It is a matter of seeing what kind of problem is involved. The choice of strategy can be hard to make or select

That choice-points for selecting paths for thinking are crucially important was seen centuries ago by Francis Bacon (1561–1626). Bacon coined the term 'crucial' experiment by analogy with cross-roads. Hints from related knowledge he called 'finger posts', like our sign posts.[8] Francis Bacon was surely right to say that for puzzle- or problem-solving there are crucial choice points requiring special care, and sometimes new experiments at cross-roads of possibilities.

This is related to the 'paradigms' of the American philosopher of science Thomas Kuhn (1922–1996).[9] Paradigms are implicitly held assumptions necessary for interpreting observations and experiments. When assumptions change, observations can be transformed. Conversely, observations may challenge and occasionally kill off paradigms. Thus phlogiston and caloric died from counter-evidence; and against human pride, the Earth was removed from the centre of the Universe.[10]

Vision is generally checked by other senses, especially by touch. But mirrors give vision without touch—the opposite of blindness. This is so, too, for any picture. So images and pictures can free the imagination from the confines of verification by touch and the other senses. But this has a down-side: one may read almost anything into a picture. Pictures relate to the object world but tenuously, by suggestion rather than literally. So usual tests for truth are misplaced for pictures. For a long time mirrors were mistrusted for science, as purveyors of illusion and even as deceits of necromancy. Now mirrors are indispensable components of scientific instruments, and their study has opened our eyes to the nature of light—and of eyes.

An elementary point we have found (page 79) is that there is *no image* from a mirror without an eye—or other focusing optics such as a camera. So the mirror's virtual image is very different from a real image, projected on a screen—a virtual image depends on the false assumption that light goes through the mirror. The same assumption is made—this time correctly—for windows; so the assumption for a part-reflecting mirror (or for Pepper's Ghost) is false for the reflection and true for the transmission.

A virtual image is no more than an object displaced by the bending or bouncing back of light. A virtual image is a view of an object in a 'wrong' place. If the visual brain could make use of this simple optical understanding we would not see images *through* mirrors. Then vision and touch would coincide, as they normally do; but the *visual* fact that mirror images do not coincide with their object-origins—even though we understand *conceptually* why the object is displaced—tells us that conceptual understanding is largely separate from perception. This is an important lesson from all manner of illusions: even though we know the answer we can be fooled every time. This uncomfortable fact, that perceptual experience is not tied to conceptual understanding, has implications for science, art, education and politics.

It is clear that vision in a mirror can not be direct, as the object is not seen where it is known to be. What is not so obvious—indeed this has very often been rejected by philosophy and by science—is that *all* perception is indirect. This rejection, even fear, of the indirectness of perception flouts what is undeniably known of our basic physiology: that vision and all the other senses have many stages of signal processing. And they need memory to make sense of the present and to predict the immediate future, for survival.[11]

Vision is predictive in two ways: it predicts unsensed features of objects, such as hardness and weight, and it predicts the immediate future. We are aware that a table is hard and scratchable even though its retinal image is not hard or scratchable. And we act not to the present (except for certain reflexes, such as the startle reflex of blinking to a sudden loud sound), but rather to what is probably about to happen.

The future cannot be signalled directly, as it has not yet happened, so there is nothing to signal. The out-of-this-world power of perception comes from transcending and very often ignoring sensory data. Illusions jolt us out of naive acceptance that seeing is direct, reliable knowledge. Vision serves remarkably well for survival in a hostile world, but there is no biological reason for perceptions to reflect deeper truths than our ancestors needed to survive. The senses are easily fooled: it is this that confers the power of pictures. When we see a table in a painting, we do not put a coffee cup on it. We see it *as* wood though we recognise that it is *not* wood, but paint on canvas. This double reality of a great deal of perception saves us from being chained to reality—whatever this, in ultimate terms, may be. Mirror images and pictures are strangely both in and out of reality. Our normal predictions are changed when we realise it is a picture, or a mirror image, that we are seeing. However, mirror images can very easily be confused with object reality (which makes large mirror-windows such a threat to flying birds), and it is interesting that *trompe-l'oeil* painting (see page 28) can fool other artists and animals.

Play

Alice played with all manner of things: words, ideas, paradoxes, absurdities, jokes—situations of many kinds. Her adventures appeal to us as we can share her games. Play may *look* trivial (and no doubt sometimes it is), yet it is through play that children discover the object world, themselves and each other. It was child-like playing with attractions and repulsions of odd pebbles, by curious Greeks over two thousand years ago, that transformed our world and explained ancient mysteries, including the nature of light and why mirrors reflect. The greatest scientist of modern times was not averse to playing with 'trivial' things. Newton famously said:

I do not know what may appear to the world, but to myself I seem to have been only a boy playing on the seashore, and diverting myself in now and then finding a smoother pebble or a prettier shell than ordinary, whilst the great ocean of truth lay all undiscovered before me.

The smoother pebble or a prettier shell may be a fossil of ancient life, or a crystal revealing atomic structure, perhaps having optical properties so bizarre they defeat Newton's theory of light, or an obsidian mirror whose images go deep into the glassy rock. Whether these are trivial depends upon how they are seen and what emerges after hundreds or thousands of years of science and technology. The achievements of science are the unpredictable consequences of play.

Play often needs toys. These extend the functions of the hands (as do tools), and they may demonstrate principles. At the dawn of science, the Greeks had a love of elaborate mechanical toys such as automata and singing birds.[12] They got their act together to produce remarkable achievements by combining their skills in co-operative effort over a long period of time. This resulted in theories of the Universe, measuring the size of the Earth and the distances of the Sun and the Moon, and designing and building sophisticated instruments. The Antikythera Mechanism, of 80 BC, was found in AD 1900 as a lump of bronze in the wreck of a ship sunk over two thousand years ago, off the small Greek island of Kythera. It is the most remarkable known toy of ancient times. X-rays have revealed over thirty meshed gear wheels comprising an astonishingly elaborate calendrical computer, for representing astronomical cycles with high precision.[13]

This mechanism must have required centuries of development through still earlier devices, and there are records of these back to the time of Plato and Aristotle and even earlier.[14] Together with early references, this wonderful finding of marine archaeology shows that the Greeks must have had an elaborate infra-structure of technology combined with mathematics and astronomical measurements, which we know went back to the Babylonians. It now looks as though much of Greek philosophy and scientific concepts were derived from experience of mechanical models and working toys: Ptolemy's epicycles for the planets was a machine much simpler than the Antikythera Mechanism.[15]

The significance of games of many kinds for cognitive development has a substantial literature.[16] The American psychologist Jerome Bruner suggests some of play's uses for children:[17]

The first is the ability to differentiate oneself from a task, to turn around one's performance, so to speak, see oneself, one's own performance as differentiated from another's. This involves self-recognition in which one, in some way, is able to model one's own performance on some selected feature of another's performance. This phenomenon in linguistics is known as *deixis*: as in learning that when I say I, it is not the same as when you say I, or that *in front* of me is not the same as *in front* of you or *in front* of the car.

Bruner outlines the functions of play:

First, it is a means of minimizing the consequences of one's actions and of learning, therefore, in a less riskful situation. This is particularly true of social play, where by adopting a play face or a 'galumphing gait' . . . the young animal signals its intent to play. . . .

Second, play provides an excellent opportunity to try combinations of behaviour that would, under functional pressure, never be tried.

Thus chimpanzees play with the components of skills, for example for poking sticks into holes in trees for extracting termites. Yes—chimpanzees do use tools! It turns out, from observing chimpanzees, that skill learning is both from watching adult expert behaviour and from individual play-practice. The use of sticks by chimpanzees as tools, especially for getting termites out of holes, has been studied extensively. Jane Van Lawick-Goodall (1968) found that part-skills, or sub-routines, are developed by repetition, then put together to be effective. Bruner says that:

One very crucial feature of tool skills in chimpanzees as in humans is the trying out of variants of the new skill in different contexts. Once Köhler's (1925) ape Sultan had 'learned' to use a stick to draw in food, he tried using it very soon for poking other animals, for digging, and for dipping it through an opening in a cesspool. Once Rana had learned to climb up stacked boxes to get a suspended piece of fruit, she rapidly tried her new climbing routine on a ladder, a board, a keeper, and Köhler himself—most often forgetting the fruit in preference for the combinatory activity *per se.* . . . It is probably this 'push to variation' (rather than fixation by positive reinforcement) that gives chimpanzee manipulation such widespread efficiency—such opportunism for dipping sticks into beehives for honey, using sticks for clubbing lizards and rodents, and using branches for striking at or throwing at big felines.

The belief is that not only are particular skills learned, but abstract concepts are also created through play—as play is unfettered from immediate need and so is free to try out new possibilities. Are abstract notions only human? Recent experiments by Sarah Boyson of Ohio State University point to a possible answer. Working with the chimps Sarah and Sheba, she found that they were able to solve simple abstract problems for sharing food, though not if they were confronted with the food itself. Sarah Boyson found that when plastic symbols were used to represent food, one chimp would point to a symbol allocating food to the other chimp, even doing very simple arithmetic—but when gum drops were used instead of symbols, greed got in the way! Joshua Fischman comments: 'During evolution, a species able to take this transcendental step could develop rules for sharing and other underpinnings of culture. And that species may have been hominids, the first non-ape primates.' Boyson concludes: 'Moving into the symbolic realm allowed them to transcend that biology, and exercise a capacity—already present—to use abstractions.'[18] Presumably this is the beginning of philosophy and science.

Do children raise philosophical questions? This has been asked, and in some degree answered, by an American teacher of philosophy at Amherst, Gareth Matthews, in *Philosophy and the Young Child* (1990). He starts with Tim, aged about six years, who while licking a jar asked: "Papa, how can we be sure that everything is not a dream?" His father said he didn't know. Tim answered: "Well, I don't think everything is a dream, 'cause in a dream people wouldn't go around asking if it was a dream." More empirical is the example of a young boy John Edgar, who had often seen aeroplanes take off and disappear in the distance as he lived near an airport. Flying for the first time at the age of four years, after take-off he turned to his father, and said in a puzzled voice: "Things don't really get smaller up here." This suggests some interesting experiments.

Ursula (aged three years four months) said: "I have a pain in my tummy." Mother: "You lie down and your pain will go away." Ursula: "Where will it go?" All children ask questions like these. They arise by analogy with toys, food, and so on going somewhere else. Indeed, children do philosophise, though perhaps most people give up philosophy by the age of ten or so. Plato approves of this:[19]

It is a fine thing to partake of philosophy just for the sake of education, and it is no disgrace for a lad to follow it: but when a man already advanced in years continues its pursuit, the affair, Socrates, becomes ridiculous; and for my part I have much the same feeling towards students of philosophy as towards those who lisp or play tricks.

Is questioning and experimenting discouraged? Is this why most of us have not grown out of the ancient 'common sense' of pre-modern science? That we are stuck conceptually in antiquity is well expressed by Bernard Cohen in *The Birth of a New Physics* (1980). Looking at how the physics of Galileo, Kepler, and Newton has revolutionised scientific perception and yet has hardly affected how most of us see the world we live in, and considering early ideas of motion, Cohen says: 'Odd as it may seem, most people's views about motion are part of a system of physics that was proposed more than 2000 years ago and was experimentally shown to be inadequate at least 1400 years ago.'[20] He continues:

In the inability to deal with questions of motion in relation to a moving Earth, the average person is in the same position as some of the greatest scientists of the past, which may be a source of considerable comfort. The major difference is, however, that for the scientist of the past the inability to resolve these questions was a sign of the times, whereas for us moderns such inability is, alas, a sign of ignorance.

Are we stuck as adults, while children at least implicitly apply simple scientific method? This is the view of Jean Piaget (1896–1980), the greatest pioneering name in the field of child development. Piaget points out that children start with 'primitive' magical notions of cause, not distinguishing between their own responses and the behaviour of inanimate objects, and they hold Aristotelian notions of physics of motion and forces, and so on. Piaget reported many investigations bearing on such questions, including the famous studies on perceived conservation (or rather lack of conservation) of matter. In *The Child's Conception of the World* (1929), he describes children as having animistic views, believing that all objects capable of movement, such as bicycles and the Sun and the Moon, are alive.

Piaget finds that most children before the age of nine, given various shapes of a lump of clay, do not appreciate conservation of substance. But how good are adults? A well-known marketing trick is to use odd-shaped bottles to make the contents look larger. Piaget has a lot to say on child development and perhaps less on why must of us are stuck in pre-modern science notions.

These are considered in *Children's Ideas in Science* (1985), edited by Rosalind Driver, Edith Guesne, and Andrée Tiberghien. It seems that children do not approach questions from a vacuum. They generally have pre-formed ideas, which though not appropriate or coherent may be held robustly enough to survive through life—in spite of school and their individual experience. Edith Guesne describes experiments with children on light and vision. She finds that many children of around fifteen years do not conceive of light as moving, and in our terms they have bizarre notions of shadows. Some children of thirteen or fourteen conceive of light as sent out from lamp bulbs—but not from other objects, such as tables or books. A French boy thought of light as going out of his eyes like a glowing stick. Seeing a cardboard box:

Here my eyes can go right up to the box . . . it's my sight. . . . If it [the box] was fifteen kilometres away, I couldn't see it, because . . . my sight isn't strong enough. . . . Because a box doesn't move, it hasn't any energy. A lamp for example moves, the light gets there. . . . The box, it's stuff that isn't alive.[21]

This is remarkably like Plato's theory of vision in the *Timaeus*.

Children often think of objects as in a 'bath of light' with no link between objects and the eyes. This is essentially the mediaeval view. Thus for Thomas Aquinas (1225–1274) seeing was *grasping* the forms of things. This is clearly an analogy to touching, implying that vision works directly, without links. This is children's view; and it is the tradition behind J. J. Gibson's (1950) account of visual perception. This mediaeval account is very different from representational views, deriving from Descartes's projective geometry, expressed by Descartes as a theory of vision in his *Optics* (1637). Here he describes the retinal image (the Sixth Discourse) and the 'multitude of small fibres of the optic nerve'. Descartes was well aware of optical means for perfecting vision (the Seventh and Eighth Discourses) and the use of refracting lenses for telescopes which he thoroughly understood (the Ninth Discourse). Perhaps his familiarity with optical instruments (he describes how to make lenses in the Tenth Discourse) might be a key to how Descartes and other practical philosophers, including Newton, broke with the mediaeval tradition—which is also children's view—to accept the notion of links of light between objects and vision, thus making vision representative, and only indirectly related to the world of objects.

Games and pretend-play in children and in other animals are safe try-outs for developing skills of response and prediction. No doubt it is true that chance favours the prepared mind, but play is needed to prepare the mind. Rather than play and toys being trivial, they seem to be essential for cognitive development and discovery, for individuals and for science. Children's toys are their laboratory.

Experiments of science are games with nature. As for all the best games there are strict rules and absolute honesty is essential. The winnings have transformed human life and how we see and think. Scientists may not be rich (they still have something of an amateur status), but the rewards are far greater than gold. The attraction of science is creating and sharing imaginative moves in the science-game, and applying discoveries to solving old and new problems. There is never a shortage of questions—never a shortage of applications.

Playing with Science

If playing is so important for discovery and learning, surely it is a logical step to develop playful 'science centres', for children and the public. Introducing the public to science and technology in this way is not a new idea. Francis Bacon, in his unfinished book *New Atlantis* (1627), describes his imaginary *House of Salomon*—a place open for all to share knowledge and harvest its benefits, through playing with the available science and technology and imagining future possibilities.

Bacon saw that science could, and should, be a social activity, with many kinds of contributions, according to individual abilities and interests.[21] His *Novum Organum* of 1620 set out rules for scientific method, with suggestions for applying it by co-operative experimenting: hence research laboratories. This inspired the foundation of the Royal Society by Charles II in 1660. Nothing much came of Bacon's *New Atlantis* dream for science centres until over three hundred years later, yet his *New Atlantis* plan made a lot of sense then and today. He proposed:

Perspective Houses, where we make demonstrations of all lights and radiations; and of all colours; and of things uncoloured and transparent, we can represent unto you all several colours; not in rain-bows, as it were in gems and prisms, but of themselves single. We represent all multiplications of light, which we carry to great distance, and make so sharp as to discern small points and lines; also all colourations of light. . . . We procure means for seeing objects afar off, and things afar off as near; making feigned distances. . . .

We have also engine houses. . . . We imitate also flights of birds; we have some degree of flying in the air; we have ships and boats for going under water, and brooking of seas; also swimming girdles and supporters. We have diverse curious clocks, and other like motions of return, and some perpetual motions. We imitate also motions of living creatures, by images of men, beast, birds, fishes and serpents. . . .

We have also a mathematical house, where are represented all instruments, as well as geometry and astronomy, exquisitely made.

Bacon was wary of errors of the senses. He distrusted the new-fangled telescope. The House of Salomon was to include warnings of perceptual errors, with demonstrations of:

... Deceits of the Senses; where we represent all manner of juggling, false apparitions, impostures, and illusions; and their fallacies. And surely you will easily believe that we have so many things truly natural which induce imagination, could in a world of particulars deceive the senses, if we could disguise those things and labour to make them seem more miraculous.

It is sad that it has taken so long to begin to make Bacon's dream for sharing science come true. The modern pioneer of hands-on science centres is Frank Oppenheimer (1912–1985), who founded the Exploratorium in San Francisco in 1969.[22] He was inspired by visiting the partly push-button, partly hands-on Children's Gallery of the London Science Museum, dating from the 1930s.[23] Oppenheimer saw phenomena of perception (especially visual illusions) as significant and useful for introducing people to the Universe through appreciating their own perceptual processes. This is an important theme in most science centres. I had the privilege of helping him with some of the first demonstrations and the philosophy of the San Francisco Exploratorium.[24] Ten years later we founded the Exploratory in Bristol, the first hands-on science centre in Britain.[25] Science centres are now a rapidly growing international movement, which is surely important for making science part of everyday life by taking children and adults through appearances with play.[26]

As we have seen (page 242), there is evidence that young children are not blank slates, but have what are often bizarre notions of physics which can be hard to shift. The 'naive notions' of children are remarkably Aristotelian.[27] Perhaps it is not clear whether children have their own thought-out theories or whether, when asked a question such as 'What holds the Moon up?', they say the first thing that comes into their heads. But whether their 'naive notions' are pre-formulated or invented spontaneously as occasion suggests, the conclusion is clear that while hands-on experience is essential, it is not *adequate* for understanding. A great deal of explanation and help of many kinds is needed. For it is absurd to expect children to recapitulate much of the history of science by their own individual efforts.

Scientist often speak of 'mere' *hand-waving*, especially when a colleague fails to give a mathematical account. And we sometimes speak of *handle-turning*, from the turning of handles of mechanical calculating machines to get answers automatically. This suggests a handy terminology for playful processes of individual and scientific discovery:

Hands-on   *Exploration*
Hand-waving   *Explanation*
Handle-turning *Computation*

Let's unpack them. *Hands-on exploration* is 'knowledge by acquaintance'—discovering properties of things by interaction. This takes us through the eye's images to non-optical properties of objects, so that we see much more than meets the eye. We learn a great deal from errors. Errors check perceptual and conceptual hypotheses; they are spurs to new ideas, and are signs of understanding and misunderstanding. But errors can be dangerous, which is a good reason for protected play. When highly developed, hands-on skill can become craftsmanship.

Hand-waving explanation is the cauldron of creativity. Freed from perceptual experience, we can create new possibilities. We wave our hands to communicate when language fails, or is inadequate. Perhaps hand-waving is intimately related to the 'brain language' of thinking.[28] When highly developed and explicit, hand-waving explanations become philosophy and concepts of science.

Handle-turning computation depends on following rules or algorithms of mathematics. Algorithms can be exceedingly hard to discover or formulate; but once selected, answers may emerge automatically by 'turning the handle'. What is striking is how bad we are at arithmetic. The cheapest pocket calculator is faster and more accurate than any human. The humble abacus of beads on strings is still used in many countries as a useful aid to monetary computations. This suggests that handle-turning is not the way the brain works: computation is unnatural. If fingernails were good at turning screws, we would not need special tools. Tools are useful because they are *not* like us. The same seems true for digital computers—their superhuman speed and accuracy suggests that they are very different from brains.

There is considerable evidence that creative scientists use hand-waving mental models, and analogies and images, for thinking. This is well described by Arthur Miller (1986) for physicists and mathematicians including Bohr, Boltzman, Einstein, Heisenberg, Hertz, Maxwell and Poincaré. Many and possibly all mathematical physicists start with hand-waving mental models before they formulate equations. This seems to be so for Newton, and was certainly true of James Clerk Maxwell, whose equations for the electromagnetic theory of light started from hand-waving mechanical models (page 131). Though hand-waving is not quite academically respectable, hand-waving mental models are extremely important for creative thinking. Presumably they have a poor press because they are not quantified and are hard to test by examination. But they are the centre of seeing and thinking, and they give meaning to equations.

Ideally a scientist should have all of the three skills, and use them to inspire and check each other: from hands-on experience from infancy, to hand-waving-speculations, to handle-turning computations, which are the visible structure and public proof of much of science and commerce.

If children and scientists learn through exploratory play, and enjoy it, why shouldn't the methods and results of science-play be shared more widely? Why shouldn't adults go on learning by more or less directed play all through their lives? This is the aim of hands-on science centres, which we may call *Exploratories.*[29]

Exploratory science centres for hands-on science-play have several aims: to make science and technology interesting; to give confidence for individual discovery; and to introduce concepts and explanations—which may always be questioned. So children and adults may come to think more in scientific terms, to create and use science and technology more effectively—and to see its potentialities and dangers. As Bacon said, science is essentially social. The most dramatic combining of skills of research and invention to achieve a specific goal was the American initiative for landing on the Moon in 1969. Another was the war-time development of the atomic bomb. Here science has gone beyond play. But it is through play we learn to cope with dangerous reality.

A tricky question is how to move from hands-on experience to hand-waving explanations. For how can we explore abstract concepts hands-on? A serious snag of science centres is the bustle and noise of exuberant youth: a necessity is oases of peace and quiet. What is needed, then, are somewhat separate, quiet, thoughtful *Explanatories.*

How can counter-intuitive ideas be revealed to children and consenting adults? It is striking how similar children's explanations are to ancient, inappropriate, notions of animism and to Aristotle's misleading pre-historic physics. This seems to be because we are misled by much of day-to-day hands-on experience. For example, Aristotle and present-day children (and most adults) think that heavy objects fall faster than light objects. Physics since Galileo tells us this is false. But it is true in much familiar experience—such as for feathers, balls of wool, pebbles in water—that heavier things fall faster than lighter things. Galileo's experiment on the Leaning Tower of Pisa is not easy to do, and for many objects (because of air friction) it doesn't work. So, we are misled by our everyday hands-on experience of falling objects. No doubt this is why Aristotle, and children and most adults, get it wrong. The snag is that a great deal of hands-on experience leads to incorrect confused hand-waving explanations. This is why science is not easy. So it does seem that we need very carefully designed science centres—Exploratories and Explanatories—to learn how to interpret everyday experience, without being misled.

What concerns us, especially, is how to move from hands-on experience and hand-waving understanding to the extremely useful, though for most of us difficult, skills of handle-turning mathematics. Computers now remove much of the sweat and tears of handle-turning. Their graphics reveal to the eye abstract principles with great beauty. They can be interactive, and so hands-on. In science centres, computers can be linked to actual demonstrations and experiments, to reveal underlying mathematical principles and functions, sometimes in real time.

The emerging multi-media technologies allow individual journeys through facts and concepts. This was the basis of Seymour Papert's work on Logo, in which the computer controls a mechanical tortoise which provides interactions of the object world with the symbolic world of mathematics.[30] It has been suggested by Philip Davis and Reuben Hersh in *The Mathematical Experience* (1980) that computer interaction allows the visualisation of dimensions beyond the usual three of space and one of time. A rotating computer-generated hypercube looks meaningless, but upon taking the controls:

I tried turning the hypercube around, moving it away, bringing it close, turning it around another way. Suddenly I could feel it! The hypercube had leapt into palpable reality, as I learned how to manipulate it, feeling in my fingertips the power to change what I saw and change it back again. The active control at the computer console created a union of kinaesthetic and visual thinking which brought the hypercube up to the level of intuitive understanding.

This is truly turning minds on through hands-on experience.

Many fundamental principles which are usually masked by contaminations, such as friction, can be experienced directly by 'purifying' them in experiments and demonstrations. This, indeed, is how many basic discoveries have been made. Examples for science centres are removing air for falling bodies—when we really do see that bodies of any weight fall at the same rate—and air tracks and air tables to reduce friction, for revealing Newton's laws of motion.

There are several studies on what children and adults can recall following visits to science centres, and there are studies on visitor behaviour such as time spent on each experiment (or 'plores' as we call them in the Bristol Exploratory[31]). But here we are more concerned with *implicit* learning, which may then be made *explicit*, to become scientific understanding. Measuring explicit knowledge can be done easily, with quizzes and examinations; but implicit understanding is far more difficult to assess, though it is at least as important. Very likely exams distort science teaching towards what is easy to mark. So we need 'signs of understanding'. One such sign is *being surprised*. Failed predictions can be clear evidence of inappropriate mental models. A classical example is Aristotle's rejection of the notion that the stars are seen as moving because the Earth spins round. He jumped up—and landed in the same place—so how could the Earth have been spinning under him? What Aristotle lacked was the concept of inertia. This shows both how important concepts are and how soon we depart from common sense in science. A favourite science centre example of surprise is what happens when air is blown between a pair of freely suspended beach balls. Practically everyone expects them to fly apart—but they are drawn together by the flow of air between them. This failed prediction tells the 'explorer', as well as the teacher, his lack of appreciation of the situation. The failed prediction is a powerful internal signal of *not understanding*. From failed predictions we learn to examine assumptions; so we may correct our intuitions, or hand-waving mental models. As surprises show the limits and failures of understanding, so they are pointers to discovery, for individuals and for science itself. For scientists, failed predictions may suggest the next step for advancing knowledge. Similarly, for the child, or for the aware but not especially knowledgeable adult, failed predictions can signal the need for further experiment, to see the phenomenon in a fresh way. But questioning and restructuring require effort which is not to everyone's taste.

Another sign is *seeing analogies*. If one understands, for example, resonance, similarities are seen between what on the surface are quite different-appearing things: musical instruments, the divisions of Saturn's rings, tuned radio circuits, positions of spectrum lines from resonances within atoms, and far more. It is important to have *many examples* of different-appearing phenomena, to practise seeing analogies. This enriches hand-waving understanding, and challenges and justifies handle-turning science.

Inventing is a sign of understanding. We may look for ability to invent novel solutions and fill gaps, for these require creative understanding.

To appreciate and make *jokes* is clear evidence of understanding. With increased interest in science and technology we may expect more science 'in-group' humour, which should enliven life and literature. *Appreciating the significance of small, apparently trivial phenomena* shows that they are recognised as significant. Increasing understanding enriches experience far beyond sensory stimulation.

The most dramatic evidence of understanding is seeing significance in *nothing*. This is the point of experimental controls, and a great deal comes from nothing happening in null experiments. Only when the situation is understood conceptually is it possible to appreciate nothing. So 'seeing nothing' is a strong sign of understanding.

If such signs of understanding could be read by teachers, could we begin to escape the tyranny of traditional examinations?

Playing with Mirrors

We have throughout been playing with mirrors—with puzzles of images and light and vision. We have played with reversing and non-reversing mirrors, including the 60° corner mirrors that *don't* reverse or rotate the world, and are surprising even to experts on optics (see page 82). These games have been experiments: hopefully interesting games with nature. Here are some more.

A simple experiment is the mirror drawing shown in Figure 9.3. It is incredibly difficult to trace even a simple shape with mirror reversal, when vision and touch disagree. This is well worth trying.

In the Exploratory science centre in Bristol, one of the first plores for exploring was movable vertical mirrors on a flat table, with a shute for propelling ball bearings (see Figure 9.4). The mirrors can be adjusted to reflect a ball to a target,

FIGURE 9.3 *Mirror drawing*

Reversing vision but not touch is extremely disturbing—it is hard to trace a simple pattern.

FIGURE 9.4 *Ball game with mirrors*

This was one of the very first 'plores' in the Exploratory science centre in Bristol. The skill is to adjust the mirrors until the ball hits a small bell. This requires the strategies and patience needed for setting up optical apparatus, such as for holography. The comparison of light with a corporeal ball generalises the law of reflection; but shows its limits at small angles for the ball when energy is transferred to spin.

FIGURE 9.5 *Divided Self*
This is a vertical mirror with a horizontal rod and a two rings, one held in each hand.
When the hidden hand is moved slowly, the experience is bizarre.

which is a little bell that sounds success. When the mirrors are adjusted so that the bell rings, the path of the ball can be compared with a beam of light. At extreme angles the similarity fails, as the ball, though not the light, is affected by friction and spin and so on.

The Exploratorium science centre in San Francisco has a disturbing mirror-experience, which might be called the 'Divided Self' (Figure 9.5). It is a vertical double-sided mirror with a horizontal rod passing through its centre. On each half of the rod is a movable ring. The rings are held one in each hand. When the ring that is hidden behind the mirror is moved slowly, the hidden hand is mistaken for the visible hand and one's arm seems to be anaesthetised—and one's Self divided. It is interesting to try this with someone else moving a ring: another's moving hand may be mistaken for one's own.

The Exploratorium also has a delightful and very amusing 'Anti-Gravity Mirror' (Figure 9.6). It is simply a large vertical plane mirror. The trick is for someone to stand at its end, so that he or she is bisected. In other words, half the person is behind the mirror and so is hidden; and the other half is seen twice—directly and reflected. As people are quite symmetrical horizontally, the reflection is taken for their missing half, so they look complete. Now, if they stand

FIGURE 9.6 *Anti-Gravity Mirror*

Because we are roughly symmetrical horizontally, the reflected leg is seen as the other leg, hidden behind the mirror. So the half-reflected person seems to rise in the air, with anti-gravity. By adding a second mirror at right angles, one can see oneself floating in the air.

with the hidden leg behind the mirror and raise their reflected leg, they appear to rise into the air, entirely unsupported. This is well described by Cathy Cole:[32]

If you raise your visible leg, its reflection also rises in the mirror, and you appear to float effortlessly in mid-air. Even though it's clearly an illusion, people break into uncontrollable laughter when they see it. They react, in other words, just as they would if the image were real.

We make remarkably little distinction between objects and images. The real trick to the Anti-Gravity Mirror is that there's no trick except the same 'illusion' you see every time you look in a mirror. No-one is fooling us but ourselves.

We have already described several mirror-games of science: 'book mirrors' giving multiple images, and reversals and rotations; kaleidoscopes; and phenomena of polarisation, especially associated with mirrors. Circular polarisation is particularly intriguing: the corkscrew light gives what we may call the *Dracula Effect*. Look through a circularly polarising filter at a mirror, and the mirror looks *opaque* (polarising filters are available for photography). This is like looking at a corkscrew in a mirror: the right-hand screw is reflected as a left-hand screw. So— like a right-hand nut and a left-hand bolt—it is no-go. The reflected reversed-rotation polarised light will not pass back through the filter. What happens with a pair of 90° or 60° corner mirrors? This is left for the reader to discover.

Lewis Carroll liked word-play, and all manner of puzzles. He played with words that, surprisingly, are *not* reversed in a mirror. Try holding these words in front of a mirror and turn them upside down:

BEECH   DICE

KID   COOKBOOK

CHOICE   BOX

They look the same! This is quite different from the rotations and non-rotations we have considered—for this is not a phenomenon of nature or perception. This is an amusing trick. The unchanged symmetries are in the shapes of the words.

Virtual Reality

Alternative worlds have been presented for millennia in pictures and poetry. By preserving the past and suggesting the future they enrich each new generation. Technology of this century has added to Plato's cave of shadows (page 231) the far more dramatic, more realistic experience of cinema and television. Now interactive virtual reality (VR) promises to bring shadows and images to touchable life.

It is surprising that cinema and television work so well, for they only provide fragmentary two-dimensional pictures, which for most objects and scenes are absurdly large or ridiculously small. This has been so for all pictures, from the cave paintings of 30 000 years ago, and remains true in almost all cases. Cinema and TV provide a new challenge to perception—for cutting from view to view, and from scene to scene, gives impossibly fast changes of scale and viewpoint, and switches of where one is supposed to be. In cinemas we travel faster than light.[33] How are we able to follow these impossible sequences that we see in every film and TV programme? How do we appreciate the endings and beginnings of scenes, realising that shots belong to the same scene even though different objects are revealed?[34] Film and video editing are intuitive arts, carried out with great skill but with few explicit rules or appreciable theoretical understanding. It is surprising that the perceptual skills of the audience are not studied more fully. There seems a great opportunity here, and interactive virtual reality offers further possibilities for studying powers of perception and its limitations.[35]

Emerging in mid-shot is the computer-based technology of interactive virtual reality. It provides 3D stereo vision with a small cathode ray tube for each eye in the goggles of a helmet. One can walk around in the computer-generated world, one's position being monitored from a little aerial on the helmet. One can 'touch' and 'pick up' objects with the DataGloves, which have sensors detecting movements of the fingers. The whole system, of 3D goggles, DataGloves and computer, is known as the 'reality engine'. The explorer of virtual reality is a 'cybernaut'. It may be possible to introduce another person into the computer world: teacher, friend, lover. It is beginning to be possible to introduce one's self.

Howard Rheingold describes his first experience in *Virtual Reality* (1991):[36]

When a cybernaut shifts his gaze or waves her hand, the reality engine weaves the data stream from the cybernaut's sensors together with updated depictions of the digitized virtual world into the whole cloth of a three-dimensional simulation. The computer engine, however, contributes only part of the VR system. Cyberspace is a co-operative production of the microchip-based reality engine sitting on the floor of the laboratory and the neural engine riding in my cranium.

Co-operation with the neural cranium engine is, indeed, vital for all perception. The co-operation is greatly enhanced by hand–eye interaction, for real and for virtual reality; but at the time of writing VR has a long way to go before it is convincing or pleasant: there are disturbing visual anomalies and sad lack of definition or detail. It is certainly no substitute for experiencing reality.

Compared with computer graphics, where the computer can spend as long as necessary calculating the edges and shadows and highlights and so on of a static picture, at present interactive VR is sadly unimpressive. But could future computer worlds of virtual reality substitute for real reality in science education? By presenting alternative universes with different laws, they may help us to see our world more clearly, much as travel shows us the assumptions by which we live at home. And the computer can take us inside atoms and stars as science sees them. Schools, and also science centres for sharing resources, should benefit from these new technologies as they unfold. Conceivably they will allow children to enter and explore, interactively, the relativistic and quantum worlds of modern physics.

But who would prefer computer simulations of flowers or rainbows or bubbles to real flowers or rainbows or bubbles? Or prefer simulations to real experiments with chemicals or gyroscopes or magnets—or indeed mirrors? Mirrors look boring on a computer screen!

There are snags to VR. When we extend the senses with a telescope, or a microscope, there is no need for suspension of belief. But objects in virtual reality (somewhat like virtual images of a mirror) are seen as objects only because we ignore or reject our knowledge that they are not truly objects. The looking-glass and virtual reality are inherently paradoxical experiences which sacrifice knowledge to the altar of appearance. Indeed, this is so for all pictures. Experiencing actual objects draws information from nature itself, not from the edited and technically limited view of other people. There is much that is uniquely important in experiencing reality at first hand. Programmed computer pictures can have errors, and what they show is edited by the interests and understanding of the graphic artist. For teaching science this can be misleading, and may perpetuate serious errors for generations. This is so also for books, but an author can simply leave out what he does not know—a picture is not allowed to have such error-avoiding gaps, and so can be more misleading than writing.

It would be foolish, without very special reason, to replace real with virtual reality. VR can not substitute for direct experience, though in some ways it may go further than hands or eyes can reach, and present new worlds of imagination and insights beyond possibility of direct experience. This is the promise of future technology, when machine minds meet ours: so computer illusions change and may become our realities.

Notes

1. Cornford (1941) page 222.
2. Cornford (1941) pages 222–223.
3. Carroll's *Symbolic Logic* (1896) is available as Bartley (1977). There are plenty of puzzles but no reference to mirrors.
4. See Fisher (1976).
5. See Graham (1962). *Alice's Adventures in Wonderland* and *Through the Looking-glass* appeared in 1865 and 1872 respectively.
6. The other side of this story is preserved by Alice Raikes, a distant cousin: 'As children, we lived in Onslow Square and used to play in the garden behind the houses. Charles Dodgson used to stay with an old uncle there, and walk up and down, his hands behind him, on the strip of lawn. One day, hearing my name, he called me to him saying, "So you are another Alice. I'm very fond of Alices. Would you like to come and see something which is rather puzzling?" We followed him into his house which opened, as ours did, upon the garden, into a room full of furniture with a tall mirror standing across one corner.

    "Now," he said, giving me an orange, "first tell me which hand you have got that in." "The right," I said. "Now," he said, "go and stand before that glass, and tell me which hand the little girl you see there has got it in." After some perplexed contemplation, I said, "the left hand." "Excellent," he said, "and now how do you explain that?" I couldn't explain it, but seeing that a solution was expected, I ventured, "If I was on the other side of the glass, wouldn't the orange still be in my right hand?" I can remember his laugh. "Well done, little Alice," he said. "The best answer I've had yet."

    I heard no more then, but after years was told that he said that had given him his first idea for *Through the looking-glass*, a copy of which, together with each of his other books, he regularly sent me.' (London *Times*, 22 January 1932). Quoted by Gardner (1965) page 180 and Fisher (1973) page 72.
7. What happens with a three-dimensional object (see Kant's account of right and left hands, page 90) is more difficult to 'see' and describe, than for a two-dimensional object such as writing—as very different processes are involved for the depth dimension and for lateral or up-down reversal. The in-out depth reversal is optical: the lateral inversion isn't. So what happens with a hand is indeed confusing, but not, as Kant thought, impossible to understand.
8. Bacon (1878).
9. Kuhn (1962).
10. It is interesting to see what science was like before the great successes of the seventeenth

century—when the paradigm of alchemy inspired and limited concepts of matter and mind. It may be no coincidence that experimental science—following Francis Bacon's rules for investigation, set out in *Novum Organum* of 1620—took off just at the time when leading scientists, such as Robert Boyle and Bacon himself, abandoned alchemy. Newton spent twenty years at Cambridge trying to make gold, and he collected a huge personal library on alchemy. Finally he became Master of the Mint.

Surely it was not so much alchemy, as the related paradigm of astrology that prevented the testing of hypotheses. For given the beliefs of astrology, there were too many excuses for failure (see Gregory (1989a)). Starting about the first century AD, alchemists carried out heroic experiments to change base metals into gold and discover the secret of eternal life. But their experiments were vitiated by ever-present excuses for failures, as astrology supposed that the positions of the planets and stars were important for success; so it seemed necessary to wait for the planets, the Moon, the Sun and stars to return to the same positions in the sky, for each comparison trial. If astrology were true, the repetitions and control experiments essential for experimental science would be almost impossible. So, experimental science could not live with astrology.

But if belief in astrology provided too many excuses for failed experiments for science to be feasible, how could the ancient queen of sciences, astronomy, have been successful? Astronomy lived happily with astrology for centuries. Noted astronomers combined them. Kepler was paid as a professional astrologer. The answer might be that astronomy escaped the problem because it was a purely observational science, and could not in any case use planned controlled experiments. As its phenomena run in cycles, it could develop predictive conceptual models, to 'save the appearances'; but as a science, astronomy was not typically experimental.

Experimental science would also be extremely difficult if telepathy, or clairvoyance or psychokinesis, really happen. Surely it is not just that they are false that makes them unacceptable to science—they are incompatible with experimental science's methods. Baconian science cannot accept them and live.

11. It might be said that being 'obviously true' does not guarantee truth. But to believe that vision is direct—without retinal images or physiological links or enrichment from stored knowledge—takes us to a paradigm that flouts our most basic knowledge of eye and brain.

12. See Brumbaugh (1966).

13. Price (1975).

14. There are several earlier references of devices of this kind (Cohen and Drabkin (1958); discussed in Gregory (1981)), going back to the time of Archimedes (*c.* 287–212 BC), who is supposed to have built an elaborate mechanical working globe, and with references back to Aristotle and Plato in the fifth and fourth centuries BC.

15. The mathematician Christopher Zeeman (1986) has re-interpreted the drive gearing, and has shown how the Greeks could have calculated the gear ratios with their available mathematical techniques.

16. See, for example, Hodgkin (1985), Görlitz and Wohlwill (1987).

17. See the excellent collection edited by Bruner, Jolly and Sylva (1976).

18. Fischman (1993).

19. Plato's dialogue, the *Gorgias*.

20. Cohen (1987).

21. Science as a shared activity leading to accepted public knowledge is very cogently argued by the physicist John Ziman (1978).

22. For the history of the Exploratorium, see Hein (1990).

23. Oppenheimer wrote: 'I suspect that everybody—not just you and I—genuinely wants to

share and feel at home with the cumulative and increasingly coherent awareness of nature that is the traditional harvest of scientists and artists.' He said of his exhibits (see Murphy (1985)): 'We do not want people to leave with the implied feeling: "Isn't somebody else clever." Our exhibits are honest and simple so that no one feels he or she must be on guard against being fooled or misled.'

24. The first hands-on science centre in Britain is the Exploratory, in Bristol, which I initiated in the early 1980s, and is now in the Brunel railway station at Temple Meads (Gregory 1983, 1986, 1988, 1989b, 1993). The Bristol Exploratory started at the same time as the Launch Pad hands-on gallery for children at the London Science Museum.

25. Hands-on science centres are part of a recent drive from within science—in Britain from COPUS, the Committee on the Public Understanding of Science, of the Royal Society, the British Association for the Advancement of Science, and the Royal Institution (Bodmer 1985, 1987)—to perceive and to promote science as an essential part of our culture. There are now forty hands-on science centres and museum galleries in Britain, and four hundred in Europe. There are many more in America, India, and other countries around the world. They are coordinated by ECSITE (European Collaborative of Science, Industry and Technology Exhibitions), and the older and larger ASTEC in America.

26. Science centres are intended to be fun and to present phenomena and ideas so that they will be understood. They have, however, been criticised for appearing too trivial. Shortland (1987) criticised science centres for being like fun-fairs. This is for the reader to judge. One can learn a lot from fun fairs! And what do children learn when they are bored? Surely very little.

27. DiSessa (1982); Driver, Guesne and Tiberghien (1985); Matthews (1990).

28. See Pinker (1994). This idea is related to Chomsky's deep structure: thought is not in spoken language, but in a universal brain language Pinker calls Mentalese.

29. Just what children learn through exploratory 'play' is a matter for research to determine. This is not easily done for long-term effects, but is being attempted (Hein (1987), Stevenson (1991), Durant (1992)). Surely exploratories are ideal laboratories for research into many questions of education.

30. Papert (1980).

31. The museum word 'exhibit' is too passive for a hands-on science centre. I coined 'plore' from explore, for hands-on exhibits and experiments. This word is used in the Exploratory, and more widely though not very generally.

32. Cole (1985).

33. Film editing is a craft, not a science, and has received surprisingly little research. But see Reisz and Millar (1968) for practical experience; for cognitive implications, Hochberg and Brooks (1978), and Hochberg (1987).

34. There may be a cost. There is a suggestion (from Mashe Aronson, Sackler Faculty of Medicine in Tel Aviv University) that prolonged watching of TV may be associated with brain damage, including Alzheimer's disease. This is attributed to rapidly changing scenes, and to emotions aroused without corresponding action. The evidence may not be strong, but it is a possibility to be considered. See Vines (1993).

35. Jonathan Miller, and Julian Hochberg (Hochberg 1987a, 1987b), do appreciate that there is much to be learned here. Karel Reisz and Gavin Millar (1953, 1968) present an authoritative hand book for film makers.

36. Reingold (1991) page 132.

10

Final Reflections

> *To see a World in a grain of sand,*
> *And a Heaven in a Wild Flower,*
> *Hold Infinity in the palm of your hand,*
> *An eternity in an hour.*
>
> BLAKE

T HE world of mirror images is a curious half-way house between reality and illusion. Things look real in a looking-glass, yet we know that what we see is not there. The reflected object is somewhere else, and there is no image when no-one is looking. It needs an eye (or a camera) to make the virtual image real. What is 'real' in the image of an eye or camera? Illusion/reality debates have been going on from the dawn of philosophy. A central issue is: what exists apart from appearance? How is appearance—perception—related to whatever exists in the object world?

The English philosopher John Locke (1632–1704) started this debate of British Empiricism in his *Essay Concerning Human Understanding* (1690), which claims that all knowledge is founded on sensation and experience:[1]

Let us suppose the mind to be, as we say, white paper, void of all characters, without any ideas; how comes it to be furnished? Whence comes it by that vast store, which the busy and boundless fancy of man has painted on it with an almost endless variety? Whence has it all the materials of reason and knowledge? To this I answer in one word, from experience: in that all our knowledge is founded on, and from it ultimately derives itself.

This step away from innate ideas or inborn knowledge, to the notion that all knowledge comes from the senses, was a bold and most important step in philosophy. But what of reality is sensed or experienced? Locke suggested that *simple* ideas come directly from the world of objects—because the mind could not create them. But how do we know the limits to the mind's ability to create? Here we have argued that perceptions are active creations, quite largely fictional. How can we know which ideas, or sensations, are directly from the world and so necessarily objectively true? This central problem of empiricism has never been solved. I see perceptions as *hypotheses*: is this a solution?

Locke followed Democritus (then Galileo, Descartes, and Newton) in distinguishing between *primary* and *secondary* qualities. Primary qualities are those supposed inherent in objects; secondary qualities are those of the senses, such as colour, which depend on certain conditions, such as illumination and the state of eyes and brains, and are not inherent in objects. It is exceedingly hard to make a sharp, acceptable distinction here; but some sensations clearly are *not* in the world of objects. This has led several philosophers to suppose that *no* sensations are objective. A few go further, to say there is *no matter*. This is the position of the Irish philosopher Bishop George Berkeley (1685–1753). Berkeley denied that any sensations come directly from objects or matter. He also denied that perceptions can be inferences to causes of sensations. In Berkeley's delightful *Dialogues between Hylas and Philonous*, Philonous says:[2]

> To prevent any more questions of this kind, I tell you once for all, that by *sensible things* I mean those only which are perceived by sense, and that in truth the senses perceive nothing which they do not perceive immediately: for they make no inferences. The deducing therefore of causes or occasions from effects and appearances, which alone are perceived by sense, entirely relates to reason.

Berkeley refers to the newly invented microscope, to show that no particular sensation, for example of colour, is specially true—for a cloud at a distance, then near, or a flower viewed with or without a microscope, look very different. So where is the objective truth of a sensation? He argues similarly for sound and for touch. Of light he writes:

> HYLAS I tell you, Philonous, external light is nothing but a thin fluid substance, whose minute particles being agitated with a brisk motion, and in various manners reflected from the different surfaces of outward objects to the eyes, communicate different motions to the optic nerves; which being propagated to the brain, cause therein various impressions: and these are attended with the sensations or red, blue, yellow &c.
>
> PHILONOUS It seems, then, that light doth no more than shake the optic nerves.
>
> HYLAS Nothing else.
>
> PHILONOUS And consequent to each particular motion of the nerves the mind is affected with a sensation, which is some particular colour.

This soon leads to:

> HYLAS I frankly own, Philonous, that it is in vain to stand out any longer. Colours, sounds, tastes, in a word all those termed secondary qualities, have certainly no existence without the mind. But by this acknowledgement I must not be supposed to derogate any thing from the reality of matter or external objects. . . . Sensible qualities are by philosophers

divided into *primary* and *secondary*. The former are extension, figure, solidity, gravity, motion, and the rest. And these they hold exist really in bodies. The latter are those above enumerated; or briefly, all sensible bodies beside the primary, which they assert are only so many sensations or ideas existing nowhere but in the mind. . . .

PHILONOUS   You are still then of the opinion, that extension and figures are inherent in external substances?

HYLAS   I am.

PHILONOUS   But what if the same arguments which are brought against secondary qualities, will hold proof against these also?

HYLAS   Why then I shall be obliged to think, they too exist only in the mind.

This is Berkeley's conclusion. It inspires a typically witty comment from Bertrand Russell:[3]

George Berkeley (1685–1753) is important in philosophy through his denial of the existence of matter—a denial which he supported by a number of ingenious arguments. He maintained that material objects only exist through being perceived. To the objection that, in that case, a tree, for instance, would cease to be if no-one was looking at it, he replied that God always perceived everything; if there were no God, what we take to be material objects would have a jerky life, suddenly leaping into being when we look at them; but as it is, owing to God's perceptions, trees and rocks and stones have an existence as continuous as common sense supposes. That is, in his opinion, a weighty argument for the existence of God.

It is surely amazing that the virtual images of mirrors are very much as Berkeley saw normal objects—as mirror images do disappear when no-one is looking.

In this book I have taken a different path from Berkeley's, for—following Helmholtz over a century ago—I have allowed that perception does make inferences. Perceptual and conceptual inferences can be different—hence we experience an illusion even though we know it is an illusion—so perceptual inferences, and their accepted data, are not the same as what we call 'thinking' (page 226). Just which qualities are 'primary' or 'secondary' remains a problem, and the categories change as science changes. But in any case it now seems far more plausible to say that *no sensations are directly of objects*, rather than to say, *there are no objects*; though in a way this doubt has re-emerged with quantum physics.[4]

The English philosopher John Stuart Mill (1806–1873) made the interesting suggestion that we recognise objects as external things because they can disappear. He defined objects as 'permanent possibilities of sensation.'[5] Mill based this notion on two postulates of mind, going back to Aristotle. First, the mind is capable of expectation. Secondly, the mind can form associations of ideas—phenomena which occur together or are in close association are 'thought together', forming an 'indissoluble association.' Mill wrote: 'We see, and cannot help seeing, what we have learnt to infer, even when we know that the inference is erroneous.'

He offers as an example:

> I see a piece of white paper on a table. I go into another room. If the phenomenon always followed me, or if, when it did not follow me, I believed it to disappear *e rerum natura*, I should not believe it to be an external object.

Mill points out that these associations for seeing objects are called up so rapidly, and are so powerful, they seem innately intuitive, though they are based on experience—on growing belief through many 'positive' and few 'negative' instances: that is, by *induction*.

Mill was the first (following Bacon) to set out Rules of Induction, which can be seen as central to learning and to scientific empiricism.[6] He pushed his view of induction too far when he tried to explain *deductive* certainties as generalisations of instances. For Mill it is *certain* that 2 + 3 = 5, because as children we play with toy bricks and find by induction that this is so. Attempts to equate deduction with induction—or attempts to make inductions certainly true—are no longer accepted. It seems better to think of induction as within scientific method rather than as a kind of logic. That is—if we accept that there *is* induction. Sir Karl Popper takes the very extreme view that induction is no more than 'optical illusion.'[7] Though how one would run a railway or write a book if this were so is far from clear. Surely we would have no expectation of trains arriving, or of a book ever appearing.[8] Yet it is the external world's ability to *surprise* that forces us to believe there is something out there.

What would John Stuart Mill say of mirror images? They have *permanent possibilities of sensation*—but are they *objects*? Would Mill accept a virtual image as an object? He might, but its 'permanent possibilities of sensation' are only visual.

What would Mill say of a picture? This has the 'double reality' of the paint on a canvas, or whatever, and of the depicted scene. This is almost the opposite of a virtual image of a mirror, as its image is seen as objects lying through the glass by default—conceptual knowledge of how the light is reflected making no difference to the perception—but the picture is seen by constructing a hypothesis from the incomplete and conflicting data of its patterns of pigment. This difference is least so for *trompe-l'oeil*, and largest for minimalist painting; but all pictures have this curious double reality, and are very different from mirror images. This seems to confuse some experts writing on painting, who set up the mirror as an ideal standard for the artist.

What would Mill say of explicitly ambiguous pictures—such as the flipping Necker cube, or Rubin's vase-faces? These are switching alternative perceptions from the same retinal image; they are extremely important for research into perception, especially for separating physiological from cognitive 'software' processes and rules. An inkblot might have hundreds of different possibilities. Is each, in Mill's sense, an object? What do quantum physicists, who hold that perceptions set reality, say of flipping perceptions?

Pictures of paint—and cinema, television and mirror images—depend on inductions of visual forms associated with experience of objects by touch and their many other non-visual properties. We continue to hold these inductions from normal objects to patterns of pictures, even though pictures do not follow the inductive generalisations appropriate to normal objects. For pictures and mirrors present but ghosts—at the most, displaced ghosts of touchable things. Virtual reality may provide pseudo-touch ghosts; but these also will draw upon, yet flout, our experiences of objects.

It is paradoxical that we believe in 'reality' by induction; for inductions reduce surprise, yet we believe in objects because they can surprise us. It is a kind of psychological laziness that we accept pictures as surrogate objects; for pictures use, yet violate, our inductive knowledge of objects. So we accept a pattern of pigment as a face, even though it is flat and cannot speak or see. It is this 'laziness' of perception that representative art depends upon to work.

Quantum Reality

Berkeley's notion that reality depends on an observer (who might be God) is revived in a new form in quantum physics. This highly non-intuitive notion is basic to the standard 'Copenhagen interpretation', as observations are supposed to set reality, by 'collapsing the wave function' of possibilities (page 145). This was the view of Niels Bohr seventy years ago, and only recently has it been seriously questioned.

An immediate difficulty is that detecting and recording instruments, including our eyes and brains, are themselves subject to quantum effects. So how can they be empowered to set reality? One suggestion is that *consciousness* is the final arbiter and setter of reality. But this would imply that reality was not set before consciousness. And in any case we (or other animals?) have a far more limited range of consciousness, or knowledge, than what we believe to be the vast and ever surprising range of reality. It was the Hungarian mathematical physicist Eugene Wigner (1902–1995) who suggested that, although the eyes and the entire brain of the human observer are subject to quantum principles, *consciousness* might lie outside physics, and be the final stopping place where reality is set. But even if we suppose that consciousness is independent of physics, the consequences are bizarre in the extreme. We would have to suppose that wave packets were not collapsed in all the history of the universe before there were conscious creatures. And we would have to ask whether a mouse, or even an amoeba, can set reality, for ever. And most of what goes on is *not* observed, yet passes as causal events to set up the future. Also, instruments such as Geiger counters seem to do the trick—they collapse wave packets—but surely they are not conscious.

An alternative account has been suggested by David Bohm.[9] It has taken a long time for this to be taken seriously, and it does not resolve all the quantum 'paradoxes'. Bohm suggests that the wave–particle duality is really two aspects of one deep, essentially hidden reality. This might be thought of as different mirror views of the same object, as when we see the back of our head, while having our hair cut. As we only see our face and the back of our head in such mirrors we have to assume they are views of the same object!

The writer John Gribbin has recently described and discussed these issues, as clearly as possible.[10] Here Gribbin quotes the physicist John Bell as accepting as 'natural and simple' that waves and particles work together; and he would 'rather give up Einstein's special theory of relativity, if necessary going back to the idea of the ether (or, at least, to a preferred frame of reference) than give up the notion of reality.' Quoting Bell:[11]

One wants to be able to take a realistic view of the world, to talk about the world as if it is really there, even when it is not being observed. I certainly believe in a world that was here before me, and will be here after me, and I believe you are part of it! And I believe that most physicists take the same point of view when they are being pushed into a corner by philosophers.

To use my terms from Chapter 9—hands-on *exploration*; hand-waving *speculation*; handle-turning *computation*—we might perhaps say that quantum physics arose from hands-on surprises from experiments, and jumped straight to successful handle-turning mathematics, but missed out on developing satisfactory hand-waving mental models of what might be going on. Only now are these being developed. It seems that we will not return to 'common sense', though reality of some kind will be saved.

If reality were set by perceptions (which seems inconceivable), we might well ask: what would happen with perceptually ambiguous objects—such as duck-rabbits, vase-faces and Necker cubes? Would momentary ambiguous perceptions determine reality? Could perceptual illusions set the present and future of the universe? This would certainly give physics a strong cognitive component: close to God creating the universe in the first place, except that we would be quixotic gods creating many universes.

It is nothing short of miraculous that we live in the symbolic mental models of our minds—which set us apart from sensed reality and yet allow us to reflect upon what is out there, and add human inventions to the universe.

The Austrian physicist-philosopher Ernst Mach (1838–1916) tried to derive physics directly from perceptual experience:[12]

From sensations and their conjunctions arise concepts, whose aim is to lead by the shortest and easiest way to sensible ideas that agree best with the sensations. Thus all intellection starts from sense perceptions and returns to them. Our genuine mental workers are these sensible pictures or ideas, while concepts are the organizers and overseers that tell the masses of the former where to go and what to do.

Quite the opposite from Mach, the physics of Newton introduced 'objective' science which as far as possible banned the observer—us. So scientific instruments became very important. Some, such as telescopes, extended the senses; though now astronomers seldom look through telescopes. The most acceptable instruments reduced observation so far as possible to *nothing*. Thus, for reading the pointer of a scale, or noting that a balance is level, it is the instrument that is all-important. The observer makes a minimal judgement that could quite easily be automated.

It is in this spirit that Einstein continually refers to the use of rulers, and beams of light and clocks, as measuring rods to give meaning to concepts of space and time. But Einstein does not omit the observer:[13]

I believe that the first step in the setting of a 'real external world' is the formation of the concept of bodily [physical] objects of various kinds. Out of the multitude of our sense experiences we take, mentally and arbitrarily, certain repeatedly occurring complexes of sense impressions (partly in conjunction with sense impressions which are interpreted as signs for sense experiences of others), and we attribute to them a meaning—the meaning of the bodily object. Considered logically this concept is not identical with the totality of sense impressions referred to; but is an arbitrary creation of the human (or animal) mind. On the other hand, the concept owes its meaning and its justification exclusively to the totality of sense impressions which we associate with it.

The *pragmatism* of William James (1907) and Bridgman's *positivism* (1927) claimed that meaning is limited to and set by what can be observed. This extension of empiricism puts a lot of weight on perception and powers of experiment. The logical positivists, and especially A. J. Ayer in his seminal book *Language Truth and Logic* (1936), tried to limit meaning to what is observed, or, as a concession, to what might conceivably be observed. The meaning of a statement was sometimes described as 'the method of its verification.' If an observational test could not be devised, the statement was written off as *meaningless*, rather than false.

Developments of technology (especially of instruments such as vacuum pumps, telescopes, microscopes, balances, space probes, brain scanners and so on) make new verifications possible, or at least imaginable. So technologies extend meanings. So do new conceptual models and theories, and techniques of mathematics. Astronomy is special here as interactive experiments were not possible; so concepts far removed from observations and mathematical models were, and are, particularly important. If astrology were accepted, experimental science would be practically impossible—as it would take ages to wait for the same conditions for confirming or disconfirming observations if it were believed that the positions of the planets mattered.[14] The logical atomism of verification needed for every statement has had to be abandoned. Now we may see science as like a bridge of arches supported by occasional piers of observations and experiments.

In this book we have seen mirrors as evocative for art and literature, as well as for science. But is the creative scientist so different from the creative artist? Among the best writers on this issue is Michael Polanyi. Considering theories of physics and geometry, Polanyi wrote in 1958:[15]

We cannot truly account for our acceptance of such theories without endorsing our acknowledgement of a beauty that exhilarates and a profundity that entrances us. Yet the prevailing conception of science, based on the disjunction of subjectivity and objectivity, seeks—and must seek at all costs—to eliminate from science such passionate, personal, human appraisals of theories, or at least to minimize their function to that of a negligible by-play. For modern man has set up as the ideal of knowledge the conception of natural science as a set of statements which is 'objective' in the sense that its substance is entirely determined by observation. . . . This conception, stemming from a craving rooted in the very depths of our culture, would be shattered if the intuition of rationality in nature had to be acknowledged as a justifiable and indeed essential part of scientific theory.

We generally think of *reason* as human; but if structures of symbols of mathematics may be platonically in the world, why not also rules of *reason*? Seeing Mind as mirroring Nature, it is as hard to know which is mirroring which, as it is to know what is objective or subjective, or what is true and what is illusion. But surely Polanyi is right to include the observer with the mirror. The question now is whether the observer might be a machine. Would such a human-like machine be describable by physics?

Mental Models

It might be said that mirrors—and the enigma scales (page 227), the glass and string (page 228) and many other puzzles—are surprising because one does not have appropriate mental models for thinking about them. This suggests that we should aim at improving our mental models, by which we see and understand.

The notion that brains build models of reality, and of fantasy, was introduced by the Cambridge psychologist K. J. W. Craik (1914–1945). Kenneth Craik's short book *The Nature of Explanation* (1952) is a classic well worth reading today.[16] Written before digital computers became familiar, the notion is that the brain builds up physiologically-based *functional working models*, reflecting aspects of reality and taking off in the imagination. Craik describes what he calls 'internal models':[17]

By a model we thus mean any physical or chemical system which has a similar relation-structure to that of the process it imitates. By 'relation-structure' I do not mean some obscure non-physical entity which attends the model, but the fact that it is a physical working model which works in the same way as the process it parallels, in the aspects under consideration at any moment. Thus, the model need not resemble the real object pictorially; Kelvin's tide-predictor, which consists of a number of pulleys on levers, does not resemble a tide in appearance, but it works in the same way in certain essential respects—it combines oscillations of various frequencies so as to produce an oscillation which closely resembles in amplitude at each moment the variation in tide level at any place. Again, since the physical object is 'translated' into a working model which gives a prediction which is retranslated into terms of the original object, we cannot say that the model invariably either precedes or succeeds the external object it models.

This is very different from the later concept of the brain as a digital computer carrying out defined rules of algorithms.[18] There is now a return in the AI world to something closer to Craik's internal models notion, with neural nets (page 271).

The psychologist who has done most to develop Craik's account of thinking is P. N. Johnson-Laird, especially in his *Mental Models* (1983). Philip Johnson-Laird shows that when people are solving formal logical problems, for example with syllogisms, they do not straightforwardly follow the rules. Rather, they conceive a model of the situation, and derive the answer informally in individual ways, from their mental model of the situation. This seems central to intelligence, but it can produce startling errors, such as for generals assessing battle situations, as discussed recently by Stuart Sutherland.[19]

An important way to improve mental models seems to be through constructive physical and mental play. The mirror becomes a 'control case' as interactive experience through handling things is not available. We have stressed the difficulty of thinking about mirror images, which cannot be touched, suggesting that hands-on interactive experience is important for learning to see and think. This has clear implications for schools and science centres.

Is Science Unnatural?

The distinguished biologist Lewis Wolpert complains that science is *unnatural*.[20] He would certainly not deny the excitement of exploration, nor that there have been many attempts through recorded history and no doubt long before to explain things. But for Wolpert not much of this is 'science'. This is a matter of definition. It may be that the rigorous experimental method (formulated by Francis Bacon in the seventeenth century) is unnatural—but surely not curiosity, and love of exploring and inventing. They are human attributes, to be captured as a way of life by attractive science teaching.

Certainly many results of science are counter-intuitive, for all manner of discoveries and inventions have taken us far from traditional common sense. This is very different from saying that the motivations of science, rooted in human curiosity and inventiveness, are unnatural. This is an important issue for considering schools and science centres; though fortunately what is unnatural for children does not necessarily represent a learning-problem. Pedalling a bicycle is unnatural, yet children take to bikes as ducks to water, and often prefer unnatural pedalling to natural walking. And the counter-intuitive—the surprising, the puzzling—appeal to many people.

Lewis Wolpert doubts that the Chinese had science, and he sees the Greeks as unique in having any science before the Western science of the last few hundred years. This must surely depend on how 'science' is defined. Lewis Wolpert is in stark disagreement (though of course this does not imply he is wrong) with authorities such as George Sarton, who in the Introduction to his pioneering *A History of Science* (1952) wrote:[21]

The understanding of ancient science has often been spoiled by two unpardonable omissions. The first concerns Oriental science. It is childish to assume that science began in Greece; the Greek 'miracle' was prepared by millennia of work in Egypt, Mesopotamia and possibly in other regions. Greek science was less an invention than a revival.

The second concerns the superstitious background not only of Oriental science but of Greek science itself. It was bad enough to hide the Oriental origins without which the Hellenistic accomplishment would have been impossible; some historians aggravated the blunder by hiding also the endless superstitions that hindered that accomplishment and might have nullified it. Hellenic science is a victory of rationalism, which appears greater, not smaller, when one is made to realize that it had to be won in spite of the face of unreason.

Sarton asks:

When did science begin? Where did it begin? It began wherever men tried to solve innumerable problems of life. The first solutions were mere expedients, but that must do for a beginning. Gradually the expedients would be compared, generalised, rationalised, simplified, interrelated, integrated; the texture of science would be slowly woven. . . It might be claimed that one cannot speak of science at all as long as a certain degree of abstraction has not been reached, but who will measure the degree? When the first mathematician recognised that there was something in common between three palm trees and three donkeys, how abstract was his thought? . . .Was it pure science, such as it was, or a mixture of science with art, religion, or magic?

. . .

    Such queries are futile, because they lack determination and the answers cannot be verified.

Are these queries futile? It is through questioning that we learn how to find answers. Lewis Wolpert is quite right to ask whether science is unnatural. It is certainly true that for many people science is difficult. But children like unnatural things such as bicycles and computers, and they like games requiring hard work and discipline; so whatever the answer, the onus must be on schools and science centres to present science attractively, so that more of us can share in the greatest adventure into the unknown.

Mechanising Intelligence

Will machines become creative intelligences—scientists in their own right? This dream (for some a nightmare) of mirroring reality in a machine has a surprisingly long history upon which we can only touch.

The first calculating device—the abacus—is prehistoric. It is far more subtle than so many pebbles simply corresponding to as many other things, for the *positions* of the pebbles determine their significance. This is like units, tens, hundreds . . . columns of arithmetic. But the abacus has to be operated by a human being who knows the rules. What of self-operating mind-machines?

The Greek astronomical calendar computer, the Antikythera Mechanism of 80 BC, and its predecessors back to the time of Plato and Aristotle and before,[22] found numerical answers to fixed problems. The first handle-turning computer which could accept different problems as they were entered was invented in 1642 by Blaise Pascal (1623–1662), to help his father with his accounts. It showed that 'mental arithmetic' could be carried out with gear wheels (Figure 10.1).

Pascal's calculator was further developed around 1670 by the German

FIGURE 10.1 *'Mental arithmetic' by gears*

Pascal's calculating machine of 1642. © Science and Society Photo Library, The Science Museum, London.

philosopher-mathematician Gottfried Leibniz (1646–1716) into a practical machine which would add, subtract, multiply and divide reliably when the handle was turned. This was the first practical calculating machine, which with slight modifications remained in use for over a century, especially for computing insurance tables. Leibniz cylinders have an extra length of tooth for each number (1–9), to engage an extra tooth of an idle wheel, leading to counters. The carrying mechanism works from trips on each counter wheel, pushing a lever to actuate the next column—tens, hundreds and so on. It will add and subtract, and with a little help it will multiply and divide.

What perhaps is not so well known is Leibniz's system for computing ideas. He tried indeed to mechanise thought. One might say that Leibniz was the pioneer of artificial intelligence. His ambitions have still to be realised. The question now is: why is it taking so long? The Cambridge mathematician Charles Babbage (1791–1871) designed and largely built astonishingly sophisticated mechanical computers 150 years ago, mainly for computing mathematical tables without errors. Babbage conceived the essential principles of programmable computers, but like modern electronic computers Babbage's machines hadn't a clue what they were doing or why. We are supposed to be different. The crucial difference is meaning: how could one make a machine handle meanings? Is this uniquely and for ever a brain accomplishment? Leibniz tried to break through the meaning-barrier with his 'calculus ratiocinator.' He considered what is, and what is not, *mental*. This led him to '*semi*-mental' concepts—such as *classes* of objects. Thus a herd of sheep is *our* conceptual classification of *objects*. So classes are part object, part mind. Looking at the simplest concepts, he gave them 'characteristic numbers': a pair of prime numbers, one positive, the other negative. The characteristic number of a complex concept would be the *product* of the numbers of its components. Thus, if *animal* is $+13-5$, and *rational* is $+8-7$, then *man* will be $+104-35$. That is: $+13 \times 8-5 \times 7$, meaning a *rational animal*.

Leibniz distinguished between *form* and *meaning* in logic. For an example of truth by form:[23]

> Every metal mirror reflects,
> Some metals do not reflect,
> Therefore some metals are not mirrors.

But:

> Every mirror reflects,
> Some reflections are intelligent,
> Therefore, some mirrors are intelligent.

This needs *meaning* to be seen as true—or false.

Leibniz got stuck in his attempt to design a meaning computer, as he found that concepts do not stand alone but are *interconnected*.

George Boole (1815–1864) took a step further than Leibniz with his *Laws of Thought* (1854). The essential notion was to assign symbols to relations between propositions. There were 'unions', 'complements' and 'intersections'. Boole thought of the mind as operating on sets (classes) with rules which could be clearly described and automated. These became the OR, AND, NOT of switch positions applying Boolian algebra to circuits. This both aided digital switching circuit design, and allowed such circuits to perform logical operations. So to a large extent computers design new computers.

Boolean algebra turned out to be too limited and too inflexible for mechanising thinking. It failed to represent general or indefinite elements. This is where Gottlob Frege made his advance: introducing *predicates*. These have true or false variables. So empirical truth or falsity can be represented in a logical statement. Frege extended this to universal quantifiers. Bertrand Russell found a paradox in Frege's formulation (conflicts of classes referring to themselves), and he urged that *existence* is not a predicate. When Kurt Gödel showed that no logical system can prove itself to be consistent, he put a spanner in the works of the attempt to produce a completely consistent logical language. Alan Turing realised that some equations could not be calculated, but concluded that this did not necessarily prevent machines thinking. For him this could only be decided empirically—by developing artificial intelligence. Perhaps we don't yet know the answer.

There are growing doubts as to whether the brain is like a digital computer. The physiology does not look suitable, and seeing and thinking are much too fast to work sequentially in this way with its slow components. So it seems to work with many parallel processes going on simultaneously, and there are growing doubts as to whether it works by algorithms. Returning to ideas from the 1970s, of the Canadian psychologist Donald Hebb, it seems more likely that much of intelligent brain function is not digital, but analogue, with self-adapting highly interconnected networks of cells. A basic notion is that cells fire more easily when frequently stimulated, and errors are fed back to modify the net, so that it comes to mirror the situation dynamically. There is no programmer—it programs itself, from its own experience. Set the net to play and it will discover and learn (see Figure 10.2). Perhaps this is starting to realise Leibniz's dream of a thinking machine for solving problems, not only by the *forms* of mathematics but also by *meaning*. Is this how we see truths through the mirror of appearance?

This leads to the current debate on how children learn language, and whether there is innately inherited structure common to all natural languages. There is no direct evidence. This would be available if it were possible to bring up babies in an artificial language, but this is not ethically possible. The issue hinges on the question: what are the limits to learning? This may become the question: what are the limits to mirroring abstract structures by brain or artificial neural nets? This is more technology than philosophy, yet it has intriguing philosophical implications. It is strangely unrecognised how powerful technology is for answering (or

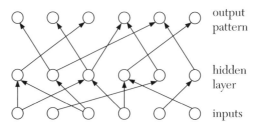

FIGURE 10.2 *Adaptive net*

*The cells become more responsive the more signals they receive. The inputs become
generalised and the system discovers patterns, sometimes over long periods of time. The
'hidden layer' is hidden to input and output—like the mind? It does not follow programmed
algorithms; it develops its own rules.*

at least providing tools for answering) the deepest questions of philosophy and
science. Conversely, limits of technology can limit imagination in science
and philosophy. At present the technical difficulty of providing rich available
knowledge to machines distorts our notions of perception and intelligence.

Intelligences

As science is co-operative it is a *shared* intelligence. One might say that with each
generation of new knowledge, science's intelligence, and so ours, increases. If we
think of intelligence as the ability to solve problems, the more knowledge and
skills we have, the easier it is to solve problems—so intelligence is needed
to increase intelligence. There is something of a paradox here: one thinks of
knowledgeable people as *more* intelligent—yet with more knowledge *less* intelligence is required. This applies not only to skills, such as the ability to do long division, but also to tools. Thus there is no great problem cutting paper or cloth with
scissors, but it is a problem without the right tools for cutting and measuring. So
in this sense, technology increases our intelligence.

The paradox starts to melt away when we realise that it requires intelligence to
learn skills and to invent devices, such as scissors. They are *stored* intelligence that
we are free to use. There are two commonly used meanings of the word 'intelligence.' One meaning is *knowledge*, as in 'military intelligence.' This does not
imply that the military are particularly bright, though they may be. It is this sense
that Shakespeare intended when Macbeth says: 'Say from whence you owe this
strange intelligence?' Here 'intelligence' clearly means knowledge. So we have
stored knowledge, and we have the appropriate *use* of knowledge (including tools)
as a kind of problem solving, and so as a kind of intelligence. The first is passively
stored; the second is actively applied.

This suggests an analogy with energy: *potential* and *kinetic* energy. For like knowledge, potential energy is built up and stored for later use. The kinetic energy required to use it may be very small. It is easy to push a stone off a cliff. The energy needed for electronic switching in computers, and neural switching in brains, is minute, though the effects can be immense. So, by analogy with potential and kinetic energy, we may suggest calling the two kinds of intelligence *potential intelligence* and *kinetic intelligence*.[24] This power of potential intelligence for making effective use of kinetic intelligence justifies learning science.

This analogy suggests that intelligence tests are suspect—because the knowledge of potential intelligence very easily dominates or swamps the relatively tiny contribution of kinetic intelligence. It is exceedingly hard to design questions so that special knowledge does not help. There are inherent dangers of circularity in claims of different, or the same, intelligences for different ages, or races, or genders. For it is all too easy to change the results by including more or less 'favouring' questions. In our culture, questions concerning motorbikes will favour men; it is still true that questions of cooking will favour women. So it is easy to make men or women come out as more intelligent by choice of questions, and very hard to know that the questions are neutral.[25]

Consciousness

Over the last few years there has been a spate of books on consciousness—by physiologists, psychologists, physicists and philosophers. What one finds is that the authors (quite naturally) approach the problems from their own points of view, bringing to bear their own expertise, expecting to find the answer further along the line of their own existing understanding. So the physiologist looks to brain structures and electrically recordable neurone functions; the psychologist to cognitive processes (something like the software of a computer); the physicist to physical mind-like phenomena that might be weird enough—hence favouring quantum phenomena. Philosophers (ideally) don't know anything. So they should lack such technical starting points. Sometimes they dismiss consciousness as an illusion of some kind. It seems better to accept that we do have qualia (sensations); but as yet we simply do not have appropriate mental models for seeing how a lump of matter, however complicated, can have qualia from the external world and awareness of itself. But if we don't look, we won't find the answer.

We have every reason to believe that consciousness is intimately associated with the brain, though not with all the brain. The cerebellum is involved in skilled performance, but the pianist is not aware of individual movements of the fingers. The awareness is at a 'higher level' of planning and co-ordinating and appreciating. If attention is paid to the fingers, the performance suffers and may break down. More prosaically, it is impossible to run up stairs fast while monitoring the movements of one's legs. One sets the general command 'run upstairs' and the cerebellum and spinal reflexes and so on do the rest. Attending consciously to 'lower level' functions gets in the way; though if one trips one is immediately aware, and can take remedial action.

Mind has often been *equated* with consciousness; but now that we are familiar with *un*conscious mental processes this has been abandoned. Hermann von Helmholtz spoke of perceptions as 'unconscious inferences' a generation before Freud, and, like Freud, he got a bad press—partly because it seemed hard to blame or praise people if they were not conscious of their actions. However, a dominating school of experimental psychology, behaviourism, set out to deny consciousness altogether. For consciousness seemed to make psychology too unlike prestigious sciences such as physics. It got in the way of making psychology a respectable science. What 'respectable' means here is 'objective'. For how is it possible to measure sensation—consciousness? Attempts were made, but they never quite captured the essentials of consciousness, now called *qualia*. These are sensations, such as red, hot, pain. Some of these have rough correspondence with 'objective' features of the world out there (wavelength of light, agitation of molecules, forms of objects). Other qualia are related to body-states: pain—tickle—nausea. Others are less clearly related: funny—shame—beauty. Fear is 'subjective', but a well-known theory ascribes it to experiencing body changes evoked by perceived danger. This is the James–Langer theory of emotions. As there are always associated bodily changes, the theory is sometimes changed from autonomic body changes to *brain* changes. This has also occurred for colour. It is now believed, from electrophysiology and PET scans, that sensations of colour are produced by certain cells (in area V4) in the brain. It is found that memories can be evoked by local electrical stimulation of certain (parietal) regions of the brain. And of course moods are changed, and visual and other experiences can be evoked, with drugs acting on the brain.

We may ask: when are we most aware? One has to resort here to *introspection*. My introspection is that one is most aware when one is surprised. The surprise can be of presence or of absence. Those of us who have ticking and chiming clocks in our sitting rooms simply do not hear them unless we are waiting for a chime—or when they stop. (Writing this, I immediately became aware of a faint ticking from my long-case clock, which was alive and ticking when Newton was living.)

Mirror images are often surprising, though frequently they are not seen as such. That is, they should be surprising, as they show objects from weird angles and separated from their surroundings. Much the same is true of windows: the scene outside has nothing to do with the interior of the room; but mirror views are more surprising as they show unusual points of view, and of course they are reversed. Why are we so often not aware of reflections? This is especially so, I suggest, when irrelevant objects are superimposed on what is relevant. For example, California has many restaurants with huge glass windows. As the outside scene fades, in the evening, the lights in the room hang in the space outside as they are reflected from the glass, but, curiously, they are seldom seen. They are ignored until attention is called to them. (I have frequently done the experiment of pointing them out, with surprise all round. This is worth trying.) The same is so for 'entoptic' phenomena of vision, such as after-images. So it is not simply the unusual that captures consciousness; surely it is what is *relevant* but *unpredicted* that captures consciousness.

While driving a car, a pedestrian's unusual movements near the road immediately evoke awareness, even though this would have no such effect on uninvolved observers. Evidently consciousness is linked to attention, to context, and to what one is engaged in doing. When lying idly on a beach, one's consciousness roams, like dreaming. Doing an unusual skilled task one is intensely aware of the task and of little else. Extremely familiar objects such as the pictures on one's walls are essentially invisible until attention is called to them. Then one may notice features never seen before, and one is surprised. Changes of attention can induce surprise in the familiar. One might, indeed, conclude that a key feature of consciousness is *surprise*. And, one is surprised by things *unusual* and *relevant*. When we attend in a new way to something familiar—generating surprise—we become conscious and we start to extract new information.

This, surely, suggests that *consciousness* is related to *information*. For the bigger the surprise, the more information is needed to signal it reliably and the more information it can convey. (So it is effectively impossible to report seeing a ghost or a Martian, or that water has frozen on a hot stove, as it would be more likely that one is dreaming, or deluded, or lying.) If a very unlikely report were believed, it would carry immense information, but it is correspondingly unlikely to be correct. This principle is true of all observations and all experiments.

Another important question is: which *regions of the brain* are associated with *consciousness*? This is discussed in a recent book by the expert on blindsight, Lawrence Weiskrantz, from the point of view of brain anatomy and losses of consciousness with brain damage.[26] He concludes that sometimes it is 'possible to say *which* lesions are critical. In amnesia [memory loss] a system of limbic lobe structures are necessary for overt recognition. In Blindsight, the primary visual cortex appears to be necessary for "seeing with awareness". . .'. Blindsight is somewhat minimal vision without awareness in a part of the visual field, associated with a lesion in one hemisphere of the visual cortex. As Larry Weiskrantz has done a great deal to show, people who experience blindsight can differentiate between stimuli but without any awareness that they are 'seeing'. Do they have full-blown perception—perceptual hypotheses? Such clinical findings can be highly suggestive and are well worth following up.

On how consciousness is related to neurones, Weiskrantz concludes:

Neurones are neurones—full stop. What we have to ask is why in certain circumstances neurones are not sufficient for awareness in isolation . . . whereas in other cases they are. The answer—if it is to be sought within a monistic realm of neural activity—must lie in their organisation, either in its dynamic and/or structural connectivity.

It has been suggested that the 'level' to look at is not the neurones or their organisation, but much deeper, into the physics of quantum mechanics. This has been developed especially by Roger Penrose, who suggests tentatively that the anatomical seat of action is the minute microtubules in cells.[27] Evoking the weird phenomena of quantum mechanics might open quite new concepts for mind. The lack of spatial localisation and action at a distance give an alternative seat of action from known physiology of neurones and their connections for considering brain function. A snag is, on this account it is not clear why mental phenomena are associated with *particular* brains: why not telepathy, telekinesis, and the rest of the bag of tricks of the occult? If indeed such phenomena do *not* occur, this might be seen as evidence *against* such a quantum account of mind and consciousness. The danger is to assume, from the mysteriousness both of quantum mechanics and of consciousness, that they are closely related, or even the same. This is not a strong argument.

Are animals conscious? Ingenious experiments by Alan Cowey at Oxford suggest that monkeys have some 'self awareness' of what they are doing. The scheme is to get a monkey to respond with keys between alternative stimuli—and have further keys for the animal to indicate whether it was 'guessing' or 'not guessing'. This is extremely interesting; but does it show that the animal is *conscious*—that it has sensations, or *qualia*? Surely not quite, for a computer might be programmed to indicate whether it was guessing or not, and we would not infer that the computer was conscious. Again, the fascinating dotted-face-and-mirror experiments initiated by Gordon Gallup (see pages #7) do not strictly prove that the animal (or the baby) has consciousness or self-awareness.

We have argued here and elsewhere that perceptions are like predictive hypotheses of science.[28] For perceptions are indirectly related to objects; they are richer than available sensory signals; they fill gaps in signals or data, and are predictive to the immediate future. On this account, perceptions of tables and people and so on are hypotheses, psychologically projected into the assumed reality of the physical world.

It is striking that phenomena of ambiguity—where perceptions flip between alternatives though the sensory signals are unchanged—show that qualia are attached to prevailing perceptual hypotheses, rather than evoked directly from sensory signals. This is also like hypotheses of science, which can change with different assumptions or 'paradigms' even without change of data; as though, as for perception, the 'flip' may suggest new places to look for further data. So hypotheses of science and perceptions do seem similar—except (and this is a big 'except') that hypotheses of science are not (we believe) conscious, though we are. And they might be held and used by presumably unconscious machines, such as advanced computers. So here perceptual hypotheses are different from science.

We may ask: what do our sensations—*qualia*—do? Here is a suggestion. The present moment is vitally important for survival; but hypotheses are essentially timeless. Is it possible that qualia serve to flag the present? Then consciousness should have become more important through evolution, as reflex behaviour gradually gave way to the intelligence (subject to dramatic errors and illusions) of cognitive brain hypotheses. Reflexes work in the here and now, because they are triggered by sensory signals; but as hypotheses depend very largely on knowledge gained from the past and do not specify time, surely they need present sensory signals—associated with qualia—to flag the present. Qualia are our subjective reality; so we seldom confuse memories, which have weak or no qualia, with perceptions. Remembered emotions, however, can have vivid qualia; perhaps because emotions can be memory-evoked sensations of bodily changes, to danger or sex or whatever. So unlike other imagination and memory, recalled emotions may have sensory signals evoking qualia.[29]

As the joke has it: the drunk who has lost his keys is silly to look under the lamppost, as this is where the light is. But in the absence of understanding, evidence or theory, where better to look? Science seeks truth where there is light from knowledge and techniques and theories. Occultism finds mystery in darkness. Paradoxically, sensations of light depend on consciousness, yet for understanding whys and wherefores of consciousness there is little or no light—or at least it is not clear under which lamppost of science or philosophy we should look. Perhaps this is like the mirror-reversal puzzle—before one sees how to see it.

What would Alice say?[30]

There was a book lying near Alice on the table, and while she sat watching the White King (for she was a little anxious about him, and had the ink all ready to throw over him, in case he fainted again), she turned over the leaves, to find some part that she could read,"—for it's all in some language I don't know," she said to herself.

ЈАВВЕRWOCKY

'Twas brillig, and the slithy toves
Did gyre and gimble in the wabe:
All mimsey were the borogoves,
And the mome raths outgrabe.

She puzzled over this for some time, but at last a bright thought struck her. "Why, it's a Looking-glass book, of course! And, if I hold it up to a glass, the words will all go the right way again."

We might add?

Then she held the page up to the light, and turned the book around. Now she

could see the writing behind the paper. The words all went the right way again—
she could read it! So she didn't need the mirror. But she couldn't see her own
smile, or her eyes. So after all Alice did need her looking-glass.

This was Alice's final reflection.

Notes

1. Locke (1690).
2. Berkeley (1963) page 152.
3. Russell (1946).
4. This position depends on considering object-perceptions as inferences, as Helmholtz did
   (and I do); and not as 'direct pick up', as held by J. J. Gibson.
5. Mill (1865).
6. I discuss this in Gregory (1981).
7. See Popper (1972): '. . . the idea of induction by repetition must be an error—a kind of optical illusion. In brief: there is no such thing as induction by repetition.'
8. The philosopher Sir Karl Popper (1902–1994) has argued very powerfully for the importance of presenting hypotheses in such ways that they can be knocked out by observations
   or experiments. Hypotheses should be framed to be vulnerable to attack by evidence. How
   does this apply to paradigm-selection? It seems that paradigm-selection is really prior to
   hypotheses and testing of hypotheses. Indeed, the manner of testing may be suggested by—
   and limited to—what is available in the accepted paradigm. So each paradigm is isolated
   from attack and discussion between paradigms is difficult.
9. Bohm (1980).
10. Gribbin (1995) Chapter 4.
11. Gribbin (1995) page 159.
12. Mach (1976) page 106. Other significant books by Mach are translated as: *The Analysis of
    Sensations* (1897); *The Science of Mechanics* (1960); *The Principles of Physical Optics* (1926);
    Popular Scientific Lectures (fifth edn,1943); *Space and Geometry* (1943). His phenomenalism is
    discussed in Bradley (1971).
13. Einstein (1936).
14. See Gregory (1989).
15. Polanyi (1958).
16. Kenneth Craik died from a cycle accident in Cambridge, tragically young. Many of Craik's
    highly original papers are available in Sherwood (1966).
17. Craik (1952) page 51.
18. The most influential account of vision in digital computing terms is David Marr's *Vision*
    (1982). I have suggested that this assumes that the brain carries out digital algorithms, when
    it would be proper to say that visual scientists *describe* what are 'non-algovistic' analogue
    processes with algorithms. There is surely a serious danger of confusing the manner of
    description with what is being described. See Gregory (1994).
19. Sutherland (1992).
20. Wolpert (1993).
21. Sarton (1952) page ix.
22. Price (1975).
23. Syllogisms were invented by Aristotle. A classical example (of the first mode BARBARA
    where all the terms are affirmative) is:

All men are mortal
Socrates is mortal
(therefore)
Socrates is a man

Another form is:

No Professors are rich
Plato is a Professor
(therefore)
Plato is not rich

This conclusion is factually false—but not logically false, for it is a valid syllogism. We often confuse logic with assumptions of knowledge.

24. I made this suggestion in Gregory (1987).

25. I discuss this in Gregory (1981) Chapter 10.

26. Weiskranz (1995). Larry Weiskranz moved from America to Cambridge, becoming head of Psychology at Oxford, where he built up a world-leading department. He is a greatly respected friend.

27. Penrose (1989, 1994).

28. Gregory (1980).

29. James (1890).

30. *Through the Looking-Glass*, Chapter 1.

References

❦

Preflections

HOPKINS, Justine (1994) *Michael Ayrton: A Biography* (London: Andre Deutsch) Chapter 23.

Chapter 1

AMSTERDAM, B. (1972) Mirror self-recognition before age two. *Developmental Psychobiology*, **5**, 297–303.

ANDERSON, James R. (1984) The development of self-recognition: a review. *Developmental Psychobiology,* **17**, 35–49.

ARISTOTLE (384–322 BC) *Parva Naturalia.* On Dreams II, 459b (Harvard: Harvard University Press, Loeb Classical Library) Volume VIII, pages 357–358.

BALINT, Michael (1968) *The Basic Fault* (London: Tavistock).

BELL, Charles (1806) *Anatomy of Expression in Painting* (London: Longman, Hurst, Rees & Orme) pages 137–139.

BENNETT, D. H. (1956) Perception of the upright in relation to the body-image. *Journal of Mental Science*, **102,** 487–506.

BERMAN, Morris (1989) *Coming to Our Senses* (New York: Simon and Schuster). Reprinted in London as an Unwin paperback (1990).

BROAD, C. D. (1929) *Mind and its Place in Nature* (London: Routledge and Kegan Paul) Chapter VII.

BROOKS-GUNN, J. and LEWIS, M. (1975) Mirror image stimulation and self-recognition in infancy. Paper presented at the Society for Research in Child Development, Denver.

CAPPON, Daniel (1973) *Eating, Living, and Dying: A Psychology of Appetites* (Toronto: Toronto University Press).

CHURCHLAND, Paul (1988) *Matter and Consciousness* (Cambridge, Mass.: MIT Press).

COHEN, Barry and COX, Carol Thayer (1995) *Telling Without Talking: Art as a Window into the World of Multiple Personality* (New York, London: W. W. Norton) page 23.

DENNETT, Daniel (1991) *Consciousness Explained* (New York: Little, Brown).

DARWIN, Charles (1872) *The Expression of the Emotions in Man and Animals* (London: John Murray). Reprinted in Chicago by the University of Chicago Press (1965).

DARWIN, Charles (1877) A biographical sketch of an infant mind. *Quarterly Review of Psychology and Philosophy*, **2,** 285–294. Reprinted in GRUBER, Howard (1974)

Darwin on Man: A Psychological Study of Scientific Creativity, together with Darwin's early and unpublished notebooks, transcribed and annotated by Paul H. Barrett (New York: E. P. Dutton) pages 464–474.

DESCARTES, René (1637) *Discourse on Method*, translated by J. Cottingham, R. Stoothoff and D. Murdoch (1985) (Cambridge: Cambridge University Press).

EKMAN, Paul (1972) *Emotion in the Human Face* (Cambridge: Cambridge University Press).

EKMAN, Paul (1973) *Darwin and Facial Expression: A Century of Research in Review* (New York: Academic Press).

GALLUP, G. G. and SUAREZ S. D. (1986) Self-awareness and the emergence of mind in humans and other primates. In: *Psychological Perspectives of the Self,* Vol. 3, edited by J. Suls and A. G. Greenwald (Hillside: Erlbaum) pages 3–26.

GALLUP, G. G. Jr (1970) Chimpanzee self-recognition. *Science*, **167,** 86–87.

GALLUP, G. G. Jr (1977) Self-recognition in primates. *American Psychologist*, **32,** 329-338.

GALLUP, G. G. Jr (1979) Self-awareness in primates. *American Scientist*, **76,** 417–421.

GOLDBERG, Benjamin (1985) *The Mirror and Man* (Charlottesville, VA: University Press of Virginia).

GOLDSTEIN, Kurt (1957) The smiling of the infant and the problem of understanding the 'other'. *Journal of Psychology*, **44,** 175–191.

GREGORY, R. L. and WALLACE, J. G. (1963) *Recovery from Early Blindness: A Case Study*. Experimental Psychology Society Monograph No. 2 (Cambridge: Heffers). Reprinted in: GREGORY, R. L. (1974) *Concepts and Mechanisms of Perception* (London: Duckworth) pages 65–129.

GREGORY, R. L. (1987) In defence of artificial intelligence—a reply to John Searle. In: *Mindwaves*, edited by Colin Blakemore and Susan Greenfield (Oxford: Blackwell) pages 235–244.

HEATH, Peter (1960) *Space and Sight* (London: Methuen) pages 326–35.

HULL, J. M. (1991) *Touching the Rock: An Experience of Blindness* (New York: Pantheon).

KRECH, D. and CRUTCHFIELD, R. S. (1962) *Elements of Psychology* (New York: Knopf).

LA BELLE, Benijoy (1988) *Herself Beheld* (Ithaca, NY: Cornell University Press) pages 16–17.

LOCKE, Don (1968) *Myself and Others: A Study of Our Knowledge of Minds* (Oxford: Clarendon Press).

MITFORD, Nancy (1945) *The Pursuit of Love* (London: Hamish Hamilton).

MOCHIZUKI, Toshiko and TORII, Shuko (1992) Perception of Mirror Image. Paper presented at the XXV International Congress of Psychology, Brussels.

MORRIS, Desmond (1967) *The Naked Ape* (London: Cape).

MORRIS, Desmond (1977) *Man Watching* (London: Grafton).

MYERS, Frederic W. H. (1915) *Human Personality and its Survival of Bodily Death* (London: Longman Green).

PARKER, S. T., MITCHELL, R. W. and BOCCIA, M. L. (1994) *Self-awareness in Animals and Humans* (Cambridge: Cambridge University Press).

PERRETT, D. I., MISTLIN, A. J. and CHITTY, A. J. (1987) Visual neurons responsive to faces. *Trends in Neurosciences*, **10**, 358–364.

RORTY, Amélie O. (1976) *The Identities of Persons* (Berkeley: University of California).

ROSENFIELD, Israel (1992) *The Strange, Familiar and Forgotten: An Anatomy of Consciousness* (New York: Knopf).

SCHILDER, P. (1935) *Image and Appearance of the Human Body* (London: Kegan Paul).

SCHWARZ, J. H. and Fjeld, S. P. (1968) Illusions induced by the self-reflected image. *Journal of Neurological and Mental Diseases*, **146**, 277–284.

SEARLE, John (1984) *Minds, Brains and Science* (London: BBC Publications).

STERN, N. Daniel (1983) The early development of schemas of self, other, and 'self with other'. In: *Reflections on Self Psychology*, edited by J.D. Lichtenberg and Samuel Kaplan (Hillsdale, New Jersey: The Analytic Press).

STERN, N. Daniel (1985) *The Interpersonal World of the Infant* (New York: Basic Books).

SUAREZ, S. D. and GALLUP, G. G. Jr (1981) Self-recognition in chimpanzees and orang-utans, but not gorillas. *Journal of Human Evolution*, **10**, 175–188.

TRAUB, A. C. and ORBACH, J. (1964) Psychophysical studies of body image. *AMA Archives of General Psychiatry*, **11**, 53–66.

UMEZU, Hachizo, TORII, Shuko and UEMURA, Yasuko (1975) *Postoperative Formation of Blind Perception in the Early Blind* (Kyoto: Psychologia Society, Department of Psychology, Kyoto University, Sakyo-ku, Kyoto 606, Japan).

VALVO, A. (1971) *Sight Restoration after Long-term Blindness: the Problem and Behaviour Patterns of Visual Rehabilitation* (New York: American Foundation for the Blind).

VERNY, Thomas (1981) *The Secret Life of the Unborn Child* (New York: Summit Books).

WALTER, W. Grey, W. (1953) *The Living Brain* (London: Gerald Duckworth).

WILLIAMS, Bernard (1973) *Problems of the Self* (Cambridge: Cambridge University Press).

WINNICOTT, D.W. (1957) *Mother and Child* (New York: Basic Books).

WITKIN, H. A. *et al.* (1954) *Personality Through Perception* (New York: Harper).

WOODWORTH, Robert S. and SCHOSBERG, Harold (1954) *Experimental Psychology* (3rd edn) (London: Methuen).

YEATS, W. B. (1983) *The Poems of W. B. Yeats: a New Edition*, edited by Richard J. Finneran (New York: Simon & Schuster).

Chapter 2

AMES, A. Jr (1951) Visual perception and the rotating trapezoid window. *Psychological Monographs* 7 (65), 1–32 (Washington, DC: American Psychological Association).

CANTRIL, H. (1960) *The Morning Notes of Adelbert Ames Jr* (New Brunswick, NJ: Rutgers University Press) page vii.

CORAN, Stanley (1992) *Left Hander* (London: John Murray).

GALLOWAY, John (1992) Reflections on handedness. *Scope*, Winter, 4–7.

GREGORY, R. L. (1968) Perceptual illusions and brain models. *Proceedings of the Royal Society B*, **171**, 179–296.

GREGORY, R. L. (1970) *The Intelligent Eye* (London: Weidenfeld and Nicolson) Chapter 6.

GREGORY, R. L. (1994) Adelbert Ames: interactions with Hermann Helmholtz, Albert Einstein and the Universe. In: *Even Odder Perceptions* (London: Routledge).

HELMHOLTZ, H. VON (1866) Concerning the perceptions in General. *Treatise on Physiological Optics*, Vol. III (3rd edn), translated by J. P. C. Southall (New York: Optical Society of America, 1925) Section 26. This classic was reprinted in New York by Dover (1962).

HELMHOLTZ, H. VON (1867) *The Recent Progress of the Theory of Vision*. Popular Scientific Lectures (New York: Appleton). This is a course of lectures delivered in Frankfurt and Heidelberg in 1867, translated by P. H. Pye-Smith.

HIGGONET, Anne (1990) The other side of the mirror. In: *Perspectives of Morisot*, edited by T. J. Edelstein. (New York: Hudson Hill's Press) page 75.

HOPKINS, Justine (1994) *Michael Ayrton: A Biography* (London: Andre Deutsch) page 372.

HUGHE, Rene (1959) *Discovery of Art* (London: Thames and Hudson).

KEMP, Martin (1990) *The Science of Art: Optical Themes in Western Art from Brunelleschi to Seurat* (Newhaven, Conn.: Yale University Press).

LEVEY, Michael (1962) *From Giotto to Cézanne: A Concise History of Painting* (London: Thames and Hudson).

READ, Herbert (1974) *A Concise History of Modern Painting* (London: Thames and Hudson).

SWINGELHURST, Edmund (1994) *The Art of the Pre-Raphaelites* (London: Peerage Books/Octopus) page 15.

URE, Peter (1956) Introduction to *The Arden Shakespeare, King Richard II* (London: Routledge) pages lxxxii–lxxxiii.

WHITE, John (1957, 1967) *The Birth and Rebirth of Pictorial Space* (London: Faber and Faber).

Chapter 3

ANNAEUS, Lucius (*c.* 5 BC–AD 65) *Questiones Naturales*, i, 17, 8.

AYRTON, W. E. and PERRY, J. (1878) The Magic Mirror of Japan, 1. *Proceedings of the Royal Society*, **28,** 127.

BESTERMAN, Theodore (1924) *Crystal-gazing: A study in the History, Distribution and Practice of Scrying* (London: W. Rider) page 47.

BOLTON, Henry C. (1893) A modern Oracle and its prototypes. *Journal of American Folklore*, **6,** 37.

BOYER, Carl B. (1959, 1987) *The Rainbow: From Myth to Mathematics* (Princeton, NJ: Princeton University Press).

BRAGG, Sir William (1933) *The Universe of Light* (London: G. Bell & Sons) pages 35–37.

BROWN, Sarah (1992) *Stained Glass: An Illustrated History* (London: Studio Editions, Princes House, 50 Eastcastle Street London WIN 7AP).

BUDGE, E. A. Wallis (1969) *The Gods of the Egyptians* (New York: Dover).

BULFINCH, Thomas (1993) *The Golden Age of Myth and Legend* [The Age of Fable] (Ware: Wordsworth Editions) pages 124–127.

CHEN-TAO SHEN KUA (350 BC) *Hou Shan Tan Tshung* (Collected Discussions at Hou-Shan).

DOUGLAS, R. W. (1958) Glass technology. In: *A History of Technology*, edited by Charles Singer, E. J. Holmyard, A. R. Hall and Trevor J. Williams (Oxford: Clarendon Press) Vol. V, Chapter 28.

FISHER, John (1973) *The Magic of Lewis Carroll* (London: Nelson).

FRAZER, Sir James G. (1923) *The Golden Bough* (abridged edn) (London: Macmillan).

FREUD, Sigmund (1919) *Das Unheimliche Image,* **5** (6-5), 297–324. English translation: Collected Papers, **4,** 368–407. Standard edition, **17,** 217–52. *Art and Literature* (London: Penguin) pages 339–376.

GOLDBERG, Benjamin (1985) *The Mirror and Man* (Charlottesville, VA: University Press of Virginia).

GOODRICH-FREER, A. (1889) Recent experiments. *Proceedings of the Society for Psychical Research*, 495, 1.

JACKSON, Anthony (1984) *The Symbol Stones of Scotland: A Social Anthropological Resolution of the Problem of the Picts* (Orkney: The Orkney Press).

JULESZ, Bela (1971) *Foundations of Cyclopean Perception* (Chicago: Chicago University Press) page xi.

KARLGREN, Bernhard (1934) Early Chinese mirror inscriptions. *Museum of Far Eastern Antiquities Bulletin (Stockholm)*, no. 6.

KEMP, Martin (1989) *Leonardo On Painting* (New Haven and London: Yale University Press).

KIRK, G. S. (1970) *Myth: Its Meaning and Functions in Ancient and other Cultures* (Cambridge: Cambridge University Press) page 181.

LI PO (1921, 1949) Character of a beautiful woman grieving before her mirror. In: *Fir Flower Tablets*, edited by Amy Lowell, translated by Florence Ayscough (Boston: Houghton Mifflin).

NEEDHAM, Joseph (1962) *Science and Civilization in China* (Cambridge: Cambridge University Press).

NICHOLLS, Richard V. (1993) *Corpus Speculorum Etruscorum. Great Britain 2* (Cambridge: Cambridge University Press).

OVID (1987) *Metamorphoses*, translated by A. D. Melville (Oxford: World Classics/Oxford University Press)

PAUSANIAS (2nd century AD) *Itinerary*, vii, 21, 5.

PLATH, Sylvia (1985) Mirror. In: *Selected Poems*, edited by Ted Hughes (London: Faber and Faber).

PLATO (1914) *Phaedrus*, ñ244, translated by Harold North Fowler (Cambridge, Mass.: Harvard University Press/Loeb Classical Library).

PLINY (Gaius Plinius Secundus) (AD 23–79) *Historia Naturalis*, xxxvi, 66, 193.

RANK, Otto (1914) Der Doppelgänger. *Imago: Zeitschrift fur Anwendung der Psychoanalyse auf die Geisteswissenschaften*, Vol. III, edited by Sigmund Freud (Leipzig: Internationaler Psychoanalytischer Verlag) pages 97–164.

ROCHE, Serge (1957) *Mirrors* (London: Duckworth).

SARTON, George (1959) *A History of Science: Hellenistic Science and Culture in the Last Three Centuries BC* (Cambridge Mass.: Harvard University Press).

SCHWEIG, Bruno (1973) *Mirrors: A Guide to the Manufacture of Mirrors and Reflecting Surfaces* (London: Pelham).

SEAFORD, Richard (1987) Pentheu's vision: Bacchae 918–22. *Classical Quarterly*, **37**(i), 76–78.

SEAFORD, Richard (1984) Corinthians XIII.12. *Journal of Theological Studies*, New Series, XXXV, 1.

THOMAS, Keith (1971) *Religion and the Decline of Magic* (London: Weidenfeld and Nicolson).

THORNDYKE, Lynn (1923–1958) *History of Magic and Experimental Science* (New York: Macmillan) 8 Vols.

TYMMS, Ralph (1949) *Doubles in Literary Psychology* (Cambridge: Bowes and Bowes).

VINCI, Leonardo da (1651) *Discourse on Painting*.

WELTON, Thomas (1884) *Mental Magic* (London: G. Ridway) page 93.

WING-TSIT CHAN (1963) *A Source Book of Chinese Philosophy* (Princeton: Princeton University Press).

WILLS, Geoffrey (1965) *English Looking-Glasses: A Study of the Glass, Frames and Makers* (London: Country Life, 2–10 Tavistock St WC2).

Chapter 4

ABBOTT, Edwin A. (1926) *Flatland: A Romance in Many Dimensions* (Oxford: Basil Blackwell).

AL-HAYTHAM, Ibn (Al Hazen) (*c.* 1040) *Optics*, translated by A. I. Sabra (1989) *The Optics of Ibn Al-Haytham* (London: The Warburgh Institute, University of London) 2 Vols.

BENNETT, Jonathan (1970) The difference between right and left. *American Philosophical Quarterly*, **VII**(3), 175–191.

BLOCK, N. J. (1974) Why do mirrors reverse right/left but not up/down? *Journal of Philosophy*, LXXI, 9 May.

BLOCK, N. J. (1981) *Imagery* (Cambridge, MA: MIT Press).

BROWN, Roger (1958) *Words and Things: An Introduction to Language* (New York: Free Press/Macmillan).

CARROLL, Lewis (Charles Dodgson) (1872) *Alice Through the Looking Glass* (London: Macmillan).

EWART, P. H. (1930) A study of the effect of inverted retinal stimulation upon spatially coordinated behaviour. *Genetic Psychology Monograph*, 8.

GARDNER, M. (1964) *The Ambidextrous Universe* (New York, London: Penguin).

GLEICK, James (1988) *Chaos: the Making of a New Science* (London: Penguin).

GLEICK, James (1992) *Genius: Richard Feynman and Modern Physics* (London: Little, Brown) page 332.

GREGORY, R. L. (1966) *Eye and Brain* (London: Weidenfeld and Nicolson) (Oxford: Oxford University Press, 1970) pages 204–207.

GREGORY, R. L. (1986) Reflecting on mirrors. In: *Odd Perceptions* (London: Methuen).

GREGORY, R. L. and HEARD, P. (1979) Border locking and the Café Wall illusion. *Perception*, **8**(4), 365–380.

HAMMOND, John H. (1981) *The Camera Obscura* (Bristol: Adam Hilger).

ITTELSON, William H., MOWAFY, Lyn and MAGID, Diane (1991) The perception of mirror-reflected objects. *Perception*, **20**(5), 567–584.

JAMES, William (1890) *Principles of Psychology* (London: Macmillan) Vol. II, page 150.

KANT, I. (1783) *Prolegomena to any Future Metaphysics*, translated by L. W. Beck, 1950 (Indianapolis: Bobbs-Merrill).

KEMP, Martin (1990) *The Science of Art: Optical Themes in Western Art from Brunelleschi to Seurat* (Newhaven, Conn.: Yale University Press).

KOHLER, I. (1951) Über Aufbau und Wandlungen der Wahrnehmungswelt. *Österreichische Akademie der Wissenschaften Proceedings* **227**, Vol. 1.

LUCRETIUS (*c.* 80 BC) *De Rerum Natura*, translated by C. H. Sisson, 1976 (Manchester: Carcanet Press).

PARSONS, L. M. (1987) Imagined spatial transformation of one's hands and feet. *Cognitive Psychology*, **19**, 178–241.

PEARS, David (1952) Incongruity of counterparts. *Mind*, **61**, 78–81.

PLATO (427–347 BC) *Timaeus*, translated by Desmond Lee, 1977 (London: Penguin).

POPPER, Karl (1959) *The Logic of Scientific Discovery* (London: Hutchinson).

POPPER, Karl (1972) *Objective Knowledge: an Evolutionary Approach* (Oxford: Clarendon Press).

DELLA PORTA, Giovanni Battista (1589) *Magiae naturalis*. English translation (1658) *Natural Magic* (London: Thomas Young and Samuel Speed, The Three Pigeons, and the Angel in St. Pauls Church-yard) pages 360–361.

RIGGS, L. A. (1965) Light as a stimulus for vision. In: *Vision and Visual Perception*, edited by C. H. Graham (New York: Wiley).

ROCK, Irvin (1974) The perception of disoriented figures. *Scientific American*, January; reprinted in: *Psychology in Progress: Readings from the Scientific American*, edited by Richard C. Atkinson (1971) (San Francisco: Freeman).

RONCHI, Vasco (1957) *Optics: The Science of Vision*, translated from the Italian *L'Ottica scienza della visione* by Edward Rosen (New York: New York University Press). Reprinted in New York by Dover (1991).

SHEPARD, Roger N. and COOPER, Lynn A. (1986) *Mental Images and their Transformations* (Cambridge Mass.: MIT Press).

SHEPARD, Roger N. and METZLER J. (1971) Mental rotation of three-dimensional objects. *Cognitive Psychology*, **3**, 701–703.

STEWART, Ian and GOLUBITSKY, Martin (1992) *Fearful Symmetry* (London: Penguin) Chapter 1.

STRATTON, G. M. (1897) Vision without inversion of the retinal image. *Psychological Review*, **4**, 341 and 463.

TAYLOR, James G. (1962) *The Behavioural Basis of Perception* (New Haven, Conn.: Yale University Press).

WHORF, B. L. (1956) *Language, Thought, and Reality* (Cambridge Mass.: Technology Press).

Chapter 5

BARLOW, H. B. (1982) What causes trichromacy? A theoretical analysis using comb-filtered spectra. *Vision Research*, **22**, 635–643.

BARLOW, H. B. and MOLLON, J. D. (1982) *The Senses* (Cambridge: Cambridge University Press).

BERRY, Michael (1995) Natural focusing. In: *The Artful Eye*, edited by Richard Gregory, John Harris, Priscilla Heard and David Rose (Oxford: Oxford University Press) Chapter 15.

BREWSTER, Sir David (1831) *Treatise on Optics* (London: Longman, Rees, Orme, Brown, and Green).

DAVIES, P. C. W. and BROWN J. R. (1986) *The Ghost in the Atom* (Cambridge: Cambridge University Press).

DAWKINS, Richard (1986) *The Blind Watchmaker* (London: Longman).

DIRAC, P. A. M. (1982) *The Principles of Quantum Mechanics* (4th edn) (Oxford: Oxford University Press).

EINSTEIN, A. (1936) Physics and reality. In: *Albert Einstein: Essays in Physics* (New York: Philosophical Library at 200 W. 57th Street, New York NY 10019).

FEYNMAN, R., (1970) *Lectures in Physics*, Vol. I (Reading, Mass.: Addison Wesley).

FEYNMAN, R. (1985) *QED: The Strange Theory of Light and Matter* (Princeton, NJ: Princeton University Press)

GAMOW, G. (1966) *Thirty Years That Shook Physics: The Story of Quantum Theory* (New York: Dover).

GRIBBIN, J. (1984) *In Search of Schrödinger's Cat: Quantum Physics and Reality* (London: Corgi).

GRIBBIN, J. (1992) *In Search of the Edge of Time* (London: Bantam).

HALL, A. Rupert (1993) *All was Light: an Introduction to Newton's* Opticks (Oxford: Oxford University Press) pages 96–112.

HEAVENS, O. S. (1955) *Optical Properties of Thin Solid Films* (London: Butterworth). Reprinted in New York by Dover (1991).

HECHT, S., SCHAER, S., PIRENNE, M. H. (1942) Energy, quanta, and vision. *Journal of General Physiology*, **25**, 819–840.

ISENBERG, Cyril (1972, 1992) *The Science of Soap Films and Soap Bubbles* (New York: Dover).

LLOWARCH, W. (1961) *Ripple Tank Studies of Wave Motion* (Oxford: Oxford University Press).

LUCRETIUS (*c.* 60 BC) *Of the Nature of Things*, translated by W. E. Leonard, 1921 (London: Everyman's Library/J. M. Dent) pages 45–89.

OEREN, Michael and NAYAR, Shree K. (1994) Seeing beyond Lambert's Law. In: *Lecture Notes on Computer Science*, edited by Olof Eklunh (Berlin: Springer-Verlag).

PIRENNE, M. H. (1948) *Vision and the Eye* (London: Pilot).

RONCHI, Vasco (1957) *Optics: the Science of Vision* (New York: University Press). Reprinted in New York by Dover (1991).

SABRA, A. I. (1967) *Theories of Light From Descartes to Newton* (London: Oldbourne).

SIEGAL, Daniel M. (1991) *Innovation in Maxwell's Electromagnetic Theory: Molecular Vortices, Displacement Current, and Light* (Cambridge: Cambridge University Press).

SQUIRES, Euan (1986) *The Mystery of the Quantum World* (Bristol: Adam Hilger).

WOOD, Robert (1934) *Physical Optics* (3rd edn) (London: Macmillan) page 348.

ZEKI, Semir (1993) *A Vision of the Brain* (Oxford: Blackwell).

Chapter 6

BREWSTER, D. (1858) *The Kaleidoscope: its History, Theory, and Construction* (2nd edn) (London: John Murray). Facsimile reprint, 1987 (Holyoke, Massachusetts: Van Cort) page 4.

BREWSTER, D. (1856) *The Stereoscope: its History, Theory, and Construction* (London: John Murray). Facsimile reprint, 1971 (Hastings-on-Hudson, NY: Morgan & Morgan).

CHARLESTON, R. J. and ANGUS-BUTTERWORTH, L. M. (1957) Glass. In: *A History of Technology*, edited by Charles Singer, E. J. Holmyard, A. R. Hall and Trevor J. Williams (Oxford: Clarendon Press) Vol. III, Chapter 9.

DARIUS, Jon (1984) *Beyond Vision* (Oxford: Oxford University Press).

DAUMAS, Maurice (1972) *Scientific Instruments of the Seventeenth and Eighteenth Centuries and their Makers* (London: Portman Books).

DOUGLAS, R. W. (1958) Glass technology. In: *A History of Technology*, edited by Charles Singer, E. J. Holmyard, A. R. Hall and Trevor J. Williams (Oxford: Clarendon Press) Vol. V, Chapter 28.

GOLDBERG, Benjamin (1985) *The Mirror and Men* (Charlotesville: University of Virginia) Chapter 9.

GOMBRICH, E. (1995) *Shadows: the Depiction of Cast Shadows in Western Art* (London: National Gallery).

GREGORY, R. L. (1970) *The Intelligent Eye* (London: Weidenfeld and Nicolson) pages 92–96.

GREGORY, R. L. (1974) *Concepts and Mechanisms of Perception* (London: Duckworth) pages 501–581.

HAMMOND, John H. (1981) *The Camera Obscura* (Bristol: Adam Hilger).

HAMMOND, John H. and AUSTIN, Jill (1987) *The Camera Lucida: in Art and Science* (Bristol: Adam Hilger).

HOWARD, I. P. and ROGERS, B. J. (1995) *Binocular Vision and Stereopsis* (Oxford: Oxford University Press).

ISRAELI, Yael (1991) The invention of blowing. In: *Roman Glass: Two Centuries of Art and Invention*, edited by Martine Newby and Kenneth Painter (London: Society of Antiquaries, Burlington House, Piccadilly, London W1V 0HS) pages 46–55.

KING, Henry C. (1955) *The History of the Telescope* (New York: Dover) page 401.

LAND, M. F. (1966) A multilayer interference reflector in the eye of the scallop Pecten maximus. *Journal of Experimental Biology*, **45**, 433–437.

LAND M. F. (1972) The physics and biology of animal reflectors. *Progress in Biophysics and Molecular Biology*, **24**, 76–106.

LAND, M. F. (1984) Molluscs. In: *Photoreception and Vision*, edited by M. A. Ali (New York: Plenum) pages 699–725.

MANLY, Peter (1991) *Unusual Telescopes* (Cambridge: Cambridge University Press) page 12.

PEPPER, John Henry (c.1877) *Cyclopaedic Science Simplified* (London: Frederick Warne).

DELLA PORTA, Giovanni Battista (1589) *Magiae naturalis*. English translation (1658) *Natural Magic* (London: Thomas Young and Samuel Speed, The Three Pigeons, and the Angel in St. Pauls Church-yard).

RAMACHANDRAN, V. S. and ROGERS-RAMACHANDRAN, D. (1996) Synaesthesia in phantom limbs induced with mirrors. *Proceedings of the Royal Society of London B*, **263**, 377–386.

ROCHE, Serge (1956) *Miroirs* (Paris: Paul Hartmann); and in English as (1956) *Mirrors,* translated by Colin Duckworth (London: Gerald Duckworth) page 12.

SCHWEIG, Bruno (1973) *Mirrors: A Guide to the Manufacture of Mirrors and Reflecting Surfaces* (London: Pelham) page 24.

Sky and Telescope (1969) January, page 14 and May, page 300.

Sky and Telescope (1984) September, page 267.

TALBOT, Henry Fox (1844) *The Pencil of Nature.*

WADE, N. J. (1983) *Brewster and Wheatstone on Vision* (London: Academic Press/Experimental Psychology Society).

YOUNSE, Jack M. (1993) *IEEE Spectrum*, November, 27–28.

Chapter 7

AVETISOV, Vladik A., GOLDANSKI, Vitalii I. and KUZ'MIN, Vladimir V. (1991) Handedness, origin of life and evolution. *Physics Today*, July, 33–41.

BLOCK, N.J. (1974) Why do mirrors reverse right/left, but not up/down? *Journal of Philosophy*, LXXI, 9 May.

CORAN, Stanley (1992) *Left Hander* (London: John Murray) page 32.

CRICK, Francis (1953) The packing of α-helices: simple coiled coils. *Acta Crystallographica*, **6** (8–9), 689–697.

EMMONS, T. P., REEVES J. M. and FORTSON E. N. (1983) Parity-non-conserving optical rotation in atomic lead. *Physical Review Letters*, **51**, 2089–2092.

DARWIN, Charles (1888) *The Movements and Habits of Climbing Plants* (London: John Murray).

FRANK, F. C. (1953) On spontaneous asymmetric synthesis. *Biochimica Biophysica Acta*, **II**, 459–463.

GALLOWAY, J. W. (1991) Molecular assymetry. In: *Biological Asymmetry and Handedness*, edited by L. Wolpert (Chichester: Wiley) CIBA Foundation Symposium 162, pages 16–35.

KIM, Scott (1981) *Inversions* (New York: McGraw Hill).

KONDEPUDI, Dilip K., KAUFMAN, Rebecca J. and NOLINI, Singh (1990) Chiral symmetry breaking in sodium chlorate crystallization. *Science*, **250**, 975.

LACKNER, J. R. (1992) Spatial orientation in weightless environments. *Perception*, **21**, 803–812.

LEE, T. D. and YANG, C. N. (1956) Question of parity conservation in weak interaction. *Physical Review*, **104**, 254–258.

MASON, Stephen F. (1991) Origins of the handedness of biological molecules. *Biological Asymmetry and Handedness*, edited by L. Wolpert (Chichester: Wiley) CIBA Foundation Symposium 162, pages 2–15.

PAGELS, Heinz R. (1982) *The Cosmic Code* (London: Penguin).

STUART, Ian, and GOLUBITSKY, Martin (1992) *Fearful Symmetry* (London: Penguin).

YOKOYAMA, Takahiko, COPELAND, Neal G., JENKINS, Nancy A., MONTGOMERY, Charles A., ELDER, Frederick F. B. and OVERBEEK, Paul A. (1993) Reversal of left-right asymmetry: a situs inversus mutation. *Science*, **260**, 679–682.

WHISTLER, Rex (1946) *OHO!* (London: Bodley Head).

Chapter 8

BERKELEY, G. (1963) *Dialogues between Hylas and Philonous* (London: Dent).

ELLIS, W. H. (1938) *Source Book of Gestalt Psychology* (London: Kegan Paul).

GIBSON, J. J. (1950) *The Perception of the Physical World* (Boston: Houghton Mifflin).

GIBSON, J. J. (1966) *The Senses Considered as Perceptual Systems* (Boston: Houghton Mifflin).

GOMBRICH, E. (1995) *Shadows: the Depiction of Cast Shadows in Western Art* (London: National Gallery).

GREGORY, R. L. (1963) Distortion of visual space as inappropriate constancy scaling. *Nature,* **199**, 678–691.

GREGORY, R. L. (1966) *Eye and Brain* (London: Weidenfeld and Nicolson) (Oxford: Oxford University Press, 1970).

GREGORY, R. L. (1968) On how so little information controls so much behaviour. In: *Towards a Theoretical Biology*, Vol. 2, edited by C. H. Waddington (Cambridge: Cambridge University Press).

GREGORY, R. L. (1970) *The Intelligent Eye* (London: Weidenfeld and Nicolson).

GREGORY, R. L. (1974a) Choosing a paradigm for perception. In: *Handbook of Perception*, edited by E. C. Carterette and M. P. Friedman (New York: Academic Press), Vol. 1, Chapter 3.

GREGORY, R. L. (1974b) The grammar of vision. In: *Concepts and Mechanisms of Perception* (London: Duckworth).

GREGORY, R. L. (1980) Perceptions as hypotheses. *Philosophical Transactions of the Royal Society of London B,* **290**, 181–197.

GREGORY, R. L. (1981) *Mind in Science* (London: Weidenfeld and Nicolson).

GREGORY, R. L. (1993) The unnatural science of illusions. *Royal Institution Proceedings,* **64**, 93–110.

GREGORY, R. L. (1994) Adelbert Ames: Interactions with Hermann Helmholtz,

Albert Einstein and the Universe, Essay 26. In: *Even Odder Perceptions* (London: Routledge).

GREGORY, R. L. and HARRIS, J. P. (1975) Illusion destruction by appropriate scaling. *Perception*, **4**, 203–220.

GREGORY, R. L. and HEARD, P. (1979) Border locking and the Café Wall illusion. *Perception*, **8**(4), 365–380.

GREGORY, R. L., WALLACE J. G. and CAMPBELL, F. W. (1959) Changes in the size and shape of visual after-images observed in complete darkness during changes of position in space. *Quarterly Journal of Experimental Psychololgy*, **11**(1), 54.

HUBEL, D. H. and WIESEL, T. N. (1962) Receptive fields, binocular interaction and functional architecture in the cat's visual cortex. *Journal of Physiology*, **160**, 106.

ITTELSON, W. H. and KILPATRICK, F. P. (1951) Experiments in perception. *Scientific American*, **185**, 50–55.

JOHNSON-LAIRD, P. and WASON, P. C. (1977) *Thinking: Readings in Cognitive Science* (Cambridge: Cambridge University Press).

KAHNEMAN, D., SLOVIC, P. and TVERSKY, A. (1982) *Judgement Under Uncertainty: Heuristics and Biases* (Cambridge: Cambridge University Press).

LINDBERG, David C. (1976) *Theories of Vision from Al-Kindi to Kepler* (Chicago: University of Chicago Press).

METELLI, F. (1974) The perception of transparency. *Scientific American*, **230**, 90–98.

MILLER, Arthur (1987) *Imagery in Scientific Thought* (Cambridge, Mass.: MIT Press).

PIATELLI-PALMARINA, M. (1994) *Inevitable Illusions: How Mistakes of Reason Rule our Minds* (New York: Wiley).

PINKER, S. (1994) *The Language Instinct* (London: Allen Lane/Penguin).

RAMACHANDRAN, V. S. and GREGORY, R. L. (1991) Perceptual filling-in of artificially induced scotomas in human vision. *Nature*, **350**, 6320.

ROCK, I. (1983) *The Logic of Perception* (Cambridge, Mass.: MIT Press).

RUSSELL, Bertrand (1946) *History of Western Philosophy* (London: Allen & Unwin) pages 623–633.

Chapter 9

BACON, Francis (1878) *Novum Organum*, edited by Thomas Fowler (Oxford: Oxford University Press).

BACON, Francis (1915) *New Atlantis* (Oxford: Oxford University Press).

BARTLEY, William Warren III (1977) *Lewis Carroll's Symbolic Logic* (Hassocks: Harvester Press, 2 Stanford Terrace, Hassocks, Sussex, England).

BODMER, Sir Walter, *et al.* (1985) *The Public Understanding of Science* (London: Royal Society).

BODMER, Sir Walter (1987) The public understanding of science. *Science and Public Affairs*, **2**, 69–89.

BRUMBAUGH, Robert S. (1966) *Ancient Greek Gadgets and Machines* (Westpoint, Conn.: Greenwood).

BRUNER, Jerome S., JOLLY, A. and SYLVA, K. (1976) *Play: Its Role in Development and Evolution* (New York: Viking-Penguin) pages 38 and 410.

COHEN, Bernard (1987) *The Birth of the New Physics* (London: Penguin) page 3.

COHEN, Morris R. and DRABKIN, I. E. (1958) *A Source Book of Greek Science* (Cambridge Mass.: Harvard University Press).

COLE, C. K. (1985) *Sympathetic Vibrations* (New York: Morrow) page 241.

CORNFORD, Francis (1941) Plato's *Republic* (Oxford: Oxford University Press) Chapter XXV (vii. 514-521B) pages 222–223.

DAVIS, Philip J. and HERSH, Reuben (1980) *The Mathematical Experience* (Boston: Houghton Mifflin).

DI SESSA, Andrea A. (1982) Unlearning Aristotelian physics: a study of knowledge-based learning. *Cognitive Science*, **6**, 37–75.

DOBBS, Betty J. T. (1975) *The Foundations of Newton's Alchemy: Or, The Hunting of the Green Lyon* (Cambridge: Cambridge University Press).

DURANT, John (1992) *Museums and the Public Understanding of Science* (London: Science Museum/COPUS).

DRIVER, Rosalind, GUESNE, Edith, TIBERGHIEN, Andrée (1985) *Children's Ideas in Science* (Oxford: Oxford University Press).

FISCHMAN, Joshua (1993) New clues surface about the making of mind. *Science*, **262**(1517), 3 December.

FISHER, John (1976) *The Magic of Lewis Carroll* (London: Nelson) pages 168–169.

GARDNER, Martin (1965) The Annotated Alice (London: Penguin)

GALLUP, G. G. Jr (1970) Chimpanzees: self-recognition. *Science*, **167**, 86–87.

GIBSON, J. J. (1950) *The Perception of the Physical World* (Boston: Houghton Mifflin).

GÖRLITZ, Dietmar, and WHOHLWILL, J. F. (1987) *Curiosity, Imagination, and Play: On the Development of Spontaneous Cognitive and Motivational Processes* (London: Lawrence Erlbaum).

GRAHAM, Eleanor (1962) Introduction to Lewis Carroll's *Alice's Adventures in Wonderland* and *Though the Looking-glass* (London: Penguin) pages 169–170.

GREGORY, R. L. (1981) *Mind in Science* (London: Weidenfeld) (London: Penguin, 1984).

GREGORY, R. L. (1983) The Bristol Exploratory – a feeling for science. *New Scientist*, **17** November, 484–489.

GREGORY, R. L. (1986) *Hands-on Science: An Introduction to the Bristol Exploratory* (London: Duckworth).

GREGORY, R. L. (1988) First hand science: the Exploratory in Bristol. *Science and Public Affairs*, **3**, 13–24 (London: The Royal Society).

GREGORY, R. L. (1989a) Alchemy of matter and minds. *Nature*, **342**, 471–473.

GREGORY, R. L. (1989b) Turning minds on to science by hands-on exploration: the nature and potential of the hands-on medium. In: *Sharing Science,* (London: The Nuffield Foundation Interactive Science and Technology Project on behalf of the Committee on the Public Understanding of Science) pages 1-9.

GREGORY, R. L. (1993) Exploring science hands-on. *Science and Public Affairs,* **3** (London: The Royal Society).

HEIN, Hilde (1987) The museum as teacher of theory: a case study of the Exploratorium Vision Section. *Museum Studies Journal,* **2**(4), 30–39.

HEIN, Hilde (1990) *The Exploratorium: The Museum as Laboratory* (Washington: Smithsonian Institution Press).

HOCHBERG, J. and BROOKS, V. (1978) The perception of motion pictures. In: *Handbook of Perception,* edited by E. C. Carterette and M. P. Friedman (New York: Academic Press).

HOCHBERG, J. (1987) Perception of motion pictures. In: *Oxford Companion to the Mind,* edited by R. L. Gregory (Oxford: Oxford University Press) pages 604–608.

HODGKIN, Robin A. (1985) *Playing and Exploring* (New York: Methuen).

KUHN, Thomas (1962) *The Structure of Scientific Revolutions* (Chicago: University of Chicago Press).

MATTHEWS, G. B. (1990) *Philosophy and the Young Child* (Cambridge, Mass: MIT Press).

MILLER, Arthur I. (1987) *Imagery in Scientific Thought: Creating Twentieth Century Physics* (2nd edn) (Cambridge, Mass.: MIT Press).

MURPHY, Pat (1985) *The Exploratorium* (San Francisco: The Exploratorium) Special Issue March

PAPERT, Seymour (1980) *Mindstorms: Children, Computers and Powerful Ideas* (New York: Basic Books).

PIAGET, J. (1929) *The Child's Conception of the World,* translated into English by Joan and Andrew Tomlinson (London: Routledge and Kegan Paul).

PIAGET, J. (1972) *The Child and Reality: Problems of Genetic Psychology,* translated into English by Arnold Rosin (London: Frederick Muller).

PINKER, Steven (1994) *The Language Instinct: The New Science of Language and Mind* (London: Penguin).

PIZZEY, Stephen (1987) *Interactive Science and Technology Centres* (London: Projects Publishing, 67 Eccles Road, London SW11).

PRICE, Derek de Solla (1975) *Gears from the Greeks: The Antikythera Mechanism—A Calendrical Computer from c. 80 BC* (New York: Science History Publications/ Neale Watson, 156 Fifth Avenue, New York NY 10010).

REISZ, K., and MILLAR, G. (1953, 1968) *The Technique of Film Editing* (London: Focal Press).

RHEINGOLD, H. (1991) *Virtual Reality: The Technology of Computer-Generated Artificial*

Worlds—And how it Promises and Threatens to Transform Business and Society (New York: Summit).

SHORTLAND, Michael (1987) No business like show business. *Nature,* **328,** 213.

STEVENSON, John (1991) The long-term impact of interactive exhibits. *International Journal of Science Education,* **13**(5), 521–531.

VAN LAWICK-GOODALL Jane (1968) Early tool using in wild chimpanzees. In: *Play: its Role in Development and Evolution,* edited by J. S. Bruner, A. Jolly and K. Sylva (London: Penguin) Chapter 10.

VINES, Gail (1993) TV's electronic assault on the brain. *New Scientist,* 13 December, page 10.

ZEEMAN, C. (1986) Gears from the Greeks. *Proceedings of the Royal Institution,* **58,** 137–156.

ZIMAN, John (1978) *Reliable Knowledge: An Explanation of the Grounds for Belief in Science* (Cambridge: Cambridge University Press).

Final reflections

AYER, A. J. (1936) *Language, Truth and Logic* (London: Gollancz). Reprinted in London by Penguin (1971).

BERKELEY, G. (1963) *Dialogues between Hylas and Philonous* (London: Dent).

BOHM, David (1980) *Wholeness and the Implicate Order* (London: Routledge and Kegan Paul).

BRADLEY, J. (1971) *Mach's Philosophy of Science* (London: Athlone).

BRIDGMAN, P. W. (1927) *The Logic of Modern Physics* (London: Macmillan). Reprinted in Salem, New Hampshire by Ayer (1993).

CRAIK, K. J. W. (1952) *The Nature of Explanation* (Cambridge: Cambridge University Press).

EINSTEIN, Albert (1936) Physics and Reality. *Franklin Institute Journal,* **221,** 349–382.

GREGORY, R. L. (1980) Perceptions as hypotheses. *Philosophical Transactions of the Royal Society of London B,* **290,** 181–197.

GREGORY, R. L. (1981) *Mind in Science* (London: Weidenfeld and Nicolson) pages 239–243.

GREGORY, R. L. (1994). What is the catch in neural nets? *Even Odder Perceptions,* Essay 18 (London: Routledge).

GREGORY, R. L. (1987) Intelligence based on knowledge—knowledge based on intelligence. In: *Creative Intelligences,* edited by Richard L. Gregory and Pauline K. Marstrand (London: Francis Pinter) pages 1–8.

GRIBBIN, John (1995) *Schrödinger's Kittens: And the Search for Reality* (London: Weidenfeld and Nicolson).

JAMES, William (1890) *Principles of Psychology* (London: Macmillan) Vol. 2, pages 449–450.

JOHNSON-LAIRD, P. N. (1983) *Mental Models* (Cambridge: Cambridge University Press).

LOCKE, John (1690) *Essay Concerning Human Understanding* (Oxford: Clarendon Press) Book II, Chapter i, Section 2.

MACH, Ernst (1976) *Knowledge and Error* (Dordrecht-Holland: Reidel).

MARR, David (1982) *Vision* (New York: W.H. Freeman).

MILL, J. S. (1865) *An Examination of Sir William Hamilton's Philosophy* (London: Longman) Chapter X.

PENROSE, Roger (1989) *The Emperor's New Mind: Concerning Computers, Minds, and the Laws of Physics* (Oxford: Oxford University Press).

PENROSE, Roger (1994) *Shadows of Mind: A Search for the Missing Science of Consciousness* (Oxford: Oxford University Press).

POLANYI, Michael (1958) *Personal Knowledge* (London: Routledge and Kegan Paul) page 15.

POPPER, Karl (1972) *Objective Knowledge: an Evolutionary Approach* (Oxford: Clarendon Press) pages 6–7.

PRICE, Derek de Solla (1975) *Gears from the Greeks: The Antikythera Mechanism—A Calendrical Computer from c. 80 BC* (New York: Science History Publications/ Neale Watson, 156 Fifth Avenue, New York NY 10010).

RUSSELL, Bertrand (1946) *History of Western Philosophy* (London: Allen & Unwin) page 623.

SARTON, George (1952) *A History of Science: Hellenistic Science and Culture in the Last Three Centuries BC* (Cambridge, Mass: Harvard University Press).

SHERWOOD, Stephen L. (1966) *The Nature of Psychology: A Selection of Papers, Essays and other Writings by Kenneth J.W. Craik* (Cambridge: Cambridge University Press).

SUTHERLAND, Stuart (1992) *Irrationality: the Enemy Within* (London: Penguin).

WEISKRANTZ, L. (1987) Neuropsychology and the nature of consciousness. In: *Mindwaves*, edited by Colin Blakemore and Susan Greenfield (Oxford: Blackwell) Chapter 21.

WEISKRANTE, L. (1997) *Consciousness Lost and Found: a Neuropsychological Exploration* (Oxford: Oxford University Press).

WELLS, Stanley and TAYLOR, Gary (1986) *The Oxford Shakespeare* (Oxford: Oxford University Press.

WOLPERT, L. (1993) *The Unnatural Nature of Science* (London: Faber).

Index